Place-Based Methods for Researching Schools

BLOOMSBURY RESEARCH METHODS FOR EDUCATION SERIES

Edited by
Melanie Nind, University of Southampton, UK

The *Bloomsbury Research Methods for Education* series provides overviews of the range of sometimes interconnected and diverse methodological possibilities for researching aspects of education such as education contexts, sectors, problems or phenomena. Each volume discusses prevailing, less obvious and more innovative methods and approaches for the particular area of educational research.

More targeted than general methods textbooks, these authoritative yet accessible books are invaluable resources for students and researchers planning their research design and wanting to explore methodological possibilities to make well-informed decisions regarding their choice of methods.

Also available in the series:

Research Methods for Pedagogy, Melanie Nind, Alicia Curtin and Kathy Hall

Forthcoming:

Research Methods for Education in the Digital Age, Maggi Savin-Baden and Gemma Tombs
Research Methods for Understanding Practitioner Learning, Vivienne Baumfield, Elaine Hall, Rachel Lofthouse and Kate Wall

BLOOMSBURY RESEARCH METHODS FOR EDUCATION

Place-Based Methods for Researching Schools

PAT THOMSON AND CHRISTINE HALL

BLOOMSBURY
NEW DELHI • LONDON • OXFORD • NEW YORK • SYDNEY

BLOOMSBURY INDIA
Bloomsbury Publishing India Pvt. Ltd
Second Floor, LSC Building No. 4, DDA Complex, Pocket C–6&7,
Vasant Kunj, New Delhi 110070

BLOOMSBURY, Bloomsbury Academic India and the Diana
logo are trademarks of Bloomsbury Publishing Plc

First published in 2017
Reprinted 2019
First Published in India 2023

Library of Congress Cataloging-in-Publication Data
A catalog record for this title is available from the Library of Congress

ISBN: 978-93-94701-47-2

Typeset by Fakenham Prepress Solutions, Fakenham, Norfolk NR21 8NN
Printed at Manipal Technologies Limited, Manipal

To find out more about our authors and books visit www.bloomsbury.com
and sign up for our newsletters.

CONTENTS

LIST OF FIGURES

LIST OF TABLES

ACKNOWLEDGEMENTS

We would like to thank our colleagues Ken Jones, Susan Jones, Jane McGregor, Nick Owen, Lisa Russell and Ethel Sanders, all of whom contributed to the production of some of the data used in this book. Jan Nespor and Barbara Comber provided detailed feedback on our first manuscript and we are very grateful for their interest and help. We also owe a huge debt to the schools and school staff who allowed us to research with them and to take and use images and data in our publications.

Thanks to Melanie Nind for inviting us to develop our passion for place into a methods book, and to Rachel Shillington and Maria Giovanna Brauzzi at Bloomsbury for support and encouragement.

SERIES EDITOR'S PREFACE

The idea of the *Bloomsbury Research Methods for Education* series is to provide books that are useful to researchers wanting to think about research methods in the context of their research area, research problem or research aims. While researchers may use any methods textbook for ideas and inspiration, the onus falls on them to apply something from social science research methods to education in particular, or from education to a particular dimension of education (pedagogy, schools, the digital dimension, practitioner learning, to name some examples). This application of ideas is not beyond us and has led to some great research and also to methodological development. In this series, though, the books are more targeted, making them a good place to start for the student, researcher or person wanting to craft a research proposal. Each book brings together in one place the range of sometimes interconnected and often diverse methodological possibilities for researching one aspect or sector of education, one research problem or phenomenon. Thus, readers will quickly find a discussion of the methods they associate with that bit of education research they are interested in, but in addition they will find less obvious and more innovative methods and approaches. A quick look at the opening glossary will give you an idea of the methods you will find included within each book. You can expect a discussion of those methods that is critical, authoritative *and* situated. In each text the authors use powerful examples of the methods in use in the arena with which you are concerned.

There are other features that make this series distinctive. In each of the books the authors draw on their own research and on the research of others making alternative methodological choices. In this way they address the affordances of the methods in terms of real studies; they illustrate the potential with real data. The authors also discuss the rationale behind the choice of methods and behind how researchers put them together in research designs. As readers, you will get behind the scenes of published research and into the kind of methodological decision-making that you are grappling with. In each of the books you will find yourself moving between methods, theory and data; you will find theoretical concepts to think with and with which you might be able to enhance your methods. You will find that the authors develop arguments about methods rather than just describing them.

In *Place-Based Methods for Researching Schools*, Pat Thomson and Christine Hall bring a particular methodological outlook to the challenge of researching schools. You will find fresh ways of positioning school-based research alongside plenty of solid good advice and detailed illustrations. Pat and Christine write in an open, accessible and straightforward style, which complements their highly engaging content. They seem to build a relationship with you, the reader, just as they advocate you build a relationship with the school(s) you are studying. Their approach almost disguises the academic weight of the ideas they discuss, as they ever so deftly ease you into complex territory. In common with other books in the series, these authors make powerful use of examples of studies from around the world in your sphere of interest. In this book in particular, these studies will become almost like old friends as you are helped to appreciate their qualities.

This book (nor any in the series) cannot be the only book you need to read to formulate, justify and implement your research methods. Other books will cover a greater range or methods and, others still, more operational detail. The aim of this series, though, is to provide books that take you to the heart of the methods thinking you will want and need to do. They are books by authors who are equally passionate about their substantive topic and about research methods and they are books that will be invaluable for inspiring deep and informed methods thinking.

Melanie Nind
Series Editor

GLOSSARY OF RESEARCH METHODS AND APPROACHES

This glossary comprises only those methods and approaches covered in this book. These words/terms will appear in bold on their first occasion of use in the text.

Action research: A systematic approach, often used by practitioners to understand and improve their own practice through a focus on their own practical actions and their own reflections on data about the effects of those actions. Action research involves cycles of planning, implementing, recording and analysing a change in practice.

Assets mapping: A way of assessing the economic, cultural and social composition of a neighbourhood by systematically driving or walking around.

Case study: In-depth, intensive analysis of the single (or multiple) case within its naturalistic context, valuing its particularity, complexity and relationships with the context. This approach uses multiple methods and perspectives to look at the case holistically.

Critical incident analysis: A method to focus the researcher on a critical incident or turning point, exploring people's behaviour and experience before, during and after the incident to analyse its meaning for those involved. Incidents are usually explored via interview and are significant or revelatory in relation to what interrupts or enables everyday practices.

Dérive: A walk designed to explore a terrain, which simultaneously disrupts familiarity and emphasizes the psychogeographical, not simply the material.

Discourse analysis: A term given to various approaches to the analysis of texts (which can be spoken, verbal or written) but which communicate something of what is taken for granted in the social situation. Discourse analysts, for example, examine texts for what they say about what is doable, sayable and thinkable in a classroom situation.

Documentary analysis: More often used by social science researchers as a supplementary rather than main method, this involves analysis of documents (pre-existing artefacts or written texts) for what they can tell us about the phenomenon under study.

Drawing: A visual method used particularly with children and young people to offer an alternative or supplement to verbal or written accounts. Participants may be asked to draw a picture to depict the phenomenon, e.g. classroom, lesson, learning support teacher. Drawings can be analysed alone or alongside recorded conversations to offer another perspective on what is under study.

Ethnographic case study: A type of case study using an ethnographic approach. This usually involves a shorter, less intensive degree of immersion in the context by the researcher than in an ethnography. The focus is on the case – the individual, event or phenomenon – rather than on the culture of the group.

Ethnography: A research approach aimed at understanding an insider perspective on a particular community, practice or setting by focusing on the meaning of social action from the point of view of the participants. Methods of progressively focused observation and interview are used by the researcher who is immersed in the situation, generating complex, detailed data to enable deep descriptions and theorization of the cultural context.

Field notes: Often thought of as simply jotting in a notebook, the term covers the range of ways in which researchers record their observations and experiences in the research site.

Focus group: A group interview method in which participants are invited to explore a given topic in group discussion. Participants respond to each other, to activities or stimuli rather than just to the researcher's questions. The researcher aims to facilitate discussion as much as direct it.

Historical/archival analysis: A systematic approach to the analysis of primary sources such as meeting minutes, first-person writings, newspapers and other media, registers and roll books. Historical analysis is often based in libraries but is now equally undertaken online, using digitized records.

Inclusive research: An umbrella term for research approaches that respond to the call for democratization of the research process. This includes, for example, participatory, emancipatory and partnership research. The emphasis is on ensuring the relevance of the research to the people concerned, so that it is important and beneficial to them, so that they are involved in the process and decision-making, and so that their views and experiences are treated with respect.

Insider research: The term used to describe those who research in their own workplace. Familiarity is both a strength and limitation. The antonym, outsider research, has the corollary asset/weakness of distance and lack of knowledge.

Interview: The method of asking participants to respond to questions, usually by reflecting on their experiences or views. Interviews may be structured, semi-structured or unstructured and conducted with individuals or groups.

Longitudinal research: Research conducted over an extended period of time, in which time is a unit of analysis. Examples include cohort studies, in which individuals experiencing the same event are observed at repeated intervals to examine changes; panel studies, involving a cross-section of a population surveyed at multiple points in time; and qualitative longitudinal research, involving returning to interviewees on multiple occasions over time.

Mapping: A visual method in which participants individually or in groups map out (write or draw) their experiences, often including a space/time dimension. The researcher may record and explore the production of these maps alongside the maps produced.

Mosaic approach: A combination of participatory and visual methods designed to bring together data generated by young children and adults, making sense of their everyday experiences. The resulting mosaic is co-constructed by the participants and the researcher.

Multi-modal analysis: An approach that takes into account multiple modes of communication (gesture, gaze, movement, speech, drawing, etc.) without taking for granted that any is the most important. The researcher reads different texts and embodied actions for what they say about the phenomenon under study.

Narrative research: The researcher focuses on the ways in which research participants 'story' their lives and work practices. The researcher might look for plot and character as well as critical events. Narrative researchers often look for ways in which narratives 'work' in an organization, how they assist in identity formation, or how narratives conform to archetypal structures.

Observation: A method for recording what can be seen in the research site. Observation can be naturalistic, conducted by participant or non-participant observers. It can also be systematic and structured, using time or event sampling and pre-prepared schedules.

Participatory/partnership research: A research process that involves those being researched or implicated in the research in the decision-making and conduct of the research.

Photo ethnography: The use of digital or mobile technology to visually record ethnographic data and experiences.

Practice-based inquiry: A research strategy for practitioners (individually or collectively) to systematically and rigorously study their own practice. Related to action research, this is a way to support the development of knowledge contextualized within specific contexts of practice, emphasizing the role of collaboration and reflection in the inquiry and learning process.

Semiotic analysis: An approach which focuses on meaning-making processes through reading cultural and social signs, usually using either discourse or narrative analysis.

Sensory research: A method which focuses on lived experience, recording data gained through multiple senses.

Shadowing: An approach in which the researcher follows the participant around to get a sense of their experience by 'walking in their shoes'. Shadowing can occur for various length of time depending on the purpose.

Spatial research methods: Methods employing physical, social, temporal, experiential and/or virtual aspects of space to understand the experiences of participants in a research site.

Survey: An approach used to discover broad, general or comparative information on a selected topic by surveying a (frequently large) number of participants. This may involve no personal contact between researcher and participant.

Transcription: A method of deciding what is described and how it is represented so that audio or video data are transformed for the purpose of analysis.

Video methods: Methods that allow researchers to produce and analyse audiovisual data including pre-existing video data, video diaries, researcher produced or elicited video films, etc. Analysis may treat the video as record or as an impression of events.

Video stimulated recall/reflection/dialogue: Video of participants in action is used to stimulate their recall of, or reflection and dialogue about, the recorded event or interaction. It is used to probe what participants were thinking or feeling at the time. Control of the selection of units of analysis can be shared or handed over to participants.

Introducing the book

We imagine you, the reader of this book, as someone who has already decided to research a school, or a set of schools. We are not therefore going to spend time arguing that researching a school is a good thing. Our task, as we see it, is to present some strategies for how such research can be conducted. In doing so, we suggest to you that thinking of the school as a 'place' and using 'place-based methods' can be very helpful.

This book is organized in the order in which a research project might be undertaken. However, the book is not a step-by-step guide or a blueprint. It is not a list of methods to use. We focus instead on the issues that researchers need to think about when organizing their school study. Each chapter begins with a key question and then offers strategies that can be used in order to address it. Some of these strategies involve discussion of particular research methods, but these are placed in the context of the practicalities of researching a school. Examples from research studies are also provided to illustrate what particular strategies can accomplish. These examples are not intended to be models to be followed, they are not 'best practice' or heuristics. They are stories to learn with, and should be read in this light. We therefore sometimes accompany a story with some questions that you might consider in relation to your own research.

We have avoided writing a how-to book, or a compendium of research tools. We wanted to write about research as we understand it and as we teach about it. Throughout the book we engage in some detail with the work of a few researchers. We are in conversation with their discussions of, and reflections on, their research. Our concern is to show the kinds of decisions that researchers make about their projects. You will quickly see these threads running across the book. At the end of Chapter 1, you will find a list of the texts we have used intensively. We also draw heavily, and we hope honestly, on our own work undertaken over the last twelve years. We have layered our research projects across the chapters. We have included an Appendix at the end of the book, which lists our projects, relevant websites and publications.

This book is written by two researchers living in England. This is not an unimportant matter. In England, when we use the term school, we do not mean university or college, as is often the case in the USA, even though many of the approaches we suggest could be modified for further and higher education. We usually call those who lead schools headteachers, not principals, as they are referred to in Australia. We talk about primary not elementary schools. We also talk about high schools and academies and sixth form colleges. Our very English use of terminology points to one of the characteristics of 'place' – places are associated with particular ways of naming things, and thus with the ways in which we think about the world. We chose not to try to develop an unplaced and generic approach to our text – for instance writing headteacher/principal all the time – understanding that this decision might mean that readers from outside 'our place' might sometimes have to think about an equivalent term used in their home territory. We hope that translating the language from one place to another is not too arduous a task.

You may want to read the book from start to finish. We conceived of the text as a whole. We do think that the book can be read in a linear fashion, but it can also, of course, be read in any order, as and when the questions that are covered match the reader's interests and needs. The book proceeds in this way:

Chapter one: Studying a school

This chapter asks you to consider the ways in which you think about the school that you want to study. It makes the case that a school is not an island, cut off from other schools, a black box only marginally affected by its context. A school is, we suggest, a place which is both patterned and unique. We offer some key theoretical tools that will be used throughout the book to shape a study of a school and show an extended example of what this kind of approach can achieve.

Chapter two: Getting into school

In this chapter we argue that it can be problematic to think of the school as a 'site' and focus on gaining 'access' to it. We propose that you think of setting up a relationship with the school, and adopting an appreciative, albeit still critical, stance towards it. We address how you might think about strategically selecting your school or schools, the kinds of concerns schools have about letting researchers 'in', the potential for difficult issues to arise, and ethical questions of anonymity and confidentiality. We also briefly discuss questions of **insider research**.

Chapter three: Getting to know the neighbourhood

We show how explorations of local place can be helpful in approaching a school. We use methods drawn from urban planning, community development, geography and demography to show how existing data and local investigations (walking around and windscreen surveys, for example) can be used to understand local histories, challenges and assets.

Chapter four: Reading the school

We demonstrate how websites and prospectuses, visual surveys, official data, **mapping** and student guided tours can be used to get an initial picture of the material, symbolic and social landscape of the school. We also discuss how this can be enhanced by examination of other artefacts such as timetables, organizational charts, budgets, minutes of meetings and annual reports.

Chapter five: Living with the school

We examine the issue of short-term versus longer-term engagement with schools and what can be gained from each. We consider the kinds of attitudes and orientations that are conducive to long-term relationships.

Chapter six: Multiple perspectives on the school

We discuss the importance of hanging about and chatting and consider the ways in which these can be recorded. We also consider some of the issues involved in using conventional research tools such as **interviews** and **focus groups.**

Chapter seven: Analysing complex data sets

We address the vexed issues involved in bringing diverse data together into one corpus, and consider the strategies that might be used to take first steps and to get a sense of the whole. We discuss the importance of arriving at the Big Idea about the school.

Chapter eight: Writing the school

We discuss questions of representation, audiences and the variety of texts that might be used to write about the school. We consider the range of dilemmas that can arise through the writing process. We argue that writing the school is integral to the kind of research relationship that is established and is an important part of the process of exit.

CHAPTER ONE

Studying a school

So you want to research a school. That sounds pretty straightforward. A school is a school is a school. Or is it?

In the spirit of 'making the familiar strange' we suggest that, before you plunge in, it is important to consciously reflect on what you think a school actually is. So we want to ask you, right at the start of our book and your project, to do a small mental exercise. We know it's not the way that books, especially research methods books, usually start. But humour us, just for a moment.

First of all we want you to think about the word 'school'. Who goes to school? What happens in a school? What images come to mind when you think of the word school?

The chances are that you have summoned up a general idea of children or young people, perhaps in uniform. They are likely to be in classrooms, perhaps sitting in rows. They are writing in exercise books or on paper, or reading from the board. Maybe the school building has long corridors which the students rush along in between lessons, banging into each other and their lockers as they go. Maybe there is a gym and a field outside; these are variously full and empty at specific times of the day. There are teachers too, standing at the front of the room, speaking – a lot. The teachers tell the students what to do and when to do it.

It hasn't been hard to summon up a generic image of a school. After all, we all know what a school is. We all went to one. Indeed. So now we want you to think about your school in particular. What comes to mind when you put the word 'my' in front of the words 'school'? What do you think of when you say the words 'my school' to yourself?

You will now be able to put specific details into the more general picture that you first thought of. The school you went to had a particular design. It was built in a particular period. There are some things about it that are memorable. Perhaps you recall a particular part of the school – the remote reaches of the field, the rabble of the changing rooms, the quiet of the library, the shade of the tree in the playground – that has special meaning for you. There are bound to be some specific people in your remembered school too – your best friends, teachers that were kind or comical or deeply eccentric, other students who were ' the cool' kids or the frightening ones you didn't want to meet on the way home. You might also remember particular events that happened while you were at school. The time when the teacher ...; the time that ...; oh and that day when ... Some of these moments might be very funny and still bring a smile to your face. Others will perhaps be sad, shaming, embarrassing. Not all of your school thoughts will be pleasant or pleasing. Some will bring back the feeling of being you, being at your school, as this memory does for the English food writer Nigel Slater:

> 'No, thank you,' I say to the tight-lipped prefect who is ladling great splodges of ivory-grey tapioca into shallow bowls and passing them round the table. 'I'm full.' Her eyes narrow and one corner of her mouth turns up. 'Sorry, you have to eat it, it's the rules.' The guy opposite me, who smells like digestive biscuits and I think lives on the council estate I am not allowed to go to, is wolfing down his down like it was warm treacle sponge or trifle, or maybe chocolate sponge pudding. But it's not. This is the most vile thing I have ever put in my mouth, like someone has stirred frog-spawn into wallpaper paste. Like porridge with bogeys in it. Like something an old man has hockled up into his hanky.
>
> When I get home I am going to tell Mum to write a note letting me off this stuff. The stew wasn't that bad, apart from the swedes which were bitter and something flabby that could have been fat but felt more like a big fat slug. I spread the spittle-coloured glue around my dish right up the side in the hope I will have to eat less of it. 'You must show me your bowls before you leave the table,' says Tight Lips. 'They must be clean, otherwise you'll be here all afternoon.'
>
> Considering we have an outdoor PE lesson this afternoon,

> staying in the warm, playing with a bowl of rice doesn't seem such a bad option. (Slater, 2003: 82–3)

Many of us have our equivalents of these moments: times when we feel out of place, times when we are bewildered. We have these moments as students, and as teachers too. These moments are pivotal and stay with us; they epitomize being there, in that school, in that place – and we know that they have helped make us who we are now. Whenever we think of such deeply charged events, they always occur somewhere, and where matters.

The point of this exercise is to show the differences between thinking about a school as a generic entity, and thinking in particular about your own experiences. These differences are not simply in the level of detail – when we think of 'my school' we are able to imagine a place that we know, and describe its actual physical features rather than produce something that is generalized. The differences are also in the life and meaning and emotions that are associated with our own experiences. When we think about our own school and our own schooling, we bring specificity, particularity and complexity to the near-universal experience of being in school, of being educated. Neither of these two imaginings is wrong. There *are* things about schools which are the same, just as there are things about all of them that are distinctive.

Schools and schooling

When you think about 'the school' at first, the chances are that you will think generally. This means that the students may be more regimented, the classrooms less or more disciplined, the buildings older, the lessons less varied and more text-based than many actually are. When we think less specifically about schools, we often produce a kind of archetype. This is not unusual. When Sandra Weber and Claudia Mitchell (1995) asked children to draw a teacher and a classroom, all of them produced pictures of rows of desks with teachers standing at the front, even though this was not their actual situation. Your imaginary teachers and students may be similarly 'typical', even stereotypical – teachers may be more caustic, more domineering, more like Miss Trunchbull than Miss Honey (Dahl, 1989), more Dolores Umbridge than Dumbledore (Rowling, 2003).

Producing this kind of generalized picture is not necessarily a problem. In these archetypical/stereotypical imaginings there are significant truths – the institutional nature of schooling, the dominance of particular transmission patterns of teaching and learning, the ongoing monitoring of student behaviour, the division of the day into lessons and the necessary transitions between them. There is something very recognizable about schooling, regardless of what part of the world you are in. You can usually tell a school building: it is set apart from neighbouring housing and often fenced off; it is large and surrounded by both space for parking and (usually) green space. Students may or may not be uniformed, but they will arrive in the morning and leave in the afternoon en masse, and in between times will be largely confined to the school environs. Their day will be organized as 'chunks' of time and space. They will move between designated learning spaces, classrooms, specialist rooms and the outside areas at predetermined times. Learning largely involves cerebral work, encountering knowledge in spoken and written forms, with some time given to more active forms of knowing, such as making and moving.

We could go on, but you get the picture. After all, you imagined this when we suggested you think of 'the school'.

By contrast, when we asked you to think about 'my school', our hunch is that you focused on the particular ways in which your own experience sat within these overall institutional patterns. That is to be expected. When memories are put into words and communicated, it is both the similarities and singularities that are important. Nigel Slater's story of his experience of school dinner works for us as readers because we too have experienced less than appetizing institutional food, we have known a prefect-figure who was unreasonable and self-important, we have faced a lesson that we didn't want to do and where punishment seems a preferable alternative. Slater's account depends on our understanding of the general in order to appreciate its specific details.

This book addresses exactly this sense of individual difference loaded with meaning, of singularity existing within commonality. However, schools are very often talked about in general terms.

These days, policymakers nearly always address schools as generic institutions (Sahlberg, 2012). Their concern is to improve the ways in which schools, as a conglomerate, support students to learn the designated curriculum. The focus is on those schools that do worse than the average, and particularly on those at the bottom of the systemic bell curve. In some countries, targets for system improvement are set, and a range of incentives and punishments are meted out through the regular rhythm of inspections, tests and exams. Individual schools *are* singled out in this kind of policy regime – those that do very well are hailed as the epitome of the good (generic) school, and held up as examples of what all other schools should become. Schools at the bottom are named and shamed; they are too far from the universal norm and have done too little to make themselves like all of the rest. Their very difference is a problem; it is assumed that they should be more like other schools.

Educational research literatures also often address schools as generic entities in a system or as aggregates of shared characteristics. We might think here of research that discusses 'effective' schools in order to identify the common characteristics of schools where students' tested learning is deemed superior to others (Teddlie and Reynolds, 2000); or school improvement, where the focus is on the strategies that effective schools use in order to better students' learning, teacher performance and leadership quality (Hopkins et al., 1994). We can easily think of, for example, meta-studies which discuss the relative benefits of various classroom strategies (e.g. Hattie, 2008), the 'right' approaches to teacher professional development (e.g. Cordingley, 2005) and large-scale studies which attribute success to particular types of leadership behaviours (e.g. Leithwood et al., 2006).

Ironically, some of these studies are based on research designs which position schools as islands, so that the ways in which individual schools are connected, even in highly devolved systems, are left out of the scope of the inquiry. Such studies may ignore the ways in which schools are linked together, say for example through enrolment policies which pit one school against another in reputational competitions which are both produced and reproduced through the workings of residential housing markets (Gorard et al., 2003). **Case studies** and **ethnographies** also often treat their study site as discrete entities. But, as Jan Nespor (2002) argues, seeing the school as a separate thing unto itself reduces the capacity of researchers to understand the detailed lives that they seek to examine. He suggests that drawing the boundaries tightly around 'the school' as the object of study

> ... allows social and economic problems to be re-territorialized as 'school problems,' deflects attention from the role of the state and the corporate sector in shaping educational possibilities, and generates an image of children as partial beings understandable in terms of their narrowly defined, school-inscribed attributes.

Nespor argues that the boundaries around individual schools create 'abstract pupils':

> that is the deletion of everything kids do outside school: their activities with friends, family life, engagements with entertainment media and popular culture, paid and unpaid work, religious participation, sports, activity in the arts, the neighborhood organizations they belong to; the public spaces they have access to or appropriate, their friendship networks and peer groups, and on and on. (p. 484)

This lacuna is ironic in ethnographic and case study research, Nespor notes, as this kind of abstraction is exactly the same as that accomplished by government policies that see students only in terms of narrow educational outcome, attendance and exclusion data.

However, other educational research, often smaller in scale, sees the school differently. It tells another story. Case studies and ethnographies of schools *can* show difference that is patterned in ways that connect the school and its teachers and students to a larger world. There are, for example, studies which document the variable take-up of policies in different schools and their different results (Ball et al., 2011a; Thomson, 2002; Tittle, 1995). This differential adoption and adaptation of policy is not because the staff or the leadership team at the school are underperforming or wilful, cut from an 'ineffective' cooker-cutter mould. Rather, variable school policy take-up and enactment result from the complex interactions and dynamics of different school populations – the 'school mix' (Thrupp, 1999), the different resources that the schools have at their disposal, the stability or instability of staff, the demands and expectations of the local community, the state of the buildings and equipment, the serendipity of misfortune, even the history of the particular school system. All of these things affect the ways in which policies are able to be implemented and the ways in which schools are variously able to make a difference in student learning (Thomson, 2000).

Our interest in this book is in understanding how to find, understand and work with these differences, to make sense of the particularities of individual schools and to comprehend why they do what they do. To acknowledge and understand these kinds of differences is not to make excuses for schools, as some policy-makers and educational researchers suggest. Rather, it is to enter into the ways that the people in the school make sense of where they are, and to recognize the kinds of spatial, temporal, material and discursive processes that shape the school world.

Why? Why should educational researchers attempt to grasp a school at this level of detail? The first answer to this question goes to the ways in which the research knowledge that we generate might be used. It is only on the back of specific understandings, we suggest, that appropriate support and development can be provided. Generic support or interventions are not nearly as acceptable or effective as those which are bespoke to the actual school and people. The importance of local circumstances, context and detail is something that all good consultants and district advisers know is crucial to their work.

But there is another reason for wanting to understand a school in detail. We can only really understand what is common to all schools, no matter where they are and who is in them, if we also deliberately seek out what is special and unique to each of them. Rather than attempting to statistically remove difference, or to thematize it out of existence, we argue that it is important for researchers to find approaches that simultaneously allow them to see both the bigger picture and the small one.

Pauline Lipman's (1998) *Race, Class, and Power in School Restructuring*, a place-based study of two low achieving junior high schools in a southern city in the USA, illustrates the importance of understanding both **history** and local nuance. Lipman argues and shows through her book that what happens in her two study schools cannot be understood without a knowledge of the history of US schooling, the push for desegregation and the history of mandatory desegregation within the broader locality. Each school in the district she studied had experienced the move to desegregation differently, and they served different populations who were differently and differentially affected.

One of Lipman's research schools, Gates, served a solidly middle-class and working-class population, had a good reputation in the district and did well in standardized achievement tests. The other school, Franklin, which served a low-income, predominantly African-American population, had a 'checkered past' and a somewhat tarnished reputation. Lipman followed both schools through a compulsory district restructuring programme: she carefully traced and analysed the dissimilar effects in each of the two schools. The end result of the restructuring programme was that both schools emerged with their reputations in the same relative position, and without achieving the desired improvements in the learning of the poorest, largely African-American, students. However, the district and parents saw these results in another light, as Lipman explains:

> At both schools, the concern was with formal and superficial signs of integration, not racism and inequality. At Franklin, educators directed their attention to visible signs of racial balance, while critiques of racism and talk about race were silenced. I witnessed Franklin being viewed with alarm in the district because it was becoming overwhelmingly African American (segregated) rather than because of the students' poor educational outcomes. On the other hand, at Gates, despite dramatic racial disparities in academic achievement and discipline, teachers voiced satisfaction with their school because excellence (as they saw it) was maintained for a sizeable proportion of those students who are at the centre of Gates. Physically, African Americans were in the building, though few were part of it. (pp. 289–90)

Lipman's book carefully unpacks why district policy and the difficult history of desegregation combined with local sites and their people and practices to replicate the existing status quo. Readers might well conclude that, had the school district not treated all of its schools as if they were the same, and instead offered tailored support and interventions, something other than this depressing and inequitable result might have been possible.

Lipman's study has what we call an 'eagle's eye view'. She is able to keep one eye on the horizon and the other focused on the life between the blades of grass. She places the particularities of each of her two study schools in the context of their district and in larger social, economic, cultural and political frames. Her study is also firmly anchored in time: she provides an **historical analysis** which explains why the schools in the city were established to serve both particular neighbourhoods and local and national political concerns. This layered view of schooling is what we aim to do too, in our own research. And, in this book, we offer a range of research strategies that you can use to achieve a view of schools that has the same kind of global/local resolution.

The notion of 'place' captures the idea of a school that is one of a kind, simultaneously both patterned and distinctive. Place, we argue and will show in this book, is a very helpful lens through which to examine schools. Our first step is to begin to consider the theoretical resources we can use to conceptualize and theorize place. We then conclude the chapter by showing some more of what a place-based analysis can reveal.

What is 'place'?

We frequently use the notion of place. We have 'our favourite places', we feel 'out of place', we have a 'place' in the world. We can think of place as being as small as a chair in a room – this is my place to sit each night – or as large as a part of the world which is 'my place'. We have a 'sense of place'. Place can be intimate, public, manufactured or natural. However, when we attempt to pin down the meaning of the word 'place', it becomes elusive and somewhat obscure.

One thing that holds these various uses of place together is that place is something that we experience. It is something we make meaningful and particular (Tuan, 1977/2011). The meaning that people attribute to a particular place is often understood and expressed as an aspect of 'identity' – I am Australian, I am from Yorkshire, I'm an Icelander. Who we are is associated with where we are, or where we have come from. In making a place-identity claim, a person is asserting that there are particular collective practices – perhaps a way of speaking, common approaches to and beliefs about the world, experiences in common, shared history – associated with a place. Such notions are often subject to bitter contestation: see, for example, the struggles in South Africa about what it means to be part (or not) of that nation-state (e.g. Dixon and Durrheim, 2000) and that of various postcolonial societies developing their own states and communities (e.g. Lewicka, 2008).

In Aboriginal communities, attachment to place is much more than identity; it is a cosmological system which encompasses the relationship between land and the life that depends on it. Belonging to country is crucial for sustaining Indigenous societies. The long battle for land rights is much more than a legal debate about ownership: it is also profoundly ontological – it is about a way of being in the world, being in and of your place (Tuck and McKenzie, 2015).

According to Tim Cresswell (2004), place is a way of understanding the world. Cresswell suggests that place can be understood in five ways:

1 A material location. A school has a specific site and a particular address, on a street, in a suburb or city or village or field. We can **map** the dimensions of this location and the school's size and built environment relative to other sites that are adjacent or far away. We address these issues in Chapter 3.
2 A locale. The implications of thinking of the materiality of the school also allow us to consider the implications of its surroundings. What does it mean for the school to be there, in that place? What kind of location is this – rich, poor, tree-lined, deindustrialized, on traditional lands, a newly built estate – and what does this mean for the school? Do the students come from nearby or do they travel to this site from far away? If they are nearby, what does the neighbourhood surrounding this place have to offer them in terms of jobs, services, facilities? How did this locale get to be like this? We take these questions up in detail in Chapter 3.

3 A sense of place. What does the school mean to the people who are in it? How do they understand and experience everyday life? What are the expectations of those working there? What kinds of emotional attachments to the place are held by different school members? What language is used to describe it, officially and unofficially? We canvass ways to research these questions in Chapter 6.

4 Spatiality. Space is a more abstract notion than place. Space is relational. We share various kinds of spaces with people, institutions, networks, imagined others, trees and animals, objects, air and water. Geographers think of space/time working together. A place can thus be thought of as a stop within space/time (Tuan, 1977/2011), but this stop is not static. A place can be seen as being in movement through time, having a history, a present and a future which are interconnected and mutually productive. Understanding the school as historically situated is important, and we offer some strategies for achieving this view through Chapters 3, 4, 5 and 6.

5 Landscape. A landscape is something we look at rather than inhabit. The view of land as a material topography is relevant to schooling if we think about the ways in which the school is seen as part, or not part, of a landscape, or if we consider the aesthetics of the views that students might have out of a classroom window, or within the school itself. We cover this in Chapter 4.

We use these five understandings of place throughout the book. But Cresswell's are not the only ideas about place that are useful to educational researchers.

When we think of place we usually think of something bounded, something defined, something with edges. Here is my place, there is not. The feminist geographer Doreen Massey offers important counterpoints to common-sense understandings of place, arguing that (1) places are not discrete territories, (2) places are not equal, and (3) places are 'thrown together'. Massey argues that:

1 Places are not discrete territories, but are sites entangled in what she calls 'stretched out relations'. Rather than being confined to one small site, the relations in a site

and between the people and 'things' within/on it extend beyond the material location. People, objects and the site itself are situated in multiple, diverse flows and interconnections.

We can use this idea to help us better understand the school and its connections with other places, people and things. The school is part of a school system and is thus engaged with local and national governments. Policies, resources and interactions flow between the school staff and head office. There are multiple vertical interconnections between the school and head office and there are horizontal connections between the school and other schools and organizations. The school is not an island, cut off from its surrounds, but has many diverse relations within the education system.

From this perspective we can reject a notion of the district and the system as Russian doll style containers within which the school sits. There are complex relations between all layers of the system. The actions taken in local and national offices, enshrined as policy and administrative guidelines, have to be both translated and enacted at the school level. This is a mediated interaction. Each school, depending on its specific relations in space/time, may interpret and 'do' the same policy slightly differently. We might say that, rather than policy simply being a top-down and one-way affair, it is also bottom dependent – head office *needs* the local school in order to actually *do* anything.

Similarly, through the stretched out relations of national testing the school is also taken into the relations of international educational governance. Put another way, the global push for international student achievement comparisons not only shapes, but also depends upon, the school's actions. We can say that the global is thus not opposed to the local but that they are actually woven together in a trajectory of activity. The global can be said to be *in* the local; global actions often take place at the local level.

The temporality of the stretched out perspective of place also allows us to avoid assuming that schools are the same everywhere. School systems around the world are very different, in part because of the ways in which they were established and have been governed over time. Schoolteachers and policymakers in Scotland for instance claim that their approach to education is different from that of England; they trace their more inclusive and holistic national system back to the Enlightenment. Thus, what counts now as an *effective* school is both differently nuanced and perhaps more possible in Scotland than in England; enacting a generic global benchmark of effectiveness will mean very different things at national, district and individual school level in each country.

Understanding a school as entangled in stretched out relations disrupts the idea that the neighbourhood is simply the container, or stable unmoving context, for the school. Using the notion of stretched out relations, we can see that students, teachers and the curriculum are engaged in flows and interactions with various communities in and beyond their own and the school neighbourhood. The school gate and fence might be material barriers, but they do not prevent stretched out social relations of various and often incommensurate kinds. The school is porous and permeable, and connected to other places, things, people and times.

2 Places are not equal. They are differently positioned through what Massey calls a 'power geometry' (Massey, 1994). A place is shaped by historical and contemporary distributions of resources – both material and discursive. Some places are wealthier than others, some have higher status, some have both wealth and status. Massey argues that what happens in a place, the actions and interactions that are possible there, are shaped by its particular power geometries. How residents of a place can live their lives depends on the wider historically situated social relations of class, gender, race and dis/ability. As Massey explains:

> [A]ny 'place' (which may be a nation, a region, a city, ...) can be imagined as a unique node, or constellation,

> of social relations. Moreover, since power is constitutive of the social, these social relations are power relations.

Massey argues that it is a mistake to think of places subject to the same social phenomena as being positioned equally:

> I think it is most common in our political imaginaries to understand 'places' as the *product* of the operation of globalising forces. The place is seen in this way as an outcome; it is also often seen as a victim. From the local place one might fight to resist the wider global forces.
>
> However, the point about thinking in terms of power-geometries is that places are *differentially* located within those geometries. Chad is in a very different position from the UK; Oldham in a very different position from London. And in thinking in this way of the UK and London, in these two comparisons, it becomes evident that it is inadequate simply to analyse all places as 'victims' (on the receiving end) of globalisation, for some of them are also the loci of the *production* of globalisation. This is especially important to note when those places are powerful nodes within global geometries. (http://www.signsofthetimes.org.uk/massey[textonly].html (accessed 27 February 2016)

Applying power-geometry thinking to schools means considering that they are not all equal. It is to consider the power geometries at work between – and within – them. The school and its people are not simply acted upon; they also have the capacity to act. However, they act variously, according to who they are, where they are from, what they know, their formal position and so on. To make this concrete, consider national testing and inspection regimes. Using Massey's power-geometry conceptualization would lead us to think about the various ways in which schools are located within the social relations of audit, and to ask questions about whether some schools are victims and others are complicit in the (re)production of hierarchies.

The understanding that all schools are not the same is often (but not always) lacking from school effectiveness and improvement research, which can assume that all schools are equally placed within the various flows and interconnections they have to national government.

3 Places are 'thrown together'. In saying this, Massey means both that a place is not planned and rational, but is the result of ongoing processes of arrival, departure, disruption and intervention. A place, Massey argues, can be thought of not as a thing, but as a constellation of processes that have happened over time/space. Place can be understood as a 'coming together' of trajectories. Place is thus unique, but it is also always unpredictable. As Massey puts it, 'There can be no assumption of a pre-given coherence, or of community or collective identity' (Massey, 2005, p. 141).

   Furthermore, Massey suggests, we must recognize that a place is open, internally multiple and incoherent. The messiness of place, its arbitrariness and its continuing unpredictability means that, within a place, people are always working out what the place is, what is going on there and how they might live in and with it. Massey notes that 'the thrown-togetherness of place demands negotiation ... Being together in a place is a process, and one which requires consistent management and often conscious reflection.' What is at issue in a place, Massey contends, are the 'terms of engagement of those trajectories' (pp. 141–2).

If we think of the school as thrown together, we understand it as neither static nor rational, but rather as something much more organic. We also see it as constantly changing, and as being subject to chance and serendipity, albeit operating within particular logics and frames. Using this lens, we can understand school decision-making as the negotiation of a set of particular circumstances, people and things and as historically and spatio-temporally situated, rather than a rational choice process carried out in experimental laboratory conditions. We can see a school deciding to become an academy or charter school as a highly complex mediation of various flows and interactions. Whatever decision is made will be contingent not only on centralized policy pressures, but also upon the particular thrown-togetherness in that particular place. As Massey has it, in such a decision '[t]he combination of order and chance, intrinsic to space and here encapsulated as material place, is crucial' (p. 151).

The above conceptions of place can inform the practice of educational research, as we will show throughout this book. Before we begin this task, however, we want to illustrate what this kind of approach actually allows a researcher to see and say differently. We have already referred to the work of Pauline Lipman, and here we want to give a more elaborated example. It comes from Pat's doctoral research, which was a study of 20 disadvantaged schools in South Australia (Thomson, 1999, 2000; see also Thomson, 2002). Here, the 'I' in the paper refers to Pat, one of the authors of this book.

A place-based approach to understanding schools

Pat's doctoral study was about a moment in Australian education when the government decided to abolish funding specifically for schools with large concentrations of students living in poverty. It was perhaps *the* moment when the emphasis shifted to focus only on 'internal' school issues, when the notion that what was outside the school didn't matter took hold. The performance of schools was to be compared; recognition of their differences was to be achieved through the development of an index of 'like schools'. 'Like' schools were those that had statistically similar student populations. As a headteacher, Pat was worried about this as she had been a leader in three schools that would apparently be taken as the same, but actually were very different. Her experience suggested that those differences could lead to very different student learning outcomes. Her research explored the possibilities of locating and mapping some of those things that might make apparently 'like schools' the 'same, but also unique'.

The study was focused on the northern and western suburbs of Adelaide, South Australia, a region that bore the brunt of 'structural adjustment'. The wholesale exodus of the footwear and textile industry, the tenuous life of the auto-passenger industry, massive job-shedding in both the state and national public sector, slowed population growth and low rates of immigration all combined with the planned concentration of low income housing suburbs to produce a 'polarised city' (Badcock, 1997; Baum and Hassan, 1993; Hamnett and Freestone, 2000; Peel, 1995). Pat's research concentrated on how these social, economic, political and cultural changes played out in state schools and their neighbourhoods.

The empirical research consisted of a corpus of taped conversations with school administrators, youth and welfare workers, photographic observations and an investigation of public collections of educational, demographic, labour market and welfare data. She situated this work in the complex history of Australian schooling, the changing role of the Commonwealth in relation to states, and the very particular configurations of, and histories of debates about, public and private schooling.

> At the completion of my fieldwork, I was faced with a morass of particularity and specificity that also showed some evidence of the patterning I had expected. There was a common story of inadequate funding, escalating welfare and disciplinary demands and an unsympathetic policy milieu. But, scattered throughout the transcripts were stories of events and issues that school administrators claimed were not only important, but also particular to their neighbourhood and/or school. The ways in which particular social relations and practices, the locality, systemic policy and the constellation of individuals and histories coalesced in the institution of the school, all seemed to be important.
>
> The first clue I found to making sense of the pattern(s) and differences among schools and neighbourhoods came from the words of the school administrators. Whenever I listened to the tapes that constituted my research evidence, I heard, 'This school ... These kids ... This community ...' My working title for the particularity towards which I was being directed was 'thisness'. The somewhat foolish label stuck, and it seemed to make sense to the school administrators on whose words it was based. My research suggested that the capacity of 'disadvantaged schools' to make a positive difference in students' learning *is* context dependent. How this happens can be glimpsed by considering 'thisness'. 'Thisness' is about the specificity of place, and how it is that local action is framed and limited by flows of people, information and things, and by connections beyond the school gates.

The research produced three major categories of neighbourhood contexts (i.e. the local workings out of larger global, national and state processes) that had an impact on what it was that school staff could, and did, do. These were: (1) the school mix, (2) neighbourhood resources and (3) neighbourhood issues. I will spend most time discussing the school mix question, and only briefly indicate some of the issues that arise in the latter two categories.

1 School mix

Each school population was different. Students and their families in 'disadvantaged schools' in the northern and western suburbs were variously affected by:

- *Patterns of migration and diaspora*
  Several of the schools served neighbourhoods in which there were continuing intakes of refugees fleeing intolerable political situations. Others served more established populations of immigrants. All reported significant shortfalls in the community services available to children and families, and increased pressure on the school to step in as a result. Cuts in interpreter and translation services were matched by cuts in English provision for adult migrants, all of which required children to act as family interpreters. Schools in which there were significant Aboriginal populations did receive some support, but all commented bitterly on the lack of fit between the quantum of resources and community need.
- *Changes in the labour market*
  Family unemployment/under-employment/tenuous employment (the local working out of macro- and microeconomic reform) played out in schools in a range of ways – for example, many students had no money for educational expenses; some children were the only ones in their household who had to get up regularly everyday and frequently didn't; some parents showed acute levels of anxiety manifested in health problems and angry outbursts in schools. Secondary schools reported that there were large numbers of young people who firmly

believed that they would not find any work at all, and that they saw little point in compliance or application. This produced significant 'behaviour' problems, which were not addressed by vocational programmes in which the students had no faith. There was also another group who were unrealistically confident that they would easily slip into a chosen career. Earlier cohorts of this group were regular and disillusioned visitors to schools, urging their younger counterparts to join them in the mall. Many young people got part-time work as soon as they could and these wages were often a necessary addition to the family income; casual work requirements of employers however often conflicted with homework, and regular attendance requirements.

- *Changes in public policy*
  The increased costs and reduction in public services that comprise the 'social wage' (viz. health, public housing and public transport) affected families and their schools. Many schools reported escalating waiting periods for referral services, particularly for depressed and substance abusing adolescents, the de-funding of local employment and family counselling services and the mounting pressure on charities to assist. One school had to hold parents' meetings straight after school because the bus service no longer ran after six in the evening. Another school catering for adult re-entry students reported increased demand for short-term financial assistance for medical and housing expenses. Several schools reported substantive numbers of children requiring 'free' lunch from the school canteen. Several schools in public housing estates being redeveloped or slated for redevelopment were dealing with children who faced the prospect of their family home being demolished, not knowing where they would be living.
- *Demography – changes in families*
  The increases in the numbers of diverse families (described in policy as separated, blended and re-blended, and extended families), many of whom were dependent on income support transfers, particularly

those for lone parents and those designated to the 'working poor' with young children, were manifest in schools. Schools believed that significant numbers of children appeared to be dealing with the pressures of living in domestic situations which were not only unstable but also strained from financial worries. Schools reported regular incidences of 'midnight flits', 'staying with grandma' and children moving between family members. Transience and children exhibiting evidence of considerable insecurity and anxiety required regular time away from instruction, and involved classroom teachers and administrators alike.

- *Concentration of families in crisis*

  While all schools reported that the number of families under pressure had increased, some were particularly affected. One school reported unusually high numbers of children with sick and dying parents – it was next to a public hospital. A couple of schools were located next to women's shelters and an ever-changing parade of traumatized children came and went. Schools in the areas of highest unemployment also seemed to be the locations where there was emergency public housing and they dealt daily with children and parents at the end of their tether. It is important to note that these schools got no extra support in recognition of these very particular issues, and in at least three of the schools it was often as much as they could do to 'keep a lid on' the situation.

In a few schools many of these factors came together. There were three schools in the group I studied who had extraordinarily high levels of student transience – more than forty per cent of their school population came and went during the year. In a school of two hundred this amounts to eighty additional children coming and going. One of these schools had to completely reorganize its classes twice during one year. This effectively put paid to the establishment of those close teacher–student relationships that are at the heart of good teaching. In one year teachers worked with classes that went from overcrowded to small and back again. Much of their time was devoted to helping children settle in and trying to find out the extent of their formal learning. Schools affected by high transience spent funds supplying books and equipment for more children than they were funded for. Global budgets that are allocated on the basis of average enrolments are grim jokes in these schools, where staff argue that seeking recognition of their material reality is not an excuse, but a simple matter of justice.

All schools had different school mixes, different combinations of these embodied neighbourhood effects that made specific, time consuming and often unrecognized demands on staff, curriculum and time.

2 Resources available to the school in the neighbourhood

The capacity of each school to run the mandated as well as desirable co-curricular programmes and provide equally and equitably for students was tied to neighbourhood resources. The following were important:

- *Employment and employment networks*

  Schools depended on numbers of small, medium and large businesses to provide not only jobs for parents and school leavers, but also work placements and mentoring for students and civic leadership in the local area. Such businesses also made contributions to the micro-economy through local purchasing arrangements, creating more work opportunities as they did so. The long-term downturn of manufacturing and small business in the western and northern suburbs of the city meant that local schools were variously able to offer such networks and opportunities to students.

- *Community infrastructure*

  Schools and students relied on local health and welfare services, public library provision, neighbourhood houses, youth services, migrant support programmes, recreation facilities and organizations, and public transport. These are part of the neighbourhood assets (McKnight, 1995) that not only support learning in and out of school but also general well-being. In neighbourhoods made poor, many of these services were routinely underfunded, and many had been rationalized, regionalized and cut back. The cultural and social capital available in poor neighbourhoods varied according to locations, with newly established localities by far the worst off.

- *Age of locality – age of school facilities*

  Because schools are generally built to coincide with the establishment of a particular suburb, there were numbers of postwar schools in desperate need of renovation, unable to compete with newly furbished, government-funded, low fee non-government schools. They were also unable to provide the same levels of learning support as those in more wealthy localities where parental contributions and School Council 'clout' resulted in better facilities. In a few locations, school plant was hopelessly out-dated: one school in the study could not operate its small bank of computers at the same time as the air conditioning, for fear of complete power failure.

- *Parent fundraising*

  The differences in resources available to schools who can and do ask parents to contribute A$400 per annum and those who can and do ask for A$150 and often don't get it, seems obvious to everybody except policymakers. Lack of funds caused numbers of secondary schools to reduce practical activities in home economics and technical studies, and all 'disadvantaged schools' found excursions and school sporting programmes increasingly difficult to maintain.

- *Availability of voluntary labour*

  The addition of unpaid voluntary labour can make significant differences in school programmes. On the one hand, in areas where there were high numbers of parents engaged in shift and casual work, schools found it impossible to engage parents in school activities. On the other hand, some poor schools did have numbers of under-employed parents demanding adult and community education, rather than the more conventional parental involvement. Such programmes rely on specifically argued for government largesse, since they were not seen as 'core business', even though parent re-schooling can have powerful positive impacts on their children.

The study suggested that schools in more established locations in the western suburbs that were close to regional centres and adjacent to gentrified suburbs were able to marshal a greater range of resources, networks and services. Even if on the surface they were identical in socio-economic composition to schools in outlying and newer areas, the actual locality did make a difference.

3 Neighbourhood issues that impacted on the school

There were unique local events that impacted on specific schools. Some of these could not be foreseen, whereas others seemed more predictable. Each such event consumed a school's energy and time for considerable periods, making it very difficult to concentrate first and foremost on instruction. These idiosyncratic events often related to:

- *History*

  The place of the school in the regional hierarchy produced long-term patterns of enrolment and expectations that were hard to disrupt. Only very concerted and expensive public relations and image management could rapidly make inroads into the local 'grapevine' and many schools were not willing to devote time and energy to this, as opposed to spending time and energy on more substantive learning issues.

- *Neighbourhood change*

  Increasing or declining enrolment in schools is a direct consequence of the age of the neighbourhood and its birth rate, but this can be compounded by the impact of school choice policies. In this study, there was evidence of the long decline of schools under constant review, which played out in a politics of 'voice and exit' (Hirschman, 1970) that profoundly embittered teachers and families. Areas scheduled for redevelopment, changes in demographics, external review, and possible closure, all created anxiety and uncertainty which not only affected enrolments but also the capacity and willingness of the school to plan ahead. Commonwealth initiatives to fund low-fee private schools in working class suburbs in addition to those in the city and more middle class neighbourhoods produced ongoing competition for students.

- *Neighbourhood factions*

  There were a few incidents of local racist gang activity and attacks that spilled over into harassment and fights in particular schools. There were also schools in which a spate of lighting fires and vandalism took whole blocks of classrooms out of operation, destroying years of teacher resources and a year of students' work. Such events profoundly disrupted the smooth flow of learning. The disputes between families in particular houses in particular streets could also spill over into nearby schools.

The issues listed above (and others) came together in specific ways and constituted important aspects of thrown-togetherness. Imagine a school with high transience, in an area slated for redevelopment, with low standing on the local grapevine, that then experiences a significant fire. Imagine another school in an area of high chronic unemployment, with a significant and politically active Indigenous population, ageing buildings, and a rapidly diminishing set of public agencies and infrastructure around them. Imagine a school with a poor but stable population, in an area recently redeveloped, close to the city. These are some of the differences that sit behind the notion of 'like' schools. What can be done and what needs to be done are very different in each of these circumstances, and the schools need different kinds of support. What is important, however, is that none of these matters beyond public policy at the time – or indeed now. Combinations of labour market, health, housing, social welfare and transport policies can make quite an impact on a number of these issues, and consequently change things for the better in so-called 'disadvantaged schools'.

There were, however, also patterns that were institutional in nature, that delimited what these schools could do. Unlike their specific neighbourhood places, these were issues directly amenable to intervention through educational policy – and indeed were also often directly caused by educational policymaking. The capacity to effect change in 'disadvantaged' schools is dependent on the actions of mediating actors. In addition to those students and parents who walk in through the gate, the embodied neighbourhood, there are also the school staff. The number of staff is of course a key issue, and South Australian school administrators are quick to point to research from the United States (Achilles, 1999; Achilles et al., 1997) about the positive impact of reduced class sizes in 'disadvantaged' schools. Other resources such as funding and provision of information technologies are important too, but there are specific variations that, even in an inadequate resourcing situation, still make differences amongst disadvantaged schools, and contribute to 'thisness'.

In public education systems, even those that are devolved, there are systemic policies that shape and frame what it is that the schools can do. In my study these included: staffing turbulence and turnover; staffing 'fit' with the school; the nature and type of system-based professional development and support on offer to teachers; budgetary allocations and the additional amounts allowed for the extra demands of working with children and young people with troubled lives; the official discourse of equity and social justice, and how holistic, instrumental or welfarist it was; support for school recruitment of staff; and support for participatory decision-making with teachers, families and the community.

In this doctoral research Pat came to understand the school as a local place which had various capacities to make the local count. Drawing on Appadurai (1996), she argued that the contemporary nation-state was stripping local places of their capacity to make their own context. In schooling, this could be seen in the processes of centralization and in the ways in which schools were positioned as an identical mass whose overall performance was useful to the standing of the nation as a signifier of status in a globalized economy. Appadurai suggests that the neighbourhood (and places within neighbourhoods, places such as schools) can be thought of as simultaneously 'context derived' and 'context generative'. He proposes that:

> ... the very capability [of neighbourhoods] to produce contexts (within which their localising activities acquire meanings and historical potential) and to produce local subjects, are profoundly affected by the locality-producing capabilities of larger scale formations (nation-states, kingdoms, missionary empires, and traditional cartels) to determine the general shape of all the neighbourhoods within reach of their powers. (p. 186)

While at first sight 'neighbourhoods seem paradoxical because they both constitute and require contexts' (p. 186), Appadurai argues that the capacity of a place/school to make a difference (to generate context) is completely imbricated with context dependent factors, mediated by the actions of local subjects. This capacity is something for school researchers to investigate.

This is not, of course, a complete list of issues facing local schools. It was the set that came to Pat's notice as she looked at the evidence from certain schools and neighbourhoods in one Australian city, the 'thisness' of that particular context and time. What is important about the list, though, is its approach. Examining the particularity and patterning of a school as a place suggests that the capacity to deal with the everyday demands of managing unequal relations, the capacity to take on systemic reform policy and the adoption of the principles of doing justice *are shaped and delimited* by neighbourhood *and* system. This is a perspective lacking from much of the research which focuses on the school as generic. It is also a perspective missing in research which simply sees the school as singular. Place-based methods allowed both the generic and the particular to be seen and understood, and the complex interactions between the two to be tracked, in order to show the different ways in which schools cope, struggle and flourish.

'Thisness' is just one take on place-based methods. We don't want you to assume that Pat's set of categories are the ones that *you* will find, or that her approach to field-work is the only one possible. You will find your own ways to research and analyse your data. In order to help you, we will introduce you throughout this book to more ways to research the school as a 'place'. All of these approaches, however, will combine the 'eagle's eye' and 'up close' view that we argued was important at the beginning of this chapter.

A final note

This chapter offers a different take on the school. We have argued, unlike a lot of educational research and policy, that schools are both the same and different. Their patterning and singularities can be understood by taking a place-based approach. Seeing schools as being engaged in stretched out social relations in space/time, as unequal and different from each other and as messy and highly contingent is, we suggest, the way to go.

Further reading

You may want to follow up and read some place-based studies at this point to see the range of different approaches and accounts that are used. While not all about school, the following are good places to start.

Clift Gore, Elaine (2007). *Talent Knows No Colour: The History of an Arts Magnet High School*. Charlotte, NC: Information Age Publishing.

An historical study spanning thirty-five years of one public school for the arts. It has a short but pointed discussion on the use and limitations of archival data to understand school as place.

Corbett, Michael (2008). *Learning to Leave: The Irony of Schooling in a Coastal Community*. Toronto: Fernwood Publishing.

A study of young people in a part of one Canadian province. The book is not about a school per se, but about education in a larger place with a rapidly changing local economy.

Hall, Julia (2001). *Canal Town Youth: Community Organisation and the Development of Adolescent Identity*. Albany: State University of New York Press.

A study focused on young people in a specific deindustrializing neighbourhood, interesting in particular for Hall's decision to find out about school by observing and talking to young people in a youth centre.

Kenway, Jane, Anna Hickey-Moody and Anna Kraack (2006). *Masculinity Beyond the Metropolis*. London: Palgrave.

A multi-sited **ethnography** which shows how the patterned particularities of place position young men seeking employment in hard times.

Parsons, Carl (2012). *Schooling the Estate Kids*. Rotterdam: Sense Publishers.

An historical case study which uses documents, personal association and oral histories to trace the entwined fates of a school and its students.

Thomson, Pat (2002). *Schooling the Rustbelt Kids: Making the Difference in Changing Times*. Sydney: Allen & Unwin.

A study of schools across two regions of an Australian city which shows 'thisness' at work.

Books and papers we have used in this text

Throughout this book we are in conversation with a small group of researchers whose work either involves the use of place-based methods, intensive engagement with a school, or both. Rather than repeatedly list these researchers and their texts, we have put them here, at the start of the book. We have not said anything about them here as you will meet them in detail as you read further. We recommend these books as integral to your reading list about place and education.

Bailey, Simon (2013). *Exploring ADHD: An Ethnography of Disorder in Early Childhood*. London: Routledge.

Comber, Barbara (2015). *Literacy, Place and Pedagogies of Possibility*. London: Routledge.

Gregory, E. and A. Williams (2000). *City Literacies: Learning to Read Across Generations and Cultures*. London and New York: Routledge.

Kerr, K., A. Dyson and C. Raffo (2014). *Education, Disadvantage and Place: Making the Local Matter*. Bristol: Policy Press.

Lawrence-Lightfoot, Sara (1984). *The Good High School: Portraits of Character and Culture*. New York: Basic Books.

Lipman, Pauline (1998). *Race, Class, and Power in School Restructuring*. New York: State University of New York Press.

Lupton, Ruth (2003). *Poverty Street: The Dynamics of Neighbourhood Decline and Renewal*. Bristol: Policy Press.

Nespor, Jan (1997). *Tangled up in School: Politics, Space, Bodies, and Signs in the Educational Process*. Mahwah, NJ: Lawrence Erlbaum.

Nolan, K. (2011). *Police in the Hallways: Discipline in an Urban High School*. Minneapolis: University of Minnesota Press.

Springgay, S. (2008). *Body Knowledge and Curriculum: Pedagogies of Touch in Youth and Visual Culture*. New York: Peter Lang.

CHAPTER TWO

Getting into school

Once you have decided you want to research a school, the problem is how to choose the school to work in, and then how to get the school's agreement to your research. This is generally called 'gaining access' in the methods literature. We suspect that this is not the most helpful way to think about the initial stage of your research, and that it is always preferable to have in mind the notion of a research relationship. We expand on this point and why we think it matters later in this chapter.

However, first we want to think a little about place based research designs. We then go on to consider the basis for choosing a school, the problem(s) and benefits of working in one, two or many schools and the actual process of making contact. A discussion of mutual benefit, damage and risk is followed by some signposts to issues that need to be thought about before you set foot on the premises. We conclude the chapter by exploring the twin notions of 'outside in' and 'inside out' research.

Designing a place-based research project

Place-based methods are most useful in projects that focus on a school or a carefully delineated set of schools. There are some common designs that you might want to consider at the outset.

1 A single case study, school history, extended **action research** project or school ethnography, perhaps an **ethnographic case study**. The purpose of such a study is to engage, over time and in depth, with a particular school

and its community. The researcher might have a particular interest – looking at youth cultures in the school for example, or exploring how a school responds to a specific reform initiative. For example, Jan Nespor undertook an in-depth single school study and reported it in the book *Tangled up in School: Politics, Space, Bodies, and Signs in the Educational Process* (Nespor, 1997). Nespor's interest was in part to 'subvert the common focus on schools and classroom as privileged sites of education work' and instead to show the ways in which 'political, cultural and economic forces shape school practices' (p. xiii). We discuss Nespor's study in some detail later in the book.

2 A study of two to six schools within the same location. The research might focus on students' learning and achievement; particular groups in the school population; a curriculum emphasis; an approach to social justice; or the ways in which a particular policy is taken up within a school. For example, Pauline Lipman's (1998) study of two junior high schools in a reforming school district, discussed in Chapter 1, was directed to 'the role restructuring played in teacher's beliefs about and practices with African American students, who as a group, were intellectually, culturally, and politically marginalized, and who were in greatest danger of dropping out' (p. 4).

3 A study of a four to six schools in different neighbourhoods. As above, the research might focus on aspects of learning, policy or what happens to particular groups within schools; there is a stronger comparative emphasis on the importance, or otherwise, of place. For example, Stephen Ball, Meg Maguire and Annette Braun examined policy enactments in 'four co-educational, moderately successful, non-denominational and non-selective secondary schools'. The research, reported in the book *How Schools do Policy: Policy Enactments in Secondary Schools* (2011a), examined a school 'that is in inner-London, two in different parts of outer-London and a fourth in a county town' (Ball et al., 2011b).

4 A study of all of the schools in a particular geographical area. Such studies might for instance look at the ways in

which a district policy plays out in various kinds of schools or the ways in which changes in the local area appear and are dealt with in schools. For example, in *Education, Disadvantage and Place: Making the Local Matter,* Kirstin Kerr, Alan Dyson and Carlo Raffo (2014) examined the histories of Area Based Initiatives, drawing on research ranging from a single school research project to two local-authority-wide case studies.

5 A study of similar schools or sets of contrasting schools across a limited range of locations. The study might for instance look at advantaged and disadvantaged schools in two or three areas to see how they understand themselves, how they are affected by current policy agendas and so on. For example, Martin Thrupp and Ruth Lupton were interested in primary school composition and student progress and they conducted a mixed methods study in '44 primary and junior schools located within about twenty miles of each other in a single county in the South East of England and thus sharing some social and economic contexts at the regional level, although located in very different neighbourhoods' (Thrupp and Lupton, 2011, p. 1). Studies that compare schools in different countries might fit here too, although we note that the tendency in comparative education is to focus on differences in the nation-state rather than also at the local level. There is room, we suspect, for nuanced comparative 'place' studies which show national histories *and* local differences at work.

6 Studies of networks and virtual/material places, school/not school, which examine the ways in which young people and institutions are connected together, to form communities and identities. Research into 'local literacies' (Barton and Hamilton, 1998) and 'learning lives' (Erstad and Sefton Green, 2013) often sit in this design group because they focus on out of school learning practices as well as what happens in school. For example, in *Canal Town Youth: Community Organisation and the Development of Adolescent Identity*, Julia Hall (2001) examined the ways in which pre-internet young people living in a deindustrialized

city made sense of their world; she examined the role of a youth centre and school in the young people's lives.

Of course, these are not the only research designs where place-based methods can be used. Your study will undoubtedly vary in some way from those listed above. But you might usefully think about which of these six variations could inform your research design.

It is important to think at the outset about whether, and/or how, your research question might benefit from incorporating a focus on place. The key is to think about what kind of places you are actually looking for. Once you know this, then you have to think about how to establish contact. Before we start on the practicalities, however, we want to orient our discussion: this is as much about what we don't want to do as it is about what we do in and with the school.

Establishing a research relationship

There is a significant body of research literature about access to a research site, and about sampling. We have some concerns about these terms.

Our concerns are not about semantics. The words we use reflect deep and often implicit and unexamined positions – they are what we might think of as both ontological and epistemological; that is, they relate to the ways in which we understand the world and in which we think about research and ourselves as researchers. The words we use in research position us in particular ways. It is therefore useful to hold them up to some scrutiny.

The notion of the site, we suggest, is at best ambiguous. Dictionary definitions of the word 'site' usually highlight its material nature – it is a plot of ground, a location, a material address, a thing of some kind. Think of other words that are commonly attached to site – burial site, a building site, the site of the action, a website – and see the same kind of locational/material meaning. The site is where the action takes place. It doesn't include the action or the people taking it. As we suggested in Chapter 1, this materiality is just one meaning of place. So, one problem with 'site' is that it positions the school as an abstract object. 'Site' dehumanizes what researchers hope to study.

However, the more serious problem with 'site' is that there is no 'site' until the researcher declares it so. The school is simply a school. The people there see it as a school, and they were acting in it before the researcher came, and will do so after he or she leaves. The term 'site' fails to acknowledge that the school is not simply the ground on which the researcher walks, the material location for his or her activity, but is also in its own right and in its own terms, people, social relations, history/ies and stories. The term 'site' privileges research and the researcher, and positions them/us as the most important partner in the research process. As we will argue in more detail soon, this loses sight of the school and the decision it takes to host our research activities.

Further, a 'site' suggests something boundaried and discrete. But, as we argued in Chapter 1, the school is not an island. It is engaged in multiple 'stretched out relations' in time/space. Where it is cut off from 'an outside' is something for us to investigate, not replicate.

Research literature also often refers to access and gatekeepers. These are subsidiary terms that support the notion of a site as simply a material location.

The term 'sample' also objectifies the school. The dictionary definition is helpful here too. A sample is defined as a small part of something intended to illuminate the whole; it is a piece of something larger, which is to be analysed. The passive sentence construction here is revealing. If we make the above phrases active – a sample is something the researcher has selected and worked on in order to illuminate the whole; it is a piece which the researcher will analyse – then the agency of the researcher and the inert and passive nature of that which is sampled are clear. But a school is not inert. It is not the same as a sample of tissue or soil or handwriting. There are people in the school who have their own analyses of what is going on there, and why, and they will choose what about themselves and their organization we can see and interact with.

The terms 'site' and 'sample' are drawn from laboratory research. It is therefore not surprising that they have these connotations of inert research objects and an active researcher. They are applicable in those circumstances. We find ourselves using the terms 'site' and 'sample' too sometimes, when it is necessary for us to talk about research to funders who expect us to use this kind of terminology. However, our preference is to try to use alternative language that does not objectify and dehumanize and which instead acknowledges the agency of others in our research project.

We like to think about building a research relationship. To continue with definitions, a dictionary version of 'relationship' has it as both a connection between two or more people or things, and the ways in which people or groups behave with, feel about, deal with, interact with and regard each other. Relationships are not fixed. They can be good or bad, exciting or dull, productive or unproductive, sad or happy, long lasting or short lived, faulty or perfect. The way that they work out depends on the ways in which the initial encounter occurred, the expectations and agreements that were made about conduct and ongoing interactions, and so on. If this is a capital R Relationship, then it is also worth remembering the old truism that it takes two to make one work, and that keeping the Relationship going requires continuous attention. A relationship is not a one-off event.

A consideration of these qualities of a relationship (and Relationship) – mutuality and reciprocity, contingency, requiring ongoing attention in order to be sustained, indeed a kind of fragility – are extremely helpful in orienting a researcher and a research project. If you approach a school thinking of it not just as a site, a material location, but also as a relationship, then what you do and the way that you do it will be mindful of the other parties involved and their wishes, interests, feelings, needs and ongoing programme of activities. You will be oriented towards **inclusive research**.

Thinking about a research relationship also helpfully reframes the notion of the sample, to focus on the process of choice.

Choosing your relationship

You might be surprised that we are about to spend a lot of time discussing the question of establishing, maintaining and sustaining a relationship with a school or set of schools. We agree with Cipollone and Stich (2012) who argue that there is still too little discussion of these issues, and what there is tends to be highly instrumental. We have seen many doctoral researchers come unstuck early in their research projects because they have simply not allocated enough thinking, time and effort to choosing and connecting with their chosen research school. Because this relationship is *the* key to generating data, we think it is important to spend time on it.

You will of course have read the research methods books which talk about purposeful, representative, stratified and random samples. We tend not to think in these terms. Studies which use place-based methods tend to either look for geographic areas or types of institutions. What usually governs our research projects are a combination of what is necessary to answer the question and perhaps what is strategic, always what is respectful and also what is possible.

A choice that will answer the research question

It is highly likely that some of the schools that we might want to connect with and research in don't want researchers around. This can be for all sorts of reasons. They're just too busy at present. Right now, they're in the middle of something pretty exciting, or difficult, or too intense to bother with what being a research partner might require of them. Maybe they've been involved with a researcher before and it was not a pleasant experience: they were misrepresented or trivialized or judged in an offensive way. The researcher promised to do all sorts of things and then did nothing; the school never got a copy of the report, not even a thank you letter.

Because of the difficulty of finding schools, many researchers now use personal connections, or they try to use an official endorsement that will enhance the probabilities of a school agreeing to be a research partner. This is what is sometimes euphemistically called an 'opportunistic sample'. The vast majority of researchers can rationalize why a personal connection, a pragmatic choice, or just plain serendipity is good for their research and fits the bill. However, while personal and institutional connections are sometimes necessary – a point we will take up again later – convenience should not be the reason for choosing a school, informal learning organization or set of schools to research. Geoffrey Walford (2006) argues the case against convenience.

> It is evident that studies are frequently undertaken in particular locations simply because they provide convenient sites for the

> researchers. Often, a particular local school is known to the researcher, or contacts can be made through colleagues or friends. Researchers settle for research sites to which they can easily gain convenient and ready access rather than thinking through the implications of particular choices. (p. 86)

Selection that uses convenience as the primary rationale for choice suffers, Walford suggests, from two major problems. The first is that a convenience choice may not provide the most convincing evidence and thus not produce an answer to the research question. Walford suggests that a lot of comparative work between countries, and smaller case studies such as the ones with which we are concerned, often fail to justify why a particular location was used and not others (Walford, 2010). Walford's second problem is that research locations chosen primarily for convenience also run the risk of being easily identified, as institutional affiliations and personal networks now leave easily followed cyber-tracks. This is not, however, to suggest that convenience is not important. Walford notes:

> Of course, it is understandable that academics and research students should include convenience in their considerations of which sites to approach to try to gain access. There are time, financial and personal costs to be considered, and a distant location may involve accommodation away from home. Additionally, and obviously, research can only proceed where access has been achieved, and this is not always straightforward. There are obvious temptations to accept sites that appear to be readily available rather than work harder to try to achieve access to the most appropriate sites for the research. (2006, pp. 86–7)

The implications of Walford's argument are that researchers need not only to be very clear about the key features of any school they wish to establish a relationship with, ensuring that these features are at the heart of their research question, but that they also need to allocate time to finding the best 'fit'.

A choice that's strategic

You might want, and be able, to select a school or set of schools for highly strategic reasons. We often do this. Most of our research has been in schools that are attempting to change what they do, often by working with 'outside' organizations. Our research interest is in change that will make schools better and more interesting for more children and young people, and so we look for schools where we can learn something about how this happens – and why it sometimes fails. Our aim is not generally to look for schools where there is 'best practice' that can simply be transferred to others; this is a fraught quest (Gertler, 2001; Marchington and Grugulis, 2000) and one which ignores the particularities of schools, their circumstances and their capacities to 'vernacularize' change, to make it their own.

We look instead for schools which have 'high theoretical yield' (Connell, 1995, p. 90). In other words, we look for schools that will tell us something interesting about educational change. It is important for us to make sure that we have enough in our 'set' to make sure that we can see both common practices and what is unique and special about each of them. This is more than a choice with a purpose: we hope that the research results will provide evidence that helps other schools and policymakers to rethink taken-for-granted assumptions and think instead about complexities, principles and diversity in practices.

If your choice of **research partnership** is also to be strategic, then it is very important to make explicit what this actually means you are looking for in a research site.

A choice that's respectful

It may seem odd to put the notion of respect onto an agenda related to choice. But we think it's worth approaching the school with two related issues in mind – an understanding about 'the school' and the stance we wish to adopt as researchers.

It is very important for us as researchers to remember that although we are at the beginning of a research project, schools are already and always in the middle. We are at a point, as Deleuze and Guattari (1987, p. 323) put it, whereas the school is on a 'line of becoming':

> A line of becoming is not defined by the points it connects, or by the points that compose it; on the contrary, it passes between points, it comes up through the middle, it runs ... transversally to the localizable relation to distant or contiguous points. A point is always a point of origin. But a line of becoming has neither beginning nor end ... only a middle ... A becoming is always in the middle: one can only get to it by the middle. A becoming is neither one nor two, nor the relation of the two; it is the in-between, the ... line of flight ... running perpendicular to both.

We think that this is a helpful graphic image for researchers to consider. If the school is on a particular trajectory of being and becoming, our research will intersect with it, travel along with it for a while and then leave. This has two important implications. First, in order to understand the school as we encounter it, we need to understand what happened before we met it. The school's life doesn't begin when we enter and become part of it. Second, our very presence as researchers has the capacity to affect the school's line of becoming in ways that might be productive or counter-productive, and we need to consider this very carefully at the outset and throughout our stay with and in it.

We also have to consider very carefully our stance towards the school. It is easy for researchers to be critical. That's what we are trained to do. But our critique can cause harm, just as being silent can too (we have much more to say about ethical research in Chapter 4). Generally, our own practice is in line with the view strongly expressed by Sara Lawrence-Lightfoot in her classic text, *The Good High School* (1984) – recommended reading for anyone interested in place-based methods. Lawrence-Lightfoot argues that social scientists often see schools as 'static and judge them against standards of perfection' (p. 25). Her own research was looking for 'good schools' and she saw her research as a practice which

> ... recognises the myriad ways in which goodness gets expressed in various settings; that admits imperfection as an inevitable ingredient of goodness, and refers instead to the inhabitant's handling of perceived weaknesses; that looks backward and forward to institutional change and the staged quality of

> goodness: that reveals goodness as a holistic concept, a complex mixture of variables whose expression can only be recognised through a detailed narrative of institutional and interpersonal processes. (p. 25)

Now, your research might not be looking for good schools per se. It might be looking at something which is likely to be much more mixed in value – the introduction of tests, the ways in which discipline is practised and so on. However, there is still something to be learnt from Lawrence-Lightfoot's approach to her schools, which began with an exploration of the phenomena that she was investigating, rather than from a position that was already fixed. She was not looking for 'best practice' but rather how goodness was produced and lived. In doing so, she wanted to understand the complexities of the (re)production of goodness and to understand, and appreciate, its forms and processes.

As researchers, we too like to go into schools asking not 'What's wrong here?' but rather, 'Why is this school like this? How did it get to be this way? What is life like for people who are here?' We focus on the question we are interested in, as it appears within the school and its neighbourhood. Generally, we also try to approach any presentations and writing that we do from the same kind of appreciative position, as we will explain further in Chapter 8.

Appreciation in and as research is a practice: it relates both to an attitude to the project and the ways in which we take action. Respect and appreciation need to begin the moment the researcher approaches the appropriate person or persons in the school. While it might be helpful for us to use informal contacts to make an initial approach to our strategic choice of school, it is crucial to sort things out formally, using the appropriate channels. This shows respect for the organization and its ways of operating. This usually means that the researcher must approach the school head but might in some instances include an influential school governor. In Aboriginal communities it is generally necessary to first of all get permission from the community governing body. This may take some negotiation. Indigenous communities are generally heartily sick of research which goes nowhere; too many researchers have come into their communities and schools to do research – indeed sometimes asking the very same research questions – but nothing happens as a result. This lack of impact affects the whole community, not just the school, so it is the community that needs to grant permission.

But concern about the benefits of participating in research is not just confined to Indigenous communities; this same concern is echoed in many 'disadvantaged' neighbourhoods and schools that have been researched over and over again, with little to show as a result of their generosity to researchers. It is morally incumbent on you, as a researcher, to explain what your research might do and might require. Schools offer hospitality to the researcher and it is crucial that we recognize this at the start. It is thus important that we think about what being a guest means, in the longer term, a point we take up again later in the chapter.

A choice that's possible

How then are we to approach a school? Researchers need to be canny in thinking about this.

Jan Nespor's (1997) choice of research school was, just like some of our own, somewhat unplanned, as he explains in his book, *Tangled up in School.* Nespor knew what he wanted to research, but hadn't yet found the right place and partner. We quote here from Nespor's description of the process involved in the mutual decision to start up a research partnership, providing some commentary along the way to indicate what we think are key issues.

> The principal, Mr. Watts, orchestrated my access to the school, endorsed my first proposal, presented it to the superintendent for approval, introduced me to teachers, gave me time at a staff meeting to pitch the project, and helped me send letters to parents. Later he made me a member of the school's site-based management committee and its report card revision committee. Without his help the project could never have been undertaken. (p. 203)

Getting into a school and conducting research very often depends on having some kind of internal broker, someone who is committed to your research and someone who can troubleshoot any issues. Brokers also often want you to do something for them, to 'give back' to the school the educational expertise that you have, rather than holding it all to yourself. It is crucial to get the head on side, but the head may not be your way into the school, nor the person who you most closely relate to during your research.

> I met him [Mr Watts] for the first time only a couple of weeks before I began the study. In early September 1992 Mr. Watts had approached one of my colleagues at Virginia Tech, Joseph Tlou, a social studies educator, for advice on how to introduce a global education theme into his school curriculum. Tlou had asked several of us on the faculty to meet with Watts. I went for a couple reasons: I had just finished writing a study about what it meant to learn in university programs (Nespor, 1994), and I wanted to work through the question of learning in a radically different setting. I had an inkling that my university-grounded concepts would founder in an elementary school and that in the wreckage I could learn about both the theory and the school.
>
> At the same time, I was intent on doing a different kind of ethnography than I'd done at the university, where I'd been an uninvolved outsider. I wanted to create a long term relationship that would involve me and a group of graduate students working collaboratively with teachers, kids and community members to explore how city politics, school system ideologies, parent–school relations, and kids' experiences of education came together in practice. I wanted this project to draw at least part of its agenda from teachers, parents, and students and to address them as well as a wider audience of researchers. (pp. 203–4)

Mr Watts made the first move in Nespor's research partnership. By contacting the university, he showed that he was interested in what researchers might have to offer, and wasn't hostile or indifferent to research expertise. Nespor doesn't tell us if this was the case, but we guess it is likely that Mr Watts already had some connections with the university either through teacher education, through district networks, being an alumnus or through postgraduate study.

Nespor was already positioned to take advantage of this potential connection. He knew the kind of research that he wanted to undertake, and why. He was also ready to commit to a relationship that would be reciprocal – the research wouldn't just address what he was interested in, but would also take up some of the things that people in the school were interested in too. He had already conceptualized a research project that was not only about knowledge production, but was something which would be of mutual concern. The research would not just benefit him or his graduate students.

> When it became clear as the meeting progressed that Mr. Watts was really less concerned with global education than with promoting a whole language curriculum at this school, I thought I'd found a point where his needs and mine connected ... Whole language approaches, as I understood them, required teachers and students to make their language and literacy practices objects of study and analysis.
>
> I suggested to Mr. Watts that I, and perhaps some of my graduate students, could become partners with Thurber Elementary. We could help teachers and students do the inquiry I presumed they would be initiating, and at the same time we could begin studying community and school system practices that created the contexts within which the school operated. (p. 204)

The first meeting between potential partners is often a search for the common meeting ground, the place to start, a potential activity which both parties are happy to undertake. But Nespor then went on to make a mistake that could potentially have undone the initial connection he had made.

> Not expecting Mr. Watts to agree immediately, I told him I'd write a short memo detailing the project and drop it off at his school within the week.
>
> When I wrote the memo I must have been feeling insecure about the vagueness of my plans, because I tried to hide their ambiguity behind verbiage ... A collaboration, I suggested, would allow us to study the 'literacy, linguistic and cultural practices in the community (or communities) served by the school', and to 'work collaboratively with teachers to create an environment of reflective inquiry critical to the Whole Language perspective'. I explained that the work I was proposing could lead in many directions including 'tracing out and describing family and economic networks, cultural boundaries and processes',

> studying the political and educational view of parents: doing an ethnographic survey of literacy practices in the community; doing a 'social geography' of the area serviced by the school; doing 'time geographies' of students, parents teachers; starting 'participatory action research' projects with teachers to address issues they identified as important, and on and on.
>
> Later, one of my colleagues in the teacher education programme remarked that he couldn't imagine teachers giving him the time of day if he sent them such a memo. The language was too academic and too distant from the everyday concerns of most teachers. I'd hoped of course that my assurances about the openness of the design and my promises to work collaboratively with teachers to address their agendas, would offset the language. This was not the case, but I did get permission from Mr. Watts to begin working in the school. (pp. 204–5)

It is not unusual for potential research partners to want some more details about what we want to do. The emphasis in institutional ethics forms on 'plain language' is not simply a bureaucratic requirement, but an injunction for researchers to think about who is reading what we have written about the potential research. People in schools are not likely to be as saturated in the research literature as researchers currently in that milieu. Their concerns are likely to be framed by what they think will be of benefit to the students and the school. Nespor's enthusiastic and overblown account of his project did not cost him the research partnership, but it might have.

You may not have such a lucky encounter as Nespor. You may feel that you need to go cold-calling potential strategic research partners. Cold-calling is by far the most difficult way to find your research project and partner (Anderson and Freebody, 2014). If there is a way to use the contacts and networks of your supervisors, friends, colleagues and/or institution to make contact with your strategically chosen school, do it – using an intermediary or friendly advocate who will make an introduction is better than the cold-call. However, in our experience, cold-calling can still 'work'. When you need to make this kind of approach, there are two things to do, and one thing to avoid.

1 Write to the principal/head and give a time and a date when you will call to make a time to discuss your project.

Most of these letters will go straight to the head's PA, who will probably show the letter to the boss. The PA will almost certainly field your call, but even the PA may be hard to get! Polite persistence is often required.

2 Make sure that your letter is straightforward and says, very succinctly, what you want to do, why it is important and what's in it for the school. You can discuss the actual details of what you want the school to do when you get into a real conversation. If your letter is too detailed, or too hard to understand, the answer will almost always be no. Lexi Earl found this out the hard way. Her PhD focused on the food experiences of Year 4 children in three schools: one inner city and very poor, one poor and in a market town, and one middle-class village school:

I spent a significant amount of time, during the design stages of this project, thinking about the 'ideal' school site. This site was informed by my reading of the literature on whole school approaches and in particular, the design of The Edible Schoolyard in Berkeley. I was specifically looking for schools that were already teaching cooking and gardening – schools that were implementing the recommendations of policy on food education. The schools I chose needed to provide particular cases that were 'vital to understand because of their particular significance in policy formulation and implementation' (Walford, 2008: 20).

I drew up a shortlist of twelve potential schools, using the Food For Life website and the local Eco Schools. I cross-referenced schools on the list to their school websites and Ofsted reports (which often highlight extra activities like food growing or cooking). I approached the initial twelve schools first via email (to either the general admin email address or where possible, directly to the headteacher). I suspect the initial letters were slightly too long, I made an amateur mistake. As Walford notes,

... every additional piece of information gives a chance for an objection or problem to be raised in the mind of the reader. Detailed letters make it far too easy to find a 'good reason' to object. (p. 23)

> It was perhaps unsurprising then that these schools responded negatively or not at all. (Earl, 2015, pp. 105–6)

Lexi did get her three strategically chosen schools in the end, using a combination of one school by broker (her supervisor), the second by institutional connections and the third by cold-calling. She also had to redraft her letter so that it began by addressing the school's existing interest and expertise in teaching about food and the potential for other schools to learn from their experience.

Building and maintaining a research relationship

This section of the chapter is largely practical. We first of all address three questions that you need to think about at the start of your research relationship, and then attend to as you go on – who needs to know, how you will proceed, and the process itself. We then consider some problems that might arise.

1 Who needs to know about you and what you are doing?

Just because you have formal permission to do research in a school, it doesn't mean that everyone knows and understands what you are doing.

Many schools expect researchers to present at a staff meeting, for example, as this gives everyone the opportunity to find out why you are going to be hanging around, and they can ask questions to alleviate any concerns. You can always ask if this is possible, if it is not immediately expected. You might prepare some written information for staff too, or post some information online. We often have a project blog where the research questions, design and methods are outlined, and interested people are always referred to it. You might also write something for the school newsletter, talk on the school radio station and ask to talk to the Student Representative Council or Student Forum.

You may need to ask specifically about how to get into classrooms, attend meetings or go on excursions and field trips. Big and secondary schools in particular often operate as a set of federated regions and, just because you are in one, it doesn't mean you can automatically get into another. Establishing research relationships with all of the people with whom you hope to work may well happen over time, and require you to adopt different strategies to establish different connections. Lexi Earl, who we mentioned earlier in the chapter, really wanted to conduct some of her school food research in school kitchens. However, she found that school cooks were polite but suspicious. Even though she was a trained chef it took a long time and many casual conversations before they let her put on an apron and join in the dinner preparation. It was even longer before they trusted her enough to record formal interviews.

There are likely to be key people in the school who will be able to help you. Front office staff, for example, generally know almost everything there is to know about a school and can be extremely important in making sure that your stay in the school is productive. Sometimes a particular teacher will be allocated to look after you – and of course this may not be something he or she has volunteered for. Being able to get people on side, to persuade them of the benefits of your work without being pushy or arrogant, is an important researcher skill. It is possible that some staff will feel they have been ordered to be involved in the research, and it is crucial for you to make the ethical commitment that participation is voluntary and, regardless of what the head says, they do have the right to refuse to participate. And you will need to work out how you are going to keep all these people informed about your research so that they don't lose interest or get suspicious of what you are doing.

You will of course have to get parents' permission, as well as permission from the children and young people themselves, for their active involvement in your research. We stress, however, that seeing these permissions simply as form-filling activities isn't helpful: it's the work that the conversations and the texts do together in establishing the research relationship that is important. Formal advice on these matters is already widely available, so we won't repeat it here (see, for example, Alderson, 2011; Clark et al., 2013). Other issues that need to be sorted out at the outset relate to any special requirements for time – for example, taking students or staff away from their normal routines for interviews. While schools are often happy to do this, it requires considerable organization and advance warning.

It's as well to be cognizant of potential problems related to getting permission and sharing information about your project. Caroline Wanat (2008) addresses the difference between what she calls 'access and cooperation'. She graphically describes the kind of resistance tactics that people within the school might use to make it difficult for researchers to operate. She discusses: passing the buck – not doing anything but saying it is someone else's responsibility to make a decision; controlling communication so that no one actually knows what is meant to happen when, how or why; always asking for more information rather than doing anything to help; and forgetting to do what has been promised.

We should sound a note of caution about this list. While all of these things are likely consequences of people not feeling any ownership or responsibility for your research, it is also the case that schools are big, complex and clumsy organizations. If communication is difficult, or if someone forgets that you were coming to do something and organizes an excursion the same day, this may not be malicious or resistant. It may simply be that making your research happen is not the first priority, or because this kind of thing happens sometimes in an imperfect world and organization.

However, Wanat's list does caution us to remember that establishing a relationship with a school is not simply a matter of getting formal permission from the person or people in charge. It is crucial to see the research relationship as being with *all* of the people in the school with whom you want to work and who might be affected by the research. It is important not to assume that just because you have formal permission that they will agree with this decision. They too need to be assured that what you want to do is worth some of their time and energy. This means that you will need, at the beginning of your stay in the school, to spend time explaining your research to rather a lot of people – school staff, students and maybe parents too. And you will need to keep working on sustaining all of those relationships all the way through the project.

2 What is the school going to get from the relationship?

It's not uncommon to hear something like this, 'You are the one doing the research. You get the PhD (or the grant or the publication). What's in it for the school?' While we understand the sentiment, we think that it casts research in an unfortunate transactional frame so that it seems that schools will only participate if they get something from it. Our experience is that, in fact, many schools are prepared to be the avenue and venue for research that is not of immediate benefit to them but that will contribute to the greater good. They see this as part of their wider responsibilities to education.

It is important to acknowledge this commitment to the public good. But it is also important to consider what you might offer the school by way of thanks for them allowing you to participate in their 'line of becoming'. This is not necessarily about 'getting something back' but about offering something in return for the school's cooperation, time and hospitality. It helps to think, as we suggested earlier in the chapter, that the school is not a passive location for your activities and that you are its guest. The minimum you can do, as a good guest, is to offer to provide information about your research results. This may be in the form of data (**survey** results for instance) as well as your analysis: many schools find this offer attractive.

The idea of being a guest can help us understand what we need to do in our research schools. A disrespectful guest is one who sneaks in the back door, takes up a lot of time and energy, pays no heed to the house rules, picks fights, makes a mess and then leaves without cleaning up or offering some kind of thanks. It's very important not to be a bad guest at the outset, in case the hosts decide they have a sudden and pressing appointment elsewhere and you just have to leave straight away, even though that's not what was planned. And a hospitable host is not endlessly forgiving of thoughtless behaviour, so you must continue to think about how you maintain the relationship.

Being a guest in a school not only brings with it obligations to come clean about your goals and the support that you need in order to conduct your research, but also to understand what this might mean for your host school. Many researchers offer to take on some kind of assistant or helping role. Stephen Ball reports that at Beachside Comprehensive,

> [m]y participation in the daily life of the school, apart from observing lessons etc., was by supply teaching etc., in the first year of field work, plus four periods of timetabled teaching, and three periods of timetabled teaching in the second year of field work. I also accompanied forms on school visits, went on one school trip, invigilated in exams, took registers for absent teachers, played in the staff v pupils cricket match, and so on. (Ball, 1981, p. xix)

Most researchers do not commit themselves to quite so much! However, it is not uncommon for researchers who are in the school for extended periods of time to work as teaching assistants. They might also serve on committees; offer professional development for staff about an area of their expertise; tutor students who need additional support; provide expertise for curriculum and policy development; write for newsletters and websites; and work with parents on working bees and the like.

3 What are the rules of engagement?

It is important to clarify as early as possible areas that might become important, even problematic, including, first of all, how any concerns about your presence as a researcher will be handled, and by whom.

It is crucial at the outset to clarify issues related to confidentiality and anonymity. But it is important to note that in the age of the internet it is increasingly difficult to disguise locations. Anonymizing place is particularly paradoxical and vexatious for place-based research, where details of the location are crucial to the research and the analysis and explanation. As Jan Nespor (2000, p. 549) notes, 'anonymization naturalizes the decoupling of events from historically and geographically specific locations (and with the way location or place itself is conceptualized)'. This limits the researcher's capacity to analyse, but more than that, Nespor argues, it also makes researchers complicit with the 'political projects of dominant groups and organisations' (p. 554) who see and work to produce places and spaces for their own interests and ends.

What is usually non-negotiable in conventional ethics approaches is the anonymity of individuals within the site. This can be quite difficult to manage, as naming a position rather than an individual generally gives away identity. In small schools it is virtually impossible to disguise who said and did what from those inside the organization, even though this may be less clear to the outside world. Both Nespor (2000) and Walford (2006) argue that anonymity ought not to be seen as an insurmountable obstacle, but rather as a fact of research life which forces researchers to think more carefully about the rights of participants, the practices of information-sharing and the ways in which reports and other publications are produced. Anthony Kelly (2009) disagrees with Walford and Nespor, suggesting that there are limits to guarantees of anonymity, and it is important that these are recognized and discussed to ensure that no false promises are made. We recommend you look at the papers by Nespor, Walford and Kelly, as they challenge taken-for-granted notions of anonymity and force us to clarify under what circumstances anonymity might not be ethical or empirically desirable.

Increasingly, it is common practice for researchers to offer participants the opportunity to provide their own pseudonym. Even this can be problematic, such as when people choose to adopt an identity that disguises something that the researcher considers important – their gender or race, for example (Lahman et al., 2015). It can also be difficult if people change their minds halfway through a set of publications. Following Kelly's maxim that researchers ought not to offer cast-iron guarantees, but rather stick to reasonable assurances, some conversation about pseudonyms might be in order (see also Marx, 2006). But of course this may be a topic that seems more important to researchers at the beginning of a research project, but not at all interesting to participants in the school (c.f. O'Reilly et al., 2011). In these circumstances, researchers have to remember that consent is not a one-off event, but an ongoing process; the issue of pseudonyms and other related questions may need to be revisited several times in a research project.

It is also helpful to think early in the research relationship about whether and/or when the school might use its research participation and the results for its own ends. It is not unusual these days for schools to want to be named in research, as they see some public relations advantage in being involved in professional knowledge generation. This may not sit well with you and your project. This has to be negotiated. And, of course, we can't forget the question of publication and what authorship opportunities will or won't be offered to the school and its staff, student and parent communities (we say more about this in the final chapter). It is important for people in universities to remember that sometimes school staff also want and value authoring academic and professional publications.

Anticipating problems

It is useful to spare a moment or two to worry about things that might go wrong during your research. This is not an exercise in paranoia, but rather thinking through how you might react if any of these were to happen to you.

You have probably already thought about the potential for people to tell you things that they think you want to hear. There is no way that you can actually force anyone to tell you what they really think, but getting around potential 'please the researcher' responses requires you to have a range of sources and ways to get the information you are after. It is not possible to get a balanced view by simply relying on what you are told by one person – particularly if it's a member of the leadership team. Their perspective is important, but there are bound to be others. (We deal with this in detail in Chapter 6.)

You may be the recipient of confidences that you do not want. Sometimes people tell you things that they want you to pass on to school leaders. This can put you in a difficult situation. It is important to be clear, and perhaps repeat at the time, that you are not a conduit and that what you are told is confidential. However, if you have made an agreement with the school that you will inform them about results as you go along, and if the information warrants communicating, then there may be a way for you to pass on some of these concerns without giving away your sources of information. You may also decide to shift, expand or change the focus of your study to take account of these concerns. If you are a research student, these are things you will need to discuss with your supervisor.

Many researchers find themselves in a situation where they are given information that puts them in a quandary. Vanessa Hayward found herself in just this situation. Her doctoral research was a single school ethnography, examining the ways in which the various policies around health were understood, met and used. However, when staff found out that her topic was related to health, they began to tell her about their own stress issues. It wasn't just one staff member either – it was several. What was she to do? In consultation with her supervisor, she decided that she couldn't pass the information on, but that it did seem to be crucial to her research. Even though she had initially focused on students and the curriculum, she widened the scope of her data generation to include the staff's own health. This turned out to be very important: her research eventually showed the paradoxical way in which the school's approach to health policies actually produced cynicism in students and additional demands on staff, which left many of them feeling demoralized and stressed (Hayward and Thomson, 2012; Thomson and Hayward, 2014).

Another set of problems that can arise is related to the researcher's identity. In some countries and in some schools, any new person in the school is seen either as someone who is making potential judgements about the quality of the education on offer, or someone who might want to enrol their child. Either way, this perception leads to suspicion and/or a desire to only present the very best picture possible. This kind of image management is of course a very rational response to those kinds of visitors, but it is not what a researcher wants. Overcoming this kind of response requires conversation, reassurance, time and indeed evidence that you are not in the school to be 'sold' something. If you are giving back to the school in some way, particularly by doing some unpaid work, then this certainly puts you in a different position to an inspector or a potential customer. However, doing unpaid work brings its own set of identity dilemmas.

If you have decided to work as a casual teacher or teaching assistant then this role sometimes conflicts with some of the ways in which you think about schooling and how it might be done. You may have to intervene in situations in ways in which you are more like a teacher, and this in turn may colour the ways in which students relate to you in the future. Simon Bailey found he had this problem. His doctoral research examined the diagnosis of ADHD in early childhood settings; he worked as an ethnographer/unpaid teaching assistant in one school over two school years. He often found himself working with small groups of children who had been segregated from the remainder of the class, either because they were struggling to accomplish a task or because their behaviour was 'difficult', or both. In the book of the thesis (Bailey, 2013), and writing about himself in the third person – the man he was at the time of the research – he describes one such incident:

> The library's relative seclusion from the classroom might well have worked to temporarily lower the net of surveillance on these children: the challenge of the task required Simon to guide children one at a time, which caused disruption among those waiting their turn. Simon's authority was also clearly not considered equivalent to Sarah's [the teacher], which he discovered through the effective use of Sarah as a threat if good behaviour was not restored; surveillance by proxy. Eventually, Simon was forced to complete most of the task himself in order to 'get the job done' on time. (p. 65)

While this was profoundly uncomfortable at the time, as he found himself behaving in ways he did not enjoy, Simon was able to use this experience to further his analysis of the workings of the school:

> [T]his scenario underlines fundamental connections between the school's need to perform and the kinds of disciplinary apparatus it employs to do so, while also providing an indication of the potential paucity of education experiences driven primarily by disciplinary considerations. (p. 65)

At the time, Simon believed he was working as any other teaching assistant would, as he had decided beforehand he must. Afterwards he was able to reflect on his inexperience in these kinds of situations, go back to a more focused researcher position and analyse his own behaviour and what it meant for his emerging understanding of the school as a disciplinary regime.

You can anticipate that you too may have to assume different kinds of identities during your research – teacher, confidant, publicity manager, parent, leader, counsellor, social worker (see also Thomson and Gunter, 2011). This is not unusual, and Simon's example suggests that it is not necessarily a problem, as long as you are aware of what is happening.

These problems are the same but also different for researchers who are investigating their own workplace.

A note on 'insider' research relationships

There is very helpful literature already available on 'inside' research (e.g. Anderson et al., 2008; Cochran-Smith and Lytle, 1993; Sikes and Potts, 2008) and practitioner inquiry (e.g. Menter et al., 2011; Metz and Page, 2002; Murray and Lawrence, 2000; Zeni, 2001). We do not want to repeat at length what this body of work says. Instead we want to return to the notion we posited at the start of the chapter, that research is always a relationship. This presents particular challenges for someone who is already in a relationship with a school as its leader, teacher or administrator, parent or student.

People in the school may begin to view you differently when you declare that you are doing research, as you ethically must. You might be expected to have expertise that you don't in fact yet actually possess. And it is tricky to get people to speak openly about something that you are responsible for or have advocated, or about their vulnerabilities, especially if you are in a position of power over them. It is equally tricky to persuade people that you have an open mind. They are right to be suspicious about this. Researchers working in their own schools often discuss the challenge of being two people at once – a researcher who is engaged with critical literatures, and a staff member who has no choice but to behave in some of the very ways that the literature critiques. It can also be a shock to discover that not everyone in the school feels the way that you do about it, and indeed may be distressed about or hostile to some things about which you feel the complete opposite. It is a really significant challenge to become more informed about your own organization and its workings, while at the same time continuing to do your job. It is difficult to hold a critical position towards a particular practice, for example, and an engaged one at the same time. Researching your own school can force a researcher to become a little dualistic.

The ways of addressing these issues are not dissimilar to what it is that 'outside' researchers have to do – sort out the ground rules, make sure everyone in the school is informed and on board with the research, set up ways of keeping people informed and engaged. Marilyn Cochran-Smith and Susan Lytle (2009) suggest that there is a potentially useful overlap between practitioner inquiry and professional learning communities. Insider researchers may well be in a good position to work with professional learning communities focused on related issues in their schools – and they might even set them up. This is the norm in **participatory action research**, for example. Working with colleagues in the same school or setting up reference groups of colleagues, students and/or parents is a good way to ensure communication and interaction with practitioner research. It is important, too, for dealing with potential problems that might arise at the publication stage (see Chapter 8).

Final note

We've suggested in this chapter that you need to choose your school for strategic reasons not simply for the sake of convenience, no matter how tempting that is. We've also argued that you think about your research as establishing a relationship with the school and its various people, and that your place in the school is as a privileged guest. This suggests both the kind of attitude and stance you need to take towards your research – you are interested in understanding the school, its history and its complexities.

Further reading

These four books all discuss aspect of estabishing and maintaining research relationships. They have a strong focus on ethical relationships as integral to research, and integral to the ways in which research projects are designed and enacted in schools and neighbourhoods.

Aldridge, Jo (2015). *Participatory Research: Working with Vulnerable Groups in Research and Practice*. Bristol: Policy Press.

Brooks, Rache Kitty te Riele and Meg Maguire (2014). *Ethics and Education Research*. London: Sage.

Cochran-Smith, M. and S. Lytle (2009). *Inquiry as Stance: Practitioner Research for the Next Generation*. New York: Teachers College Press.

Stoecker, Randy (2013). *Research Methods for Community Change: A Project Based Approach*. Thousand Oaks, CA: Sage.

We also recommend reading these three articles to focus your thinking about the difficulties of the ethics of anonymity:

Kelly, Anthony (2009). 'In defence of anonymity: Rejoining the criticism'. *British Educational Research Journal* 35 (3): 4331–45.

Nespor, Jan (2000). 'Anonymity and place in qualitative inquiry'. *Qualitative Inquiry* 6 (4): 546–69.

Walford, Geoffrey (2006). 'Research ethical guidelines and anonymity'. *International Journal of Research and Methods in Education* 28 (1): 83–93.

At the start of your project, it is also worth looking at journals such as *Qualitative Inquiry* and the *International Journal of Research and Methods in Education,* which have very helpful papers on research practice, including establishing relationships and relationship-building, and narratives of researcher experiences.

CHAPTER THREE

Getting to know the neighbourhood

It's very common to hear and read the words 'local school' and 'neighbourhood school'. There is often an implication, in the use of these terms, that the school exists not only in a material location, but that it also has a special association with its surroundings. The notion of 'school community' is often used to mean those who live around the school site. But school community additionally suggests a singular and homogeneous population, bound together through a meaningful association with the school (see Chapter 1 for the related notion that place is boundaried, stable and fixed).

In the first part of this chapter, we address the associated ideas of 'neighbourhood' and 'community', and suggest that the terms are not as simple as they might at first appear. We then offer some strategies that you can use to explore the locality in which a school is situated, and its inhabitants and associations.

What is a neighbourhood?

Dictionary.com defines a neighbourhood as 'the area or region around or near some place or thing; vicinity; a district or locality, often with reference to its character or inhabitants'. This is clearly referring to a place as a material location on a map.

We are very accustomed to seeing street maps with designated suburbs and areas designated as units for statistical data collection, election boundaries and so on. We are also used to government policies that work on an area basis – school catchments, regional health or employment interventions, local government service delivery areas and the like. Think for example of tourist maps where particular neighbourhoods are marked out. San Francisco, for instance, is often 'sold' to tourists on the basis of its varied and accessible neighbourhoods – North Beach, Chinatown, Nob Hill, Haight Ashbury, Fisherman's Wharf, Castro, Filmore, Mission and so on.

The general inference is that a neighbourhood has boundaries and there is something distinctive about what is inside those limits. Its people share something greater than simply being within the same area. They have some kind of experience or history or practice in common by virtue of being in the same place. For instance, sanfranciscotravel.com describes North Beach as:

> ... rich in Italian heritage, compresses cabarets, jazz clubs, galleries, inns, family style restaurants and gelato parlors into less than a square mile. A perfect spot for cappuccino and espresso, North Beach is transformed into one of San Francisco's most electric playgrounds by night; live music and dancing keep the streets swinging. In the morning practice tai chi with the regulars in Washington Square and from here, catch the No. 39 bus to the top of Telegraph Hill. Coit Tower atop Telegraph Hill offers amazing views. Thirty local artists painted murals on its ground floor walls in 1933. This hill is also laced with stairways off Filbert and Greenwich streets as well as lush gardens. (http://www.sanfrancisco.travel/explore/neighborhoods/north-beach (accessed 31 October 2015))

In this enthusiastic appeal to visitors, North Beach is characterized by a singular history (Italian heritage) and as a place for cosmopolitan consumption (coffee, clubs, galleries, restaurants), where residents do tai chi and make gardens and art.

This manufactured representation allows the artificiality of 'the neighbourhood' to be seen. It is likely that many residents of North Beach lay claim to other heritages and some of them may in fact be recent arrivals. Those cosmopolitan tourist venues may be run by people who don't actually have a residence in North Beach, but their daily work makes them part of everyday life there. And, conversely, many of the local residents probably go somewhere else in San Francisco to work. Making art and gardens and doing tai chi is hardly likely to be *all* that people do in North Beach. And what of people who live just outside the area designated as North Beach but who see themselves as part of it? These questions – what counts as being in or out, which histories are recognized, who is associated with the area and who isn't – apply to all locations, not just San Francisco.

Research on location is germane to thinking about neighbourhood. For example, Gareth Rees, Sally Power and Chris Taylor (2007) studied area-based interventions in education in England under New Labour. They argue that most area-based initiatives are flawed on several grounds. First, the rationale for intervening in a small geographical area relies on policy rhetoric which almost inevitably reproduces deficit views of particular areas, equating employment and epidemiological data with particular negative social beliefs and practices. Second, area-based initiatives tend to:

> ... reinforce the notion of homogeneity within an area, thereby ignoring the frequent coincidence of extreme wealth and poverty in urban areas and creating an exaggerated impression of the concentration of poverty within a given neighbourhood. (Power et al., 2005, p. 113)

Finally, a great deal of change in small geographical areas depends on decisions made elsewhere, for example in the commercial housing market, in regional and national employment policy and in overseas boardrooms (Thomson, 2002). Nevertheless, intervention in particular geographical areas, at the level of the city for example, as in the London and Manchester Challenges, does appear to have some purchase in redressing some of the insensitivities of national resource allocations (Ainscow, 2015; Baars et al., 2014). However, we ought nevertheless to exercise considerable caution about boundaries and resist the temptation to assume that they hermetically seal off a neighbourhood.

Where boundaries are actually drawn is often very arbitrary. They do not reflect the way that people actually live and move around their area. For example, we have undertaken participatory research with a local theatre company in a particular suburb in Nottingham (Jones et al., 2013; Thomson et al., 2014). One of the first things that the theatre company found was that, from the residents' perspectives, the suburb was actually split in two, with a major road severing one group of residents from the other. We described what this meant in the following extract:

> In some ways, the building of the motorway at the edge of this community, having initially encapsulated the optimism and aspiration its residents held for their new lives in a modern Britain, in time came to represent the beginning of change in the community, symbolising as it did a new age of mobility, both social and geographic. The impact of the mobility of this 'lost generation' is still felt in the community today, with the area having a higher than average population of elderly residents living alone, alongside a much younger demographic of families, often welfare dependent and moved into the area from other social housing across the city.
>
> Conversations with residents from across the estate revealed a tendency to maintain an exclusionary identity based on cultural essentialism rather than the social collectivism of past generations, by the marking of symbolic boundaries between areas, sometimes based on different sides of a road. Residents of the older part of the estate, built before the war, explained:
>
> We've always felt separate; we've been treated as separate. The other side of [the estate] thought we were posh – brick houses, concrete. (Member of Tenants and Residents' Association)
>
> This part of the estate had recently experienced periods of anti-social behaviour which affected its reputation and compounded the sense of separation from the more modern parts:
>
> Five years ago, this was one of the most deprived parts of the area, with 'problem families' and other social issues meaning that it had gone from being a 'lovely area' to being 'really quite rough' to now coming round again. (Field notes, 3 December 2008)
>
> The changing socio-economic context of the estate affected the ways residents identify with where they lived:
>
> Residents may have different opinions based on how long they've

> lived in the area: if they've lived here longer, they're more likely to see [the neighbouring borough] as a separate entity. [The Neighbourhood Action Officer] points out that many people in this area used to classify themselves as [another borough], until [that borough] came out quite low in a survey based on rates of deprivation. (Field notes, 21 October 2008)
>
> This reflects a community that in many ways defines itself not by 'what we are' but rather by 'what we're not', reinforcing the sense of fragmentation reported by those who worked within the community. (Jones et al., 2013)

This separation and fragmentation were commented on during three community plays, the subject of our study, but making the plays also brought the various fragments of the neighbourhood together, working on a common project. A secondary school was central to this community development project, and acted as a shared place in which collective past memories, lives in the present and hopes for the future could all be brought together.

We also can't assume that everyone in a neighbourhood experiences it in the same way. South Australian teacher Marg Wells did a classroom literacy research project that started with her class of seven- and eight-year-olds mapping their neighbourhood (see Comber et al., 2001). Marg enlarged a page from a street directory and, while still in the classroom, children marked their own houses on the map. The class then went out to draw and take pictures of their houses, the local shops and play areas that they used. This took three mornings. The children were very excited and took turns being the 'guide' as the class neared their house. They pointed out various local features that they knew.

Marg was struck by the fact that many of the children did not know that other children in their class lived nearby, and all the children were surprised by the fact that so many of them used the same park and shops but had not seen each other while there. It was as if there were shared locations, but not shared times for their use.

Children living one or two streets away did not know each other except in class: they had often not ventured past their own small, immediate vicinity. Marg and the researchers she was working with, Barbara Comber and Pat, came to understand that the lived experience of the neighbourhood varied enormously for the

FIGURE 3.1 *Marg's class, neighbourhood map*

different children in the class. The class pasted their pictures and drawings onto a very big map (see Figure 3.1), which then became the basis for further work about trees, the development of natural spaces and the urban regeneration project that was underway.

The urban generation project connected the particular neighbourhood in which Marg worked and the children lived to the wider world. The area had been deemed worthy of redevelopment by the state government, after considerable lobbying by the local authority. The company that had the contract for the redevelopment was a major national, which also operated in South East Asia. Urban planners working on the project did not live in the area, nor did many of the workers. Neither of course did many of the teachers who came in and out each day. Flows of people, information, equipment, ideas and capital entered and left. But these were not the only connections that the neighbourhood had with locations elsewhere. The area was one with a significant immigrant and Indigenous population; a range of cultural organizations supported flows of information, conversation, people and things between the neighbourhood and other far-flung locations. All of these became part of the literacy research that Marg undertook, which was both local and global at the same time, and also continually moving. (See more about Marg and other similar place-based literacy work in Comber, 2015.)

You can see, just from our examples, that there are some assumptions about neighbourhoods that don't stack up. Far from being neatly bordered areas on maps:

1. neighbourhoods are not homogeneous;
2. the boundaries of neighbourhoods are arbitrary and do not necessarily equate to the diverse ways in which residents live, work and mix or don't mix together;
3. neighbourhoods are porous – people physically move in and out of them at various times of the day/night;
4. official and market driven representations of neighbourhoods are only one version of the neighbourhood – there are others;
5. neighbourhoods are joined to other neighbourhoods near and far through the movement of people, things, images, information and so on;
6. neighbourhoods are not static, they have various histories which variously frame their present/future.

Another problem with the idea of neighbourhood is that it is a profoundly urban concept. The notion of a neighbourhood summons up images of a suburban, built environment. Whether this is 'the hood' from *Straight Outta Compton* (Legendary Pictures, New Line Cinema, Cube Vision, Crucial Films, Broken Chair Flicka 2015) the relentless sameness of the immaculate homes of *The Stepford Wives* (Deline Pictures, 2004), or something more ordinary, the location of the neighbourhood is probably neither *in* the city nor *out* of it. If you google-image the term neighbourhood, you get low-storey buildings, front fences, porches, front steps, gardens, playgrounds and small shopping centres. You don't get city apartment blocks or warehouse residences. You don't get any surrounds that suggest farming. As a popular image, neighbourhood largely leaves out villages, hamlets and market towns, regional cities and isolated country towns, municipalities, townships and settlements.

The notion then of neighbourhood schools is flawed, not simply because schools enrol students beyond their neighbourhood and children go to schools out of their neighbourhood. The notion of the neighbourhood school simply doesn't cover anything like the actual range of schools, their locations and their students. If you begin to think of the sheer range of school locations – from tiny single rooms on islands, to students studying remotely from vast but isolated stations and ranches, to schools that collect young people from a 20- to 50-mile radius each day, to the only school in the village – then it is clear that the surrounds of a school vary enormously.

And the idea of 'neighbourhood' centres on human residents. While the popular image of an urban neighbourhood might include the occasional pet, park and urban garden, the concept does not automatically attune us to the environment more generally, and the ways in which humans do and don't exist harmoniously with it. We will discuss this further in relation to 'reading the school' in the next chapter.

So, if the notion of neighbourhood is not straightforward, perhaps the idea of a school 'community' is better? Alas, the notion of 'community' is also vexed.

What is a community?

Starting again with dictionary.com, a community can be thought of as: social group of any size whose members reside in a specific locality, share government and often have a common cultural and historical heritage; a locality inhabited by such a group; and a social, religious, occupational, or other group sharing common characteristics or interests and perceived or perceiving itself as distinct in some respect from the larger society within which it exists (usually preceded by *the*). So, community can mean a geographical area, just like neighbourhood, but also the people who live there. Like neighbourhood, the people in a community are assumed to share either some kind of history or cultural characteristics. However, community can also mean people who are joined together through mutual activity or sets of beliefs which set them apart from others. These social communities are not necessarily connected to a neighbourhood, although they may have some kind of shared location associated with their raison d'être – a church, clubhouse, playing field or meeting room for instance.

If you think about yourself, then it is pretty likely that you will be able to name several different communities to which you belong. They may be about your work, home or the things that you do.

The notion that many people belong to more than one community, and only one of them might be associated with where they live or where they go to school, is important. It suggests that within a neighbourhood (and, as we will argue, within a place such as a school) there are people with multiple associations and bonds. It is not necessarily the case that living in a neighbourhood or going to a school will have the same meaning and importance for everyone. There are likely to be different kinds of attachments to and feelings about a given neighbourhood. Some attachments and bonds will also stretch well beyond the local area.

We tend to think of communities in a positive light. It you are a member of a community then the things you have in common with other people might bring conversations, pleasurable times, memories. Community members are often assumed to have regard for each other, perhaps to exercise some degree of care about each other, and to offer support. Communities might have informal rules, rituals and norms of behaviour which bind people together. David Plank (1996) argues that four types of communities are invoked in contemporary political discourse:

1 autochthonous communities – characterized by 'mutual interest and mutual concern' (p. 15) (see Tonnies, 1957/1887 on Gemeinschaft);
2 atavistic communities – those that seek to find a lost sense of community, relying on 'identity politics, exclusion, and intolerance as strategies for building or maintaining boundaries and enforcing compliance with community norms' (p. 16);
3 ascribed communities – communities that may choose to be together, but this may also serve to exclude them from wider polities and communities. Giving the example of 'the black community', Plank suggests that 'common interest and mutual concern are ascribed to these communities, or asserted by aspiring community leaders, whether or not these in fact exist' (p. 17);
4 atomized communities – which have no social solidarity nor any particular desire to regain a sense of community.

Plank suggests that politicians and policymakers of all political persuasions purport to see 'community' as desirable and remarkably easy to achieve by means of changes to public policy:

> Among conservatives, for example, the key assumption is that vital and resilient autochthonous communities remain widely available to policymakers, to be restored to power and responsibility as the powers of federal and state governments are reduced. Among progressives the analogous assumption holds that many communities have been shattered or profoundly weakened, but that they can nevertheless be summoned into service when needed to assume major political and administrative responsibilities or to enforce accountability on other levels of government. Both groups agree, however, that communities – once restored to their rightful place in the political order – will exemplify norms and values that correspond closely to the norms and values of those who are doing the calling. (p. 18)

Plank argues that education policymakers often see the school as having a prime role in producing autochthonous community/ies. Schools are positioned as being the key to the production of a stable, self-sufficient mini-polity, able and willing to look after whatever sits within its' neat and tight boundaries. We would add that this is a vision that schools often hold too.

There is an extensive literature about the idea of community, much of which addresses Plank's autochthonous and atavistic categories. The American sociologist Eli Zaretsky (1977) argues that modern life, and particularly contemporary work practices, has stripped family life and neighbourhoods of their sense of community. Robert Putnam (2000) examined economies and social relations in Italy to show that it was possible for work, family and community life to be mutually supportive. Strong social bonds and bridges can be built between neighbourhoods and layers of administration, he argues, leading to increased civic participation and responsibility. The USA needs to take note of this, Putnam suggests, because North Americans are frequently 'bowling alone', as tight-knit communities of the past give way to looser, more disparate groupings. Urban scholar Mike Davis' book, *City of Quartz* (1992) graphically demonstrates how residents in Los Angeles, the uber-city, are becoming increasingly ghettoized, with the wealthy in particular living in high security, gated communities, shut away from everyday life. The British sociologist Anthony Giddens (1990, 1991) also talks about the sequestration of experience, suggesting that modern lives are then increasingly compartmentalized; and require reflexive practices; not, disembedded in space and time, out of place; and lacking in community. And Robert Reich (1991) examines globalized workplaces, arguing that a highly mobile knowledge workforce has no allegiance to place at all.

Much of this work is critiqued as reliant on a memory of a communitarian 'golden age' which didn't really exist, a time with harmonious villages, happy workers and active citizens. Critics point to the highly gendered, classed and raced histories which belie the romantic view that glosses over the meanness, desperation and oppression that marked many neighbourhoods in the past, just as today (Driver and Martell, 1997; Frazer and Lacey, 1993). Nevertheless, the golden age notion of ideal communities imbues politics and popular imaginaries, and offers a vision of a better future that is persuasive to many (e.g. Obama, 2006).

We can see, from this discussion of the literature, that the notion of a community, when collocated with the notion of school, is likely to carry some unhelpful assumptions unless we are clear that:

- people belong to several communities at once, and these may be of different kinds and orders;
- communities are not necessarily harmonious and the social ties that are created within them are various, and not always positive;
- the notion of community is a powerful imaginary used for various political and policy ends.

Framing the school and its surroundings

In the preceding two sections we have differentiated between the neighbourhood and a community. This is because a school may not serve all of the children in its neighbourhood, many schools serve locales that cannot be understood as neighbourhoods, and a school is not simply a singular community, but many communities. We now explore these issues further.

Schools beyond neighbourhood

Schools can be thought about via several scales – as belonging to a state or religious system, perhaps some kind of regional or district organization or perhaps a 'chain' as are the academies in England and charter schools in the USA, and possibly some kind of voluntary network. It is important when beginning to think about researching a school to consider the ways in which it is part of something bigger, and what that means. Schooling in England, for example, has some historical specificities – the national system includes Anglican and Roman Catholic schools, as do many Canadian provincial systems. Until recently, English schooling was organized through local authorities, which, like North American school districts, were able to mediate national policies and make distinctive decisions about the way education was organized. For example, some English local authorities retain grammar schools while others do not and this difference does play out in local educational 'markets' (Gorard et al., 2003). In Australia, the federal government directly funds independent or 'private' schools, as they are known, whereas in England such schools, known as 'public' schools, are registered charities. States/provinces in Australia, Canada and the USA have interpreted national polices very differently, and there are distinctive and significant observable patterns between them – the histories of desegregation in the USA, for instance, were important in Pauline Lipman's study reported in Chapter 2.

Studying the local, and thinking of the school as a place, does not mean that these broader scales of activity and practice can be ignored. It is important for any researcher to understand not only what is particular about their chosen school, but also the specific history of the wider scales of activity and practice within which it operates.

A school serving its neighbourhood?

Many schools, particularly primary schools, *do* serve specific locations, often with tightly defined borders which determine who has the right to attend and who cannot. Of course, not everyone inside these 'catchment areas' or 'zones of right' actually chooses to attend. Some parents may elect to pay fees, or enter their children for competitive scholarships, or sit selective tests in order to send them to a school outside of their neighbourhood. But many schools, particularly secondary schools, serve several neighbourhoods. Students come from a range of different neighbourhoods into the one educational place. Other schools – charters, magnets and some faith schools – have no meaningful relationship with a geographical area at all, selecting students on the basis of their talent, area of interest, or their religious beliefs.

It is impossible, therefore, to draw an automatic equation between the defined material location of the school and the students who attend that school. Nevertheless there is often a relationship between the school and its surrounds, regardless of how tightly the school enrolment matches the immediate material location. Researchers can't just take the locality–school relationship for granted, but they can make it part of their formal inquiries by asking, 'How many neighbourhoods are inside this school? What is the relationship between the school and the surrounding area?'

A school made up of many communities

Even where a school does draw largely from its surrounds, or where it attracts students of a particular faith or curriculum orientation or selects on the basis of test results, there will be multiple communities within the apparent common educational frame. Students and their families will have various kinds of affiliations and associations and students will be divided along class, race and gender lines, which may also form the basis of mini-communities within the school. Other divisions might be made around youth cultures, youthful identities and sporting affiliations. The school itself, in its grouping practices, also supports the creation of mini-communities: the students in the 'top class', those who do a lot of sport, those who spend all their time on the computers, for example. Such mini-communities often have atavistic tendencies. These can map onto, for example, bullying practices. In turn, they can and do deeply influence the ways in which the school is experienced by different groups of students (Thomson and Gunter, 2008).

Because schools are not homogeneous, it is important that researchers consider which communities are represented in the school population and the nature of the wider and mini-communities to which students belong. These connections are one pointer to the kinds of trajectories of social relations in which the school is embedded. Researchers therefore can't make easy assumptions about school community, but they can make community part of their inquiries by asking, 'What are the communities in this school? How are they connected?'

Researching a local area

Having raised these challenges, we devote the remainder of this chapter to considering how to go about researching a school's relationships with its surroundings. These may be small and local, or cover a larger catchment. We begin by looking at two research studies that have investigated a local area. We then go on to consider some strategies that you might use to examine the school(s) that you plan to research.

1 *Research into place-based literacies*

Eve Gregory and Ann Williams conducted a long-term study into school literacy practices used by past and present generations of London families connected with one primary school in Spitalfields, and another nearby in the City of London. (This is research design six, a study which focuses on a geographical area and the learning practices within it, as described in Chapter 3.) This research is reported in their book *City Literacies: Learning to Read Aacross Generations and Cultures* (2000). Drawing on existing research which showed that the literacies taught in schools were not the same as the literate practices found in many communities (e.g. Barton and Hamilton, 1998), the research questions that guided their study were:

> How have children in Spitalfields and the City throughout the twentieth century set about learning to read in their homes, schools and communities? Can we discern patterns of successful early reading common to all four generations? How do parents view their role in children's literacy education? How much do teachers know about children's home literacy practices? How

> do young children set about transferring learning strategies from home to school and vice versa, and how do teachers facilitate their task in doing this? (Gregory and Williams, 2000, p. 13)

In order to answer these questions, Gregory and Williams adopted a multi-layered approach which used ethnographic methods to examine the phenomena and social context, and then moved to a detailed ethno-methodological analysis of individual reading. Our interest here is the first stage, or what Gregory and Williams call the 'outer layer' (p. 15).

In *City Literacies*, Gregory and Williams devote two chapters to social and historical context, using data from 'secondary historical sources and official education reports'. The first chapter focuses on the people in the geographical location who 'grew up in the busy cosmopolitan district that lies on the eastern borders of the city of London' (p. 19). Beginning with references to the tenth-century and medieval landmarks that can still be seen, the authors quickly sketch the development of the built environment, situating it historically as an area which accommodated 'waves of migrants' (p. 20) and where 'the city' with its wealth and enterprise rubbed up against extreme poverty and the hard work necessary to make ends meet. The Huguenots fleeing from persecution flourished, while the Irish fleeing from famine fared less well; the Jews fleeing pogroms and persecution in Europe initially kept themselves somewhat separate from everyone else. Many Spitalfields residents worked in sweatshops and lived in appalling conditions and, unsurprisingly, political dissent was rife. Bangladeshis arrived in the post-war period, and they too left their mark on the streetscape. The first chapter shows both historical and contemporary images of these various communities and their dwellings, churches and commercial buildings.

The second chapter documents the development of schools and schooling in the area. The authors focus on the area's poverty and poor educational provision. They situate one of their schools in the struggle to educate the poor:

a Church of England primary school with a philanthropic mission, which the authors say continued after it became a state funded school, and continues into the present. Their second primary school was built by the state at the turn of the twentieth century, on the site of Jack the Ripper's first murder. At that time it served a high proportion of children unable to speak English, many of whom were Jewish refugees. The authors explain the extraordinary changes the school has seen in the ethnic composition of its students, and the gradual process of the school becoming more middle class. Gregory and Williams also note the presence of both Jewish, Qur'anic and Bengali classes in the community, as well as a progressive socialist community and workers' education centre, Toynbee Hall. Toynbee Hall is strongly associated with a range of important British policies including the development of the welfare state, legal aid and free secondary education.

Now why, you might ask, have Gregory and Williams spent so much time looking at history? The authors argue that this history, this rich mix of cultures, religions and politics, was experienced by the generations still living. These experiences are not only embedded in the built environment, but also in stories, beliefs, bodies of knowledge and in literacy practices – even in vernacular expressions. These are passed on through generations (see Mannion, 2012, for more on intergenerational education). The schools had ways of 'doing literacy' that were historically inflected. And it was precisely these historically situated, place-based literacy practices that the researchers wanted to understand.

Gregory and Williams are not the only researchers to take this kind of 'place-based' approach to researching literacy and other areas of the curriculum. You might want to follow up by looking, for example, at research which examines rural literacy practices (e.g. Donehower et al., 2007; Green and Corbett, 2013; Kmetz et al., 2012) and that which investigates local/global 'funds of knowledge' (e.g. Gonzales and Moll, 2002; Gonzales et al., 2005; Gonzales et al., 1993).

2 *Research into a neighbourhood undergoing 'renewal'*

Ruth Lupton's prize-winning book *Poverty Street* (2003) reports on a study of twelve disadvantaged areas across England. The study (see research design five in Chapter 3) asked two questions:

- What was it that was causing apparently continuous decline in these areas, and an increasing gap from more advantaged areas? Is neighbourhood decline an essentially economic problem? Or has it been created by other forces, and if so what are they?
- Does it make sense to consider 'worst neighbourhoods' as though their problems are common, or are there in fact major differences between poor urban neighbourhoods and small towns, ethnically mixed areas and ethnically homogeneous ones, areas of public housing and areas of low-income private renting? What is the extent of difference and what explains it? (Lupton, 2003, pp. 12–13)

The twelve areas were carefully selected: they encompassed inner-city areas, outer estates and small towns across England and Wales. The study conceptualized three '**spatial** levels' – a neighbourhood consisting of 1,000–7,000 people and roughly equivalent to an electoral ward; a larger area of about 20,000 people; and then a city or local authority.

Two waves of quantitative and qualitative analysis were carried out. Statistics about the population, employment and welfare benefits, health outcomes, education and income were derived from a range of existing data sources, including administrative data held by local authorities. The study had a historical perspective: three census data sets were used. This statistical material was supplemented by two sets of field visits: Lupton conducted interviews with frontline and senior staff and resident representatives, collected local documents, photographs and newspaper cuttings, and observed community facilities and the physical environment.

These data allowed Lupton to discuss 'structural deprivation' and the potential for area based initiatives in a sophisticated and nuanced way. She concluded that:

> The stories of these 12 areas and neighbourhoods demonstrate very clearly the structural origins of neighbourhood 'degeneration', but also the importance of space and place. What had made the areas poor in the first place, and kept them persistently poor, was the fit between their 'intrinsic' or 'hard to change' characteristics – location and topography, housing stock and economic structure – and the demands of the economy and the housing market. The most fundamental causes of area change were, in this sense, 'externally induced' (Galster, 2001, p. 2118). They were 'macro' causes, originating way beyond the neighbourhood, but the particular spatial distribution of their impacts was also determined by 'micro' explanations: by the characteristics of the areas themselves and their particular fit with economic and housing demands. (p. 205)

The rich mix of quantitative and qualitative data, the two waves of data generation and the lens applied at different spatial levels allowed this analysis. Lupton's is an approach which would allow for a view of several schools within a local area, or a secondary school which contained students from several neighbourhoods within a region.

Both of these studies have clues for the researcher wishing to research a school:

- the importance of getting a historical perspective;
- the usefulness of seeing change over time;
- the benefits of using existing data sets;
- the possibilities for incorporating more than one spatial level of analysis;
- the detail provided by combining multiple qualitative methods;

- the different and complementary contributions of quantitative and qualitative data.

We now take these insights into the final section of the chapter, which offers some strategies that you might use to find out more about what lies beyond the school.

Exploring the school surrounds

We assume that you have selected your school (or schools) already understanding whether the student population comes from the immediate surrounds or from further afield. A couple of weeks spent researching the surrounds of the school – be they a neighbourhood or a broader region or city – while you are waiting to sort out initial meetings and formal permission will pay off hugely. Not only will you be more knowledgeable when you get to speak to the head, but you'll also know more about what you might look for when you get inside the school.

The strategies that you employ to understand the school surrounds will vary according to the ground you need to cover. We offer two approaches: (1) library work and (2) getting out and about.

1 *Library work*

   There is a great deal that can be learnt from reading about a local area and its region. We suggest:

   - a social atlas

   Our first point of call is always a social atlas, if one is available. A social atlas is a set of maps which has brought together all or some of the occupational and unemployment data, welfare payments, epidemiological data, income distribution, and data about race, ethnicity and religion, age distribution and educational outcomes. Examples of social atlases are Daniel Dorling's *A New Social Atlas of Britain* (http://www.sasi.group.shef.ac.uk/publications/new_social_atlas/index.html [accessed 12 June 2015); *The Social Atlas of Europe* (Ballas et al., 2014) and the Australian

Social Health Atlas (www.phidu.torrens.edu.au. [accessed 2 July 2016]). Using the mapping made possible by Geographic Information Systems, this data can be presented as national, regional and local area maps. If the social atlas is online, you can drill down into it and compare the surrounds of your school(s) to other areas, and situate the surrounds in larger spatial levels too.

If an aggregated social atlas is not available then each of the data sets is likely to be accessible. It may be that the local authority, city or district council will have compiled their own sets of these data and it certainly doesn't hurt to present yourself to them as a researcher and ask to see what they can provide or allow you to peruse in their office. The local library might help too. Alternatively, the university in which you are enrolled may already have much of this data available through the library or through specialist research units. If all this fails, then an online search will certainly produce some results, although you will then need to compile them.

There are also often relevant large-scale government surveys and cohort studies which can provide helpful information relevant to your work. Longitudinal youth and family studies – such as the Longitudinal Study of Young People in England (LSYPE) (http://discover.ukdataservice.ac.uk/series/?sn=2000030 [accessed 31 October 2015]), the National Longitudinal Surveys in the USA (see http://www.bls.gov/nls/home.htm [accessed 31 October 2015]) and the Longitudinal Surveys of Australian Youth (LSAY) (http://www.lsay.edu.au [accessed 31 October 2015]) – provide a national picture about education, health, cultural pursuits, friendships, and values and attitudes which you can use as a point of reference. Some of these studies can be disaggregated by region, and it is worth knowing before you begin your study whether this is possible.

Finally, it is quite likely that you are not the only person who is, or has been, interested in your particular location. It is always worth a quick search of the university library catalogue to see if anything comes up in response to a geographical search term. This is likely to be at a scale somewhat larger than a school or its immediate surroundings and will probably be anonymized. But a search of a city or region may very well turn up something quite interesting – and useful.

- browsing

There is potentially a lot of useful information online in the form of local websites. Many suburbs and towns now have their own websites which provide handy snapshots of key cultural features such as theatres, cinemas, museums and galleries. Local landmarks will also feature – and this will point to some of the history of the area. Local services and tradespeople are sometimes listed and this too tells you something about how easy or hard it might be to get to a doctor, for instance, or to get a plumber to come to fix a damaged drain. And there may well be a listing of local events, so you can see some of the churches, clubs and associations that exist – and this tells you something about some of the communities that operate around the school site.

Visiting the local newspaper website is often rewarding too. Not only are there often stories about schools, including the one you're interested in, there are also leads about cultural and social life. The newspaper headlines might, for instance, tell you something about community safety, economic development, potential tourism, new employment opportunities, or loss of jobs. There are also of course newspaper archives where you can follow up any of these leads, including stories about your school over time. It often helps, we find, to know if the school has a strong sporting tradition, if it was the subject of media attention because of some kind of perceived scandal, or if it has produced some notable alumni.

Finally, a trip to the local bookshop, if there is one, to the shelf or shelves which are devoted to the area. You may find novels, guidebooks, local histories and books about local heroes and heroines. You don't have to read these in any detail. The scholarly art of skim reading the introduction, table of contents, back cover and concluding section will probably tell you if any of the texts are worth reading in more detail. But from doing this you also know where to go back to if you later discover that any of the information is pertinent. If there is no local bookshop, then you will find some of the same texts online – we love the 'look inside' function – and of course, many of the books will be in the local library if there is one.

2 Getting out and about

There is no substitute in our view for actually getting out into the local area yourself if it is at all possible. We suggest both the immediate area surrounding the school and a somewhat bigger spatial level – the town, the city, even the region. For schools which are 'collectors' – that is, they enrol students from multiple neighbourhoods – the researcher's challenge is to understand a heterogeneous catchment area. This may take some time. It is impossible, for instance, to understand a lone Birmingham secondary school without knowing the history of schooling in the city overall. Children can go to their local Birmingham secondary school, or choose to sit for entrance examinations to a highly selective elite school. Thus, every morning, Birmingham buses are full of children from very different neighbourhoods criss-crossing the city to get to their particular school. There is no substitute for experiencing this for yourself. But do remember, before you get out and about, that it is very important to check on safety issues first by asking someone who is likely to know and give you a frank response.

When we start a research project in a primary school we always like to arrive at the school and then walk or drive the streets around it. We look at the kinds of housing in the immediate vicinity, its age, size and condition. We already have an idea from our library work of the mix of public housing, rental and privately owned dwellings, but nothing beats actually looking in situ. How modern/old is it? What are the gardens like? How well maintained is the streetscape?

We look for shops and other amenities too. Where is the bus or train stop? Where is the local shop the students might go to before or after school or perhaps at lunch time? What does it sell? Who else seems to go there? Is there a bigger shopping centre nearby or does it seem as if the local residents have to depend on small and expensive options or travel further afield? Is there a doctor handy? A dentist? Is there a local park or playground? Who seems to use it and when? Is it maintained? What churches, sporting facilities and other local amenities are there? Does it seem as if the school has to be self-sufficient, or can it use amenities in the neighbourhood?

While it is relatively easy to walk around a primary school or country town, it is harder with schools which serve multi-neighbourhoods. If this is the nature of your study, or if you are studying a group of schools in a wider region, we suggest walking around two or three contrasting neighbourhoods.

If we get to the school before the students arrive then we can see how many of them arrive on foot or by bicycle, and how many of them are dropped off. What kinds of cars do the parents drive? If they come by public transport, what routes are they using? Is there a school bus?

We like to do some mapping around the school. We take some phone photos of the built and natural environment that seem to tell us something about the locality and then stick them on a street directory page, just as Marg Wells did with her class (see earlier in the chapter). We often make a **sensory map** of the school surroundings, where we plot the sounds and smells that we encounter as we walk around. We might map spots which seem neglected, spots that are attractive to us, spots that seem to be heavily used. Now of course these initial impressions can be mistaken. But, if we are careful to record the physical details of what we see and experience, we can hold them up to critical scrutiny during the research.

Figures 3.2 and 3.3 show photographs taken outside two different primary schools. Figure 3.2 is a 1960s council housing estate,

FIGURE 3.2 *A 1960s council housing estate*

Figure 3.3 a late Victorian suburb. Both schools serve their immediate neighbourhoods. Both are made up of largely public or privately rented housing accommodating families who are struggling to make ends meet. The 1960s housing estate has more green spaces available, perhaps where children might play, but fewer trees. Both areas appear to be moderately well maintained, although it is likely that the 1960s housing is less well built than the older late Victorian terraces. If we were to show you more photographs of these two areas, then you could build a view of what it might be like to live there.

Neighbourhood first impressions can be very powerful, and telling. Ruth Lupton, whose research we described earlier in rather dry terms, begins her book *Poverty Street* (2003) describing the council estate that motivated her study. She called it Bridgefields. She was anything but dispassionate about what she saw as she walked and drove around it:

> Bridgefields is a 1970s council estate: modern three bedroomed houses in neat cul-de-sacs, backing onto pedestrian alley-ways

and communal play areas. It is right on the edge of town, and has stunning moorland views. A frequent bus service links the estate to the town centre, 15 minutes away. When I visited it, I found a strong sense of community, and a core of committed people, helping each other out and getting involved in estate life: running youth groups, social activities, pensioners' lunches, a food coop and a credit union. The facilities available to residents were extensive: a modern and well-equipped community and employment centre, workshops, a family centre, health centre, library, youth centre, award-winning youth project, church-run community house, top-quality football pitch and hard court play area, as well as two primary schools. But Bridgefields was not seen as a neighbourhood of choice for many people. In April 1999, more than one third of its houses were boarded up, with some streets almost completely empty. Some houses had been seriously vandalized, with evidence of fire-setting, missing roof tiles and fences and extensive graffiti. Piles of rubbish lay in the gardens of empty homes and there was little around the estate in general. It was an appalling living environment. (Lupton, 2003, p. 1)

FIGURE 3.3 *A late Victorian neighbourhood*

Not long after you've completed your walking around, it is very helpful to write a short description of the school surrounds as you first saw them. This is a way of bringing information together so that you can check it out and/or use it later.

You might, however, like to be a little more experimental about your exploration. You could organize a **dérive** as a way of just coming across something unexpected. Unlike an organized walk, or a more flaneur-like stroll where the whim takes you, the dérive (literally, floating freely) focuses on psychogeographic responses to a landscape (Debord, 1956/58). Guy Debord discriminates between a dérive and the exoticism of getting to know somewhere new:

> The spatial field of a dérive may be precisely delimited or vague, depending on whether the goal is to study a terrain or to emotionally disorient oneself. It should not be forgotten that these two aspects of dérives overlap in so many ways that it is impossible to isolate one of them in a pure state. But the use of taxis, for example, can provide a clear enough dividing line: if in the course of a dérive one takes a taxi, either to get to a specific destination or simply to move, say, twenty minutes to the west, one is concerned primarily with a personal trip outside one's usual surroundings. If, on the other hand, one sticks to the direct exploration of a particular terrain, one is concentrating primarily on research for a psychogeographical urbanism.

The key thing about the dérive is to clear the mind of any preconceptions. Rather than approaching the school surrounds with a set of questions already in mind (a what-is-there-in-this-locality agenda), the dérive requires you to simply walk/drive around, open and observant to the surroundings and any encounters that you have. You are more likely to stumble across something unexpected if you are not looking for anything in particular. You can actually pre-set yourself an itinerary too – something arbitrary, like 'walk for a block and then cross the road, look left, what do you see …' Debord held that the purpose of the dérive was to remap, in his case, a city. As he put it:

> The lessons drawn from dérives enable us to draw up the first surveys of the psychogeographical articulations of a modern

> city. Beyond the discovery of unities of ambiance, of their main components and their spatial localization, one comes to perceive their principal axes of passage, their exits and their defenses. One arrives at the central hypothesis of the existence of psychogeographical pivotal points. One measures the distances that actually separate two regions of a city, distances that may have little relation with the physical distance between them. With the aid of old maps, aerial photographs and experimental dérives, one can draw up hitherto lacking maps of influences, maps whose inevitable imprecision at this early stage is no worse than that of the first navigational charts.

Debord's thesis was that the physical make-up of a city, or neighbourhood, did not necessarily map onto its psychic layout. The dérive was a way to focus on the intangible and haptic.

You might also look for inspiration to the writings associated with 'literary walks' (e.g. Atkins, 2014; Hamilton and Roberts, 2014); the literature on exploring place (e.g. Marsden, 2014; Tyler, 2015); writing about psychogeographies (e.g. Ellard, 2015; Richardson, 2015); and methodological texts which explore the ways in which walking can be used to generate conversations and ideas (e.g. Back and Puwar, 2013; Ingold, 2011). You could also look for new apps that generate random instructions for you to wander or drift around a neighbourhood.

There are of course other, more systematic, ways to deal with larger neighbourhoods, cities and regions. To conclude the chapter, we focus on two – windshield surveys and **assets mapping**.

A *windshield survey* is simply a survey of an area made from a car using a street map. Plot a route around the area that covers all of the sections. Then drive the route – preferably with someone else doing the actual driving. You might want to take notes, or use a digital recorder – the method that we prefer. Things to look for include:

- the presence or absence of commercial activity;
- the location, condition and use of public spaces;
- the amount of activity on the streets at given times, and who is involved in doing what;
- the noise level in various part of the area;

- the level of traffic and frequency and accessibility of public transport and its use;
- the nature, age and condition of housing;
- the public buildings, their location, condition and use;
- differences that suggest cultural diversity or economic inequalities.

In order to understand how people use the local area, it is necessary to repeat the windshield survey at different times of the day and week. The windshield survey is very suitable for understanding larger areas and cities.

Assets mapping is a technique used by community developers; they see a community asset as anything or any person that might be interested and involved in, or is already improving, the quality of life in an area. An assets map aims to find and map influential and helpful people, services, organizations and businesses. Assets mapping is posited as an antidote to the negative view of areas that can be created through the collection of statistics that focus on poverty and on need (Kretzmann and McKnight, 1993; McKnight, 1995; McKnight and Kretzmann, 1996). The Creative Citizens project (http://www.creativecitizens.co.uk [accessed 31 October 2015]) suggested that it was helpful not only to map assets on a street map, but also to map them in relation to a project, as what is an asset in one project may not be so for another.

Figure 3.4 offers an assets map. Imagine that the school sits at the very centre of these three circles. In the inner ring are those neighbourhood organizations and institutions that have the strongest connections – these might be a church, the chip shop where students sneak off to, the factory owned by the chair of governors – well, you get the picture. In the outer circle are those 'assets' in the neighbourhood with the weakest relationship with the school.

This kind of assets mapping can be done by the researcher, but it is also very often a helpful participatory exercise conducted with various groups in the school – students, teachers, school leaders – and these can then be compared with each other. The map allows you to visualize the kinds of relations in which the school is involved and to foreground the potential flows of people, things

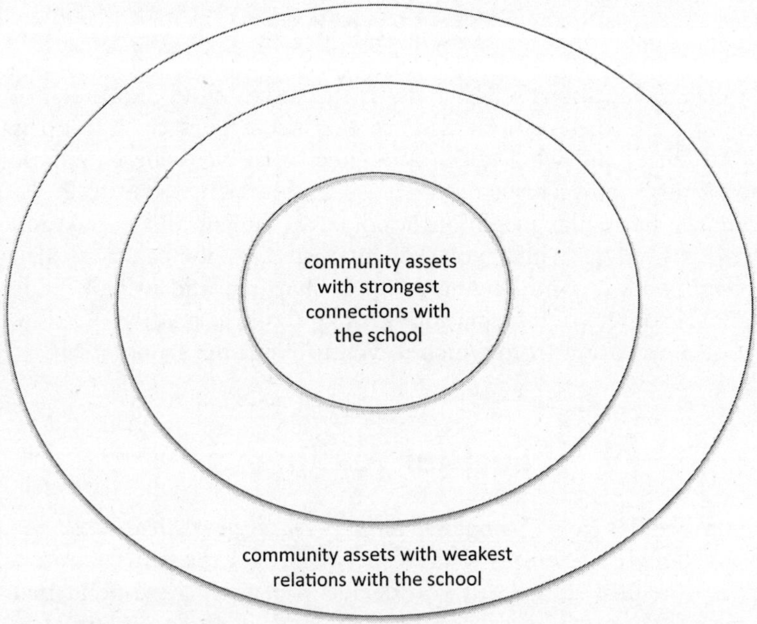

FIGURE 3.4 *Mapping a school's community assets*

and information that might accompany these relations. Using an aerial map of the school and its neighbourhood(s) and region additionally allows you to see the differences between close social relationships and material distance. You can then raise interesting questions – for example, why does the school work closely with the church a mile away and not with the one on its doorstep? This kind of relationship mapping is often helpful to the school too, as it focuses attention on potential relationships that the staff and students might want to foster.

It is also possible to do assets mapping with students themselves. This is particularly useful when working with 'collector' schools, as the students can help you to cover and understand the range of neighbourhoods that are 'in' the school.

Final note

You hear a lot about schools and their communities and much of this kind of conversation assumes that what goes on inside the school fence, and what goes on outside, is stable, coherent, static and homogenous. This is not the case, and it is important to investigate the particular neighbourhood(s), catchment and population of the school in which you are interested. A lot can be learnt through walking and driving around, chatting, and using readily available sources of information. This kind of information provides a good foundation from which to venture into the school itself.

Further reading

Emma Smith's text *Using Secondary Data in Educational and Social Research* (2008) is written specifically for the British context but is a helpful resource if you decide you want to work further with such data sets, as is Thomas Vartanian's book *Secondary Data Analysis* (2011), written for US social workers.

You might also want to examine some of the work by researchers who focus on neighbourhoods. By reading more than one of their texts you can assess the various approaches and theoretical resources that they use. We recommend three researchers to start with:

Kalervo Gulson

Gulson, K. (2011). *Education Policy, Space and the City: Markets and the (In)visibility of Race*. London: Routledge.

Gulson, K. and C. Symes (2007). *Spatial Theories of Education Policy and Geography Matters*. London: Routledge.

Webb, P. and K. Gulson (2015). *Policy, Geophilosophy and Education*. Rotterdam: Sense Publishers.

Pauline Lipman

Lipman, P. (1998). *Race, Class, and Power in School Restructuring*. Albany: State University of New York Press.

Lipman, P. (2004). *High Stakes Education: Inequality, Globalization, and Urban School Reform*. New York: Routledge.

Lipman, P. (2011). *The New Political Economy of Urban Education: Neoliberalism, Race, and the Right to the City*. New York: Routledge.

Margaret Somerville

Somerville, M. (2013). *Water in a Dry Land: Place-learning through Art and Story*. London: Routledge.

Somerville, M., B. Davies, K. Power, S. Gannon and P. de Carteret (2011), *Place Pedagogy Change*. Rotterdam: Sense Publishers.

Somerville, M. and M. Green (2015). *Children, Place and Sustainability*. London: Palgrave.

Somerville, M., K. Power and P. deCarteret (2009). *Landscapes and Learning: Place Studies for a Global World*. Rotterdam: Sense Publishers.

CHAPTER FOUR

Reading the school

We begin this chapter assuming that you have permission to research in the school. You can now take all of the things you learnt from touring the school surrounds, large or small, into the actual school site itself. This chapter works with methods that you might use *early on* in your contact with the school.

We focus here on the school and its 'discursive practices'. In the first section of the chapter we explain our usage of the term 'discursive practice' and why we think of a school as having multiple and diverse texts and discourses. We will discuss a range of written texts, and virtual ones, but we also include the school building and grounds in this discussion. We then examine research which has 'read' the school before going on to consider (1) texts produced by and about the school, (2) displays on the school walls as a text and (3) clues in the school's built environment. We conclude with a brief discussion about mapping.

The discursive practices of schools

We begin by explaining what we mean by our key terms: practice, discourse and discourse practice.

The term **practice** is often used to describe the patterned, everyday activities that are at the heart of social life. A practice approach focuses on what people do regularly, as part of their ordinary work. By looking at everyday practices we can analyse who is involved in them and why and how they were conceived, produced and patterned. If we think of a school assembly as a practice, then we can ask who decided that assemblies were needed and important, why, who is involved and how, what happens in assemblies and what happens because of them.

This approach to practice comes from a particular 'non-structuralist' approach to social theory. Practices are seen as neither individual, nor as social and cultural structures. Practices are trans-personal activities – that is, they are socially and culturally produced, framed and regulated. This means that, in relation to school assemblies for instance, there may be religious, cultural and/or historical reasons which shape how they are conducted. There may also be some kind of official regulations which govern them. What can be done in the local school assembly may not be the school's decision alone, but be partially shaped by external processes. However, local schools can adjust the usual patterns to suit themselves: what we might call local mediation and fabrication. It is that local mediation, translation and fabrication, as well as the overall framing, that interests us in relation to the school as place.

According to Schatzki (2001, p. 11). practices can be understood as 'embodied, materially mediated arrays of human activity centrally organized around shared practical understanding'. We might thus think of the school assembly as a practice which brings together a school hall, chairs, people, microphones and a regular format of activities. Schatzki points to practice as the bringing together of understandings, bodies, the material environment and activities. This 'bringing together' is something that we can systematically investigate. Furthermore, practices can be described as routines – practices are the routinized ways in which 'bodies are moved, objects are handled, subjects are treated and the world is understood' (Reckwitz, 2002, p. 250). Because practices are routinized, rather than being one-off random acts, they are potentially comprehensible and codifiable and/or already codified. School assemblies, for instance, may always start with a school song, followed by an address by the headteacher: we could, for example, code these as official, stable and/or 'common school format'. Researchers can look not only for routines but also for the ways in which these are produced and talked about – in other words, how the practices are knowable by teachers and students, and how they are categorized and rationalized by the school itself. We might see the school song and headteacher address as expressions of authority, whereas people within the school itself might see them as tradition – it's 'what we have always done'.

The notion of discourse helps us further with the task of locating and analysing the various arrangements of words, things, people and ideas which organize everyday life in the school. Discourse is most commonly understood as talk, or talk and text (a text is a body of writing as in a book or website). This is not the way in which we use the term here. According to Foucault (1972, 1980, 2001), discourse can be understood as namings, texts and sayings. So, there are talk and texts associated with a school assembly, to continue our example. These include what is said, as well as the things that are read out, that are circulated before and after the event and that refer to it. Foucault says that, together, namings, texts and sayings organize ways of being, behaviours, relationships, interactions and the arrangements of signs and material objects. What is said in – and about – school assemblies, for example, requires students and teachers to act in particular ways, to listen, to speak when spoken to and so on. A researcher might see the school assembly as part of instilling a particular form of mass discipline. Perhaps there are other things that you can think of that are also accomplished through the school assembly.

However, discourses do more than shape behaviour and what is said. Discourses, according to Foucault, are not simply practices – they also constitute, codify and legitimate a practice or set of practices. This means that they also shape what *can* be said and done – and what can't. We 'know' for instance when someone has 'misbehaved' in an assembly because they have gone against the rules that govern behaviour. If a headteacher says something which is more like staffroom talk, then he or she may have used a discourse inappropriate to the particular assembly practice. Discourse is integral to the ways in which we make sense of who we are, where we are, what we are doing, why and how. Through sense-making processes such as problematization (this behaviour is not appropriate) and categorization (that misbehaving student is put in the 'naughty' or 'troublesome' category), discourses frame not only what can be thought, said and seen but also what it is possible to be and do.

We understand discourse to include and exclude, foreground and background, and render some things important and others invisible. Moving away from the assembly, take this example. A school might make sexual harassment part of the school discipline code (it is included) but then not make it a routine part of discipline processes unless a student specifically complains about it (it is backgrounded). In this case, while there is an official discourse about sexual harassment, the discourse practice marginalizes it.

Researching with discourse as a lens means that we can think of the school as a site for particular ways of being, thinking, acting and knowing. We can look for these particularities. Particular discourse practices simultaneously make other possible ways of being, thinking, acting and knowing less likely. We can therefore also look for what is less or not possible. Researchers interested in discourse can examine practices, asking how some lines of thinking and arguing come to be taken as legitimate and as truths, while other ways of thinking/being/doing are marginalized.

We have already referred to 'official discourse' when we used the example of a school assembly, but a school's discourse practices are always much more than what is official. The school can be understood as an assemblage of discourse communities, which share some common ways of thinking, being and doing. As we saw when we looked at communities in Chapter 3, a school has an 'official' community and it has an 'official' discourse practice. But it also has within it different communities with distinctive shared ways of being, speaking, doing and believing. A school can be thought of as one discursive community, only in as much as there is recognition of the sets of discourses sutured together in place. These discourses do not necessarily cohere, but they are made to do so in temporary and fragile 'settlements' and through ongoing mediation. Researchers look for the ways in which different discourses are translated, settled and mediated.

As we have suggested, discourse is also about beliefs and values. Some discursive practices within a discourse community are normative, in that they create 'truths' about what is appropriate thought, speech and action. Discourse constructs knowledge and governs, through the projections and enactments of knowledge and assemblages of texts, what is legitimate, worthwhile and right. In other words, within a school there are both explicit and taken-for-granted ways of understanding the school as an institution and the wider world. The school rules are one way in which rights and wrongs are established, but there are always other hidden and taken-for-granted customs and rituals which are highly normative. These norms shape what it is possible to be and what it is possible to know, talk about and do in, with and for the school. Students, for instance, can be thought of as variously 'troubled', 'able' or gifted': these are normative categories which then make particular kinds of actions – exclusion, rewards, setting and so on – possible.

Foucault himself was clear that discourse practice included texts, interactions, networks and material objects. His interest was not in a text or building per se, nor in a network or set of social interactions, but in the practices through which knowledge both produces and is produced (Bacchi and Bonham, 2014). As practices, discourse re/produces knowledge and power simultaneously.

Researchers interested in discourse thus understand they are not conducting an inquiry on neutral territory. They not only look for ways of thinking, being and doing in the school, but also how power circulates through these practices and to what ends. Analysing discourse practices requires the researcher to look for patterns of category-making, asking from what broader discourse or discursive assemblage they emanate, what they omit and include, and what social work they legitimate and bring about *in* and *as* practice (see also Chouliaraki and Fairclough, 1999; Fairclough, 2003). (Discourse practice is not an easy notion to grasp, and at the end of this chapter we have suggested some further reading that you might pursue.)

In order to get to grips with what this complex theory actually means for research, we now consider two types of research projects that have looked at aspects of schools' discursive practices. We are not offering these examples as the *only* places in which it is possible to look for discourse practices. A researcher might equally look at school excursions, school assemblies, signs, yearbooks and so on. It is important to read our examples looking for the method – the approach – used by researchers with an understanding of discourse practice. Our first example looks at school websites and prospectuses, and the second at school displays.

Analysing school websites and prospectuses

There is a small body of research which analyses the various kinds of promotional materials that schools produce to 'sell themselves' to potential new enrolments and the wider world. These are often easily obtained prior to starting work in the school itself, or early in the piece. In the context of increased school choice, and the marketization of schooling, the importance of image management has become a more significant aspect of the work and budgets of schools.

We report on two research projects here, each using a different method of **discourse analysis**.

1 Andrew Wilkins (2011) conducted a discourse analysis of image and written texts. He analysed the brochures and websites of two Roman Catholic secondary schools in London. Both schools gave priority to baptized Roman Catholic children, were situated in the same borough, and both were 'voluntary aided', that is they got the majority of their funding from government with the remainder from the Church. Both schools' intakes were predominantly girls. There was some common framing of the schools' advertising materials. However, one of the schools, Elwood, had received a satisfactory inspection grading, with the report commenting on the 'dispersed' student intake and its ethnic diversity. The other school, Greendale, had an outstanding grading. The task to be accomplished by the advertising – that each was a 'good school' – was therefore different.

   Wilkins obtained permission from the schools to use images from their websites and brochures in his published work, provided he removed any obvious markers that would identify them. His analysis of their texts showed that each school positioned itself through discourses of tradition, community, curriculum and localism/globalism. These discourses shaped what could and couldn't be said. Wilkins points, for example, to the schools' references to two different religious orders:

   > Elwood locates its distinction and appeal through the enduring legacy of the pedagogic teachings of the F.C.J. [Faithful Companions of Jesus] Sisters. With ministries and professional and lay colleagues operating across the world, the F.C.J. Sisters represent a global consortium of Roman Catholics with influences that span and cultivate the ethos and organization of different public

> and private institutions, ranging from spiritual and refugee centres for women and homeless people to primary and secondary schools. Viewed through a critical discourse perspective, the F.C.J. Sisters perform the ideological-symbolic work of locating Elwood within a utopian-global religious narrative that is structured around themes of continuity, permanence and order. (Ironically, too, it doubles as a kind of utopian-local narrative in which the global translation of religious sentiment and charitable giving is transposed or re-coded into comfortable feelings pertaining to localized expressions of security, predictability, safety and settlement.) (p. 76)

Greendale offered a similar affiliation to another order. Both schools also used images of their school buildings to convey a sense of grandeur, structure, history and past order. Wilkins observes that the images used by both schools on their websites and brochures

> ... combine shrubs and small trees with a clear arching sky, thus conveying to the viewer fanciful interpretations of a calm, peaceful, idyllic setting. This has the effect of generating an inclusive notion of community: the building is imposing by the way it is presented as an enclave overseeing the space of the courtyard, with the implication that the school works to insulate people within a space built upon ideas of settlement, predictability and security. Moreover, the buildings look on to each other, fashioned as a kind of courtyard, serving to heighten a sense of inclusion and surveillance. This structure of feeling is matched by the way in which the trees and shrubs positioned in the foreground of the image have the powerful effect of making the viewer feel like an outsider looking in. (p. 80)

The schools situated themselves differently within government policy initiatives, Elwood as a specialist arts college, and Greenwood as a specialist science college with mathematics. Elwood used drama masks as its logo, while

Greendale adopted a scientific-style symbol of subatomic particles orbiting an atom. The arts/science binary is highly loaded in current English policy contexts and it is perhaps not accidental that the outstanding inspection rating went to the science specialist college.

Wilkins also locates some significant and possibly related differences in the ways in which the two schools represented their student populations, with Elwood showing photos dominated by Afro-Caribbean girls, stating a commitment to church-based 'praise' music, and thus implied connections to the local area. Greendale on the other hand positioned itself as a 'cosmopolitan' school with connotations of 'plurality, multiculturalism and globalism' (p. 82). Greendale's student photos showed a mixed student population, as well as both visual and verbal references to international connections.

Wilkins argues that his analysis of these two schools' promotional materials illuminates the official discourse practice of school choice, as mediated by the school. By looking for what was included and excluded, what was highlighted and what was selected and to what ends, Wilkins shows how schools worked through the texts to position themselves in a competitive school market. (See also work by Meg Maguire, Jane Perryman, Stephen Ball and Annette Braun (2011), who analysed school websites as part of their research into policy enactments in what they called 'the ordinary school'.)

2 Using a different method, that of rhetorical analysis, Paula McDonald, Barbara Pini and Robyn Mayes (2012) examined the prospectuses of 65 elite schools in Australia. The authors take organizational rhetoric as a discourse practice which helps to achieve closure of meanings by positioning some interpretations as legitimate and normative. This excludes other potential meanings. They argue that the interpretation of organizational rhetoric is context dependent and is not about the intentions of the speaker. The authors draw on a particular theorization of rhetoric (Cheney et al., 2004) which offers twenty specific

types of rhetorical strategy that can be used in order to support organizational strategy, vision and ambition.

The researchers had two questions:

> (1) What rhetorical strategies of persuasion do private schools use in their prospectuses to attract prospective students? What do the rhetorical strategies mask, in terms of broader education frameworks?
> (2) What are the connections between organizational rhetorical strategies and the context of broader politico-cultural discourses? What are the points of tension and concern? (p. 6)

They selected schools in three Australian states that at the time charged parents more that A$10,000 in fees. Writing to all of the potential schools produced a set of sixty-five prospectuses. As in Maguire et al.'s (2011) study,

> [t]ypically, prospectuses were in booklet or folder form on very high-quality paper and around 14 pages in length. Their structures were broadly similar and included a 'message from the principal', demographic and historical information about the school, and a description of the school's accessibility and location, religious values, curriculum and code of behavior. (p. 7)

The researchers read the texts looking for holistic understanding; a second reading was then conducted looking for any of the twenty pre-identified rhetorical strategies. We do not have space here to report all of the results of this analysis, but we would recommend reading the paper in full, particularly if you want to focus on rhetorical strategies in your research. We quote here some extracts from the analysis to show the insights that the researchers' chosen method afforded:

> *Identification* – linking one issue with another indivisible issue – was used most frequently in relation to academic achievement. Academic success was attributed to the specific pedagogical practices at the school. (p. 8)

> Prospectuses used *juxtapositioning* in aligning tradition and innovation, and religion and critical enquiry. Prospectuses often dedicated at least one page at the beginning of the document to providing a description of the history of the school, along with a statement reflecting the continuity of values and principles of a time past. (p. 10)
>
> *Bolstering or self-promotion* as a way of consolidating the status or credibility of the organization was the most frequent and salient rhetorical strategy evident in the data. Bolstering was most immediately obvious in the appearance of the prospectuses. The documents and their packaging and formats denoted sophistication, status, prestige and expense through the use of top-quality printing materials and glossy full-page photographs, often of sweeping views from the school's premises and cheerful, engaged, wellgroomed and attractive students. (p. 11)
>
> *Reframing and reversal* ... meaning an ironic or surprising shift to create a new idea (Cheney et al., 2004). Schools, by using this strategy, carefully denied that they were exclusionary and instead communicated information about their inclusivity and/or commitment to diversity, either in their fee structures, the accessibility of locations, the diversity of religious and cultural backgrounds of the student body or the occupations of parents. (p. 13)

The researchers note that their analysis allowed them to see the ways in which these schools deployed organizational rhetoric in order to promote themselves as socially just, rather than as self-serving bastions of wealth that critics would have them be, by 'writing out' references to privilege, wealth and elitism. According to the researchers, this fine-grained rhetorical analysis, while partial, opened the way for further research into the histories of this marketing discourse and the interactions with experts outside of the school. Through imprecise expression and appeals to values, the schools' brands lauded lasting positive effects on students, and dealt with contradictions between tradition and the need for young people to be adaptable.

School displays

This next example is intended to focus attention on an aspect of a school that often strikes you when you first encounter it – the way in which it looks. We approach the material environment of the school as a visual text which can be 'read' through discourse analysis, asking not just what displays say about and to the school, but how the displays were produced and read, by whom and why.

We have long been interested in school buildings and what might be learnt from them. Some years ago we conducted a three-year ethnography of Holly Tree Primary School which, at the time, was working with an artist-in-residence. One of the most striking things about the school was the sheer amount of arts-based material that was on the walls (this aspect of the study is reported in Thomson et al., 2007). On the very first day our researcher Lisa Russell spent in the school she made the following **observations** in her **field notes**:

> I stand up from the seated area and inspect the artwork that is clearly evident, displayed on the walls as you enter the school ... Two plaster of paris figures welcome visitors ... One is a female figure and one is a male, both in red school uniform, both of real child-like age and stature [see Figure 4.1]. The deputy introduces herself to me and asks two year 6 girls to give me the guided tour. H and E ... take me round each classroom, starting in the nursery. The nursery looks like an adventure play area, full of hidden dens and escape areas. They show me outside, the grassland where they do sports day, the little areas where different groups of children play, and where they get their school photo taken and perform a summer concert in front of parents, near the entrance to the school. They freely walk into the staff room to show me where the staff gather, get cups of coffee and go to the lavatory. (I'm struck by the kids' freeness, they didn't hesitate to go into the staff room, it wasn't out of bounds!) They point out the collage of a teacher displayed on

> the staff room wall along with other paintings of faces ... they point out the various artwork displayed all round the school. They show me the photographs of the annual school trip, they tell me the names of the previous year 6s who have just moved onto secondary school and point out their self-portrait work, complete with their names, on the wall ... They also point out their own work that is put on show. H shows me herself in various forms, she shows me a painted picture of her face, a photograph of herself, a drawing of herself and a sculpture. E shows me a plaster of paris outline of her face. They show me the Peter Pan figures hanging near the arts area and I note the Waterstones exhibition self-portraits evident on the wall. There are sculptures, painting and photos of present and previous children everywhere. I'm struck by all the artwork displayed in every room on almost every bit of wall! (Lisa's field notes on her first day at Holly Tree; Thomson et al., 2007, pp. 381–2)

We decided we needed to be quite systematic in the way in which we thought about the displays. We wanted to examine display as discourse practice – what *was* said and done in relation to the displays, and what was not. We took a complete photographic survey of every wall in the school and then undertook a *content analysis* (Rose, 2001) – that is, we looked to see what each of the displays was about. We also asked about the displays – we talked with the headteacher, the teaching assistant who was responsible for display, staff and three groups of Year 5 children. Lisa also observed the ways in which the displays were used in classes, and when visitors came.

We first of all saw that the most immediately public areas of the school – hall, foyer and shared work areas – were dominated by children's portraits in various media, sculpted figures, pages from a child-produced, alphabetized poetry book, and mounted pages of autobiographies and biographies. Some of the work, such as a frieze in the hall, was clearly the work of a professional artist. Classrooms typically displayed mounted collages of children's curriculum-based work, much of it with teachers' comments attesting to its worth. However, some displays were very busy, some work was more obviously teacher-developed and not all rooms were as well organized as others. We concluded that some teachers were more committed to display than others.

FIGURE 4.1 *Display at Holly Tree Primary entrance*

In talking to the head, Miriam, we discovered that she was very wedded to the display practice:

> Miriam had a strong belief in display as both the means of exhibiting the school's long commitment to artistic endeavour and also creating a stimulating learning/working context. This was manifest in a requirement that all staff should receive in-service training in the Holly Tree mode of display.
>
> Every year two of my staff, a teaching assistant and a teacher who are particularly good at it, run a course. A morning's course, and they have our teacher trainees, our new TAs [teaching assistants], any new teaching staff. And they do a whole morning's course with them. First of all showing them round the classrooms, showing them the sorts of displays that we do; giving them strategies for doing it. (Miriam, transcript 1)
>
> This in-service training came about partly by accident.
>
> [O]ne or two of the new teachers had let the TAs do the displays and they were fine but straight away I thought 'Heck! This is not right' ... they were stilted and they were not stimulating and they were not backed properly and there was just not enough of them. There were just about half a dozen pictures on a display board with lots of space between. I said to my deputy 'These are fine for any other school but they are not good enough for us'. So we took then down and did them again ... that's when I decided to do the course. (Miriam, transcript 1)
>
> Teachers were expected to maintain the 'quality' of display in their own rooms, but they could get help from TA Susan who also took a key role in managing the appearance of the shared areas of the school, including the front foyer and office area. (Thomson et al, 2007 pp. 386–7)

We also found that Miriam inspected the classroom displays regularly to see if they were up to her standard. This was because she thought that the displays acted as a pedagogic resource, which students could consult and the teachers could use both as exemplars of 'good work' and as a reward for work well done.

We did not, however, see teachers explicitly using the displays as a learning resource and we speculated that they might have thought that this use occurred informally, simply through exposure.

Miriam saw the displays as a counter to what she understood as the drab aesthetics of children's lives on their estates. She also made considerable use of them when visitors came to the school. It was as if the school walls were a living prospectus which demonstrated the standard of work that was achieved in the school, and the rich array of extra-curricular activities the school had to offer. They were tangible demonstrations of good work, good teaching and good students. There was, we concluded, a strongly normative element to the displays: they were a visual reminder of what teachers and students must do every day.

The children we spoke to had a somewhat different view. We had noted that the displays were a kind of palimpsest – some remained year on year, so layers of school activities were built up. The displays recorded regular events in the life of the school as well as special events. Our analysis was that the displays served not a curriculum, but rather an associational purpose:

> For children, the cumulative nature of the displays functioned in a diary-like manner, as a visual aide-memoire. They made the school a 'theatre of memory' (Samuels, 1994), where displays provided the resources, not for learning 'school stuff', but for the construction of a narrative of experience of schooling which was peppered with excitement, enjoyment and a sense of individual and collective achievement. Children could trace their own trajectory through the school and that of their peers via displays. We suggest that these stories of affiliation created an emotional attachment to the school, which was strongly evidenced in the children's almost unanimous liking for staff and the school itself. (Ofsted and interview data) (Thomson et al, 2007 p. 397)

We came to understand that the display in the school was a discourse practice which brought together and made sense of several strongly held discursive strands: normative views about learning and teaching 'standards'; a connection with the tradition of the 'progressive British primary school'; a middle-class sensibility of the importance of the arts and child-produced art; and the need to demonstrate/perform for visitors and inspectors. The walls organized all of these various lines of thinking: the displays were one available tool for stitching together potentially contradictory ideas – accountability for standards and a holistic concern for children, for instance. These were not the only sites where this work occurred. However, our exploration of the walls provided a very useful lens through which to focus on the ways in which the school set forms and managed competition. You may well find other school practices that are as generative.

We now turn from research that examines aspects of a school's discourse practices to some things that you might look at when you first go into your strategically chosen school (as explained in Chapter 3).

Texts produced by and about the school

Schools now produce a great deal of material for public consumption. This is because, as we have already suggested, they are now in much more marketized and audit-driven systems. It is possible to gain some understanding about schools by examining and conducting some preliminary analysis of these texts.

When we go to a new school we always look first at any system aggregator sites, such as those that list test results. The Australian myschool.edu.au site, for example, allows you to obtain a great deal of base-line information about a school's population, numbers of teaching/non-teaching staff, its recurrent income and sources of income and national test results, as well as a school-produced mission statement. This information is available from 2007, so it is possible to see any changes in student population and school size. Other data, such as enrolment in vocational courses, attendance and proximity to other schools, are also provided. In some countries, this kind of information may be scattered or unavailable, but it is always worth spending a bit of time looking to see what there is.

We then look for any inspection reports that are available. Most school systems have some way of inspecting the quality of schools, although these vary enormously. Some inspection authorities, such as Estyn in Wales, and Ofsted in England, have comprehensive websites. These websites house sets of inspection documents for each school, which, when read together, give a sense of what challenges the school has faced and what its strengths and weaknesses have been judged to be.

We then – inevitably – search online, using the school's name. That brings up the school website but also other sets of information. For instance, when we searched for the local primary school near where we both live in Nottingham we found on the first seven pages a report of a grant for recycling; two sites listing employment opportunities; a school uniform provider; seven sites which 'rated' schools; local authority school dinner menus; a Wikipedia entry; reports of various sponsored events (anti-bullying, healthy schools, arts, music); archived newspaper articles from the local paper; articles in the city newspaper; a Year 4 class blog; a Facebook page for the teachers' and parents' association; a slide show of children's art produced for a national gallery plus other sites with pictures of the children's artworks; various newspaper reports of league table results; and a pinterest board kept by a Year 2 teacher of class artwork. We also found several maps and information about location, and an architectural site on which several pictures of the Victorian building, with its distinctive bell tower, had been posted. Switching from words to online images produced a large number of pictures of children in the hall, gym, art rooms, in an orchestra, in sports teams, and more pictures of the buildings. There were also some historical photographs and these led us back to that Year 4 blog where the class had obviously been doing some local history research. Many pictures led us back to the school's own website.

These days most schools have websites, and it is certainly worth visiting them. This is not simply for content, but also for the images that they choose to present. We think it is worth spending a little time on the school website. The following questions are starters, which we hope will help orient your scrutiny of the site. These questions, similar to the ones Andrew Wilkins asked of the websites he examined, take as their starting point the notion of discourse practice as a means of producing norms, inclusions and exclusions and of projecting imaginaries.

Consider the front page.

- What is on the front page of the website? Is there anything that is obviously missing?

- If there is a building, what kind of building is it and what might it represent – is it traditional, modern and innovative, cosmopolitan, locally connected?
- If there are students, what are they doing – extra-curricular activities, celebrations, ordinary classroom work?
- What are the links that are provided in the side bar? Why do you think these have been chosen? What assumptions are embedded in this choice of links about who is reading the site?
- What is the text on the front page? What story is it trying to project about the school and to whom?
- What is the school logo and motto? What do these signify?

Now look at each webpage in turn and the various subsections, asking similar questions about what is deemed important enough to talk about and what is not, which people are shown and not shown, what people are doing and not doing, what stories are being developed about the school and the work it does.

Here are some questions you might ask:

- How does the school address its own performance on tests and other forms of external judgement? Is this explicit?
- If the school is marketing itself, what are its 'unique selling propositions' (USPs) and to whom is it aiming these?
- How does the school position itself vis-à-vis other schools? For example, does it emphasize local connections, an international orientation, a strong base in tradition, the cutting edge of innovation, multicultural dimensions, specializing in particular kinds of cultural capitals (arts, science), and, if so, to whom are these likely to appeal?

Thinking about the answers through the lens of place will alert you to the flows and framings, and the kind of mediations that might occur within the school. After getting as much as you can from these sources, you are ready to enter the school.

The built environment

We want to begin this section by acknowledging that many people visit schools and form quite distinct first impressions. Visitors leave schools saying things like 'This school feels ...' and then add a word like 'friendly', 'warm', 'happy' – or sometimes the opposite – 'miserable', 'alienating', 'cold'. These first impressions are often at the haptic level – that is, they are experienced but not articulated. The haptic response is produced through the senses. In other words, as you enter the school you are receiving visual, audio, olfactory, kinaesthetic or tactile information, or combinations of these, and these produce that first impression.

Such impressions can be wrong or only partially correct. Nevertheless, it is important to be aware of your initial responses, to note them and then try to ascertain what it is about the school that has produced this reaction. The list of possibilities for research that we provide in this section can assist in this process.

Approaching the school

When approaching the school it is instructive to look for the ways in which the school appears to the visitor.

- How welcoming is it? Is it easy to find? Is the way in for visitors clearly marked? Is there a sign? What is on it, and what does it say?
- How security conscious is the school? Is there a large forbidding fence? Is there an intercom system and how does this work for you? As a parent, would this level of security make you feel reassured or alienated?
- What about the grounds? Are they large and well kept? Or are they full of litter or badly maintained? What does this lead you to think?
- Is there enough parking? Do staff and visitors park together or separately? Does the school leadership team have marked places? What does this suggest?
- Can you find your way to the front office? Is there enough signage? Is it in multiple languages?

FIGURE 4.2 *A multilingual school sign*

Figures 4.2 to 4.4 show aspects of schools that are outside clues to follow up inside.

We might assume from sign 4.2 that there are four main language groups in the school population (these represent global flows and connections) and we might also suspect that the school is very conscious of the need to provide information in all community languages. This is something to follow up. If this is not the case, why have these languages been chosen and not others?

Schools in different countries advertise their presence very differently. Figure 4.3 is from a village school in France. The sign, which identifies first that the school is a public institution, only becomes visible when visitors have walked through the yard. Presumably everyone in the village knows where it is so it has no need to advertise its location or to solicit student enrolments. The sign in Figure 4.4, from a primary school in England, stands in an elevated and exposed position at the gate rather than by the front door, and displays the school logo and the school's affiliation to a trust and sponsors.

FIGURE 4.3 *French school sign*

FIGURE 4.4 *English school sign*

The front office

The front office is a rich site for research, but surprisingly little attention is paid to it (but see Casanova, 1991; Thomson et al., 2004). Many schools spend quite a bit of thought and money on designing their foyers, and it is worth considering what they have done and why. Here we present two separate field notes to illustrate this. These were taken by Pat during a research project which visited 40 different schools across England (Thomson et al., 2009):

> Field Note One:
> The entrance to the office is mainly glass. There is no security access. I walk straight in. The front office is a large space, comparatively empty, painted white with pale lino on the floor. The impression is one of lightness, but also 'modern'. There is a large light pine desk of the kind found in commercial offices. A woman, dressed in something that could be mistaken for a bank uniform, sits behind the desk working on a computer. Behind her on the wall is a large, clearly commercially produced sign which gives the name of the school and a list of seven 'sponsors'. These are mostly national businesses whose names I recognise. There are two smart navy blue sofas against one wall; in front a small pine and glass coffee table on which sit school newsletters and some other educational materials. A large glass cabinet full of trophies sits against one wall together with a substantial commercially produced freestanding display which has photos of students smiling, playing sport, musical instruments and generally having a fun time. It reminds me of nothing less than an insurance office crossed with the doctor's waiting room.

> Field Note Two:
> The school has no security access. The front office is painted in school colours, a rather unattractive mid-blue and yellow. The logo and motto are (a little amateurishly) painted across one wall. There are two stands which contain information about community services – health, income support, employment office, free school meals. A set of six certificates attesting to participation in various schemes – anti-bullying, healthy schools, anti-racism and so on – sit on another wall in mis-matched frames. There are three worn standard issue low chairs underneath the

school logo-ed wall. The secretarial desk sits in the middle of the room, rather like a marooned kitchen island. A student desk is placed strategically near the office desk but there is no 'naughty student' in it when I arrive. Instead, a very glum boy is hunched in one of the three chairs. I am immediately put off by the surrounds, in spite of the warm welcome I receive from the staff member seated behind the kitchen island.

It is not too hard to see from these two field notes some of the possible avenues that we wanted to follow up. Field Note One suggests a school keen to present itself as professional, businesslike, modern and forward thinking, where students excel and engage in a range of enjoyable activities. The school positions itself in a national as well as local context. By contrast, Field Note Two suggests a school that is locally focused on its community, which clearly has significant social needs. The presence of leaflets and certificates suggests that the school is making an effort to deal with some of the challenges faced by the neighbourhood in general and the students in particular. The school has clearly made a decision not to spend a lot of money on the front office, and uses the front office staff as part of its disciplinary regime. One can only wonder about what message the parents and visitors, sitting next to students who have clearly been disobedient, actually receive.

The school tour

Most schools have a printed map showing their layout and key locations such as the library and staff room, gymnasium, hall, and specialist and general classrooms. They may also show staff offices.

The location of staff offices and the staff room can be informative. How accessible is the head? Are the senior staff all positioned together close to the staff room, or are some of them 'outposted' to other parts of the school? Who is outposted and why? What is the balance of generalist to specialist rooms? Are there particularly large groups of any specialist facilities? What does this suggest? Questions that arise from looking at a school map can be followed up later in conversation.

We often ask the school to provide a guided tour at the start of the research. The guide is likely to be a person who can answer some preliminary questions that have arisen from reading documents and touring the neighbourhood. If a senior staff member takes a researcher around the school he or she will generally provide quite a lot of information about the school population, some of its history, curriculum emphases and current priorities for development.

We like to be given a tour of the school by students. Students generally don't know as much about school policies and the school history as staff, but they will have versions of these which are interesting. They are also likely to tell you much more about school food, who hangs out where, where students can and can't go, places in the school that they like and don't like, how accessible the staff are and what courses they are doing. They may also be able to tell you about any forms of student involvement in decision-making, special events and celebrations, and any particular groups or subcultures of students in the school.

After such tours it is useful to go back to the map of the school and mark on it any information that is particularly interesting or significant. An initial tour can be followed up in more detail – perhaps as a **photo ethnography** which is how many of the images in this chapter were generated – but it is usually possible during these early stages to see:

1 Areas that are out of bounds and reserved for staff

FIGURE 4.5 *Staff space away from students*

Seeing in and out of bounds areas gives some early clues about the degree of separation, or not, between staff and students (Figure 4.5). If there are dedicated smaller spaces for teachers, it is worth noting these as they may well be the material manifestations of particular teacher subcultures within the school, established and actively maintained around curriculum or age level specializations. Such 'identity' communities usually operate not simply within the school but as sites for 'stretched out social relations' and 'flows' well beyond the school itself (Hodkinson and Hodkinson, 2003; McGregor, 2003).

2 Signs that point to the disciplinary regimes at work in the school

There is much to be learnt from observing how students are disciplined – who the miscreants are, how many there are, what they appear to have done, what happens if they are withdrawn from classes, who is involved in deciding what should be done, and whether there are connections made between discipline and learning/teaching approaches and the curriculum (Armstrong, 2003; Slee, 2011).

FIGURE 4.6 *The time out room is a place where students are supervised by teachers*

FIGURE 4.7 *An unwelcoming staff room*

3 The staff room and how it is used

Some schools have attractive staff rooms where staff are encouraged to relax; others (as in Figure 4.7 above) have unloved and down-at-heel facilities with individual stores of tea and coffee, and notices urging users to tidy up. Some staff rooms are set up as professional workspaces, others are repositories of teaching materials and resources.

Some staffs have regular morning teas, or have someone employed to make the drinks. Some staff rooms are almost always empty with staff using smaller, often faculty-based, facilities located in other parts of the school. Staff rooms say a lot about the togetherness or otherwise of a staff, and how they are seen and supported by the school leadership (Penuel et al., 2009; Woods, 1983).

FIGURE 4.8 *Waiting room style staff room with work spaces*

4 Leadership offices

The office spaces of senior administrators often make for interesting analysis. The seating arrangements may allow easy or highly formal interactions with parents, staff and visitors. The bookshelves may show nothing but official folders and guidelines, or books about educational research, or links to school tradition or sporting success, or plans for future development (Prosser, 1999). Student work may or may not be on display. We have been into headteachers' offices that are full of stuffed toys, others that have shelves of counselling leaflets and boxes of tissues, some that are full of travel pictures and others that have art and craft displays. These offices all say something about the ways in the school leaders see themselves, their work, their relations with people and their connections with the outside world (Schratz, 2009).

The headteacher whose door is shown in Figure 4.9 is David Stewart from Oak Field Special School in

FIGURE 4.9 *Headteacher's door*

Nottingham. From the top, we see a photo of the participants on a special education course that David led in China; room designation and number; a photo of David in his office when he first became head of the school, with a Makaton (a system of sign language) sign underneath; a card in the shape of a spoof book called *The Grumpiest Teacher in the School*; a photo of David receiving a community education award from a television presenter; and the Makaton symbol for headteacher. From reading this visual display it is not too hard to see that tracing connections, commitment to the school and to inclusion, expertise and recognition, together with a sense of humour, might all be important to a study of the school.

5 Corridors and walls

FIGURE 4.10 *Connected to local businesses*

The corridors and walls of the school can say a great deal, as we have already suggested earlier in the chapter.

Looking at corridors allows us not only to see something about the ways in which students relate to each other as they move between lessons and in and out of the buildings, but also the ways in which students may or may not be sent out of rooms as punishment, the degree to which the school staff police in-between-lesson behaviour, and the kinds of locker storage that is available to students. The nature and types of signage are telling, as are the kinds of notices on display – student work, commercially produced materials about the curriculum (the global flow of edu-business or the work of regional consultants), 'inspirational' slogans, records of special occasions, records of attendance and behaviour and so on.

Figure 4.10, for example, shows local connections but also that the school has actively sought out 'sponsorship' and has rebadged the subject history as 'history enterprise' (a local enactment of national policy on vocational relevance).

FIGURE 4.11 *An outdoor classroom*

These initial clues can be followed up later, but preliminary discourse analysis can be very helpful at the outset of a project.

It is also helpful to examine the outside space to see whether and how it is used for sporting activities and educational purposes. What emphasis is placed on active play? How is the yard managed and by whom? The space shown in Figure 4.11 suggests regular use and a range of curriculum activities undertaken using experiential processes (outside learning is an optional approach in the English national curriculum and this indicates a local choice).

There are two further activities that are useful in getting to know the school and establishing areas to investigate further.

Participatory mapping

We have already referred to maps, earlier in this chapter and in the previous one, when we talked about street maps and maps of the school. These kinds of maps are generally schematic representations of the built environment. Here, we simply want to point to the benefits of participatory mapping conducted early in a research project.

A participatory map is a way to bring different, and often multiple, perspectives to a topic (Emmel, 2008). Participants are given the freedom to design and produce a map in response to a researcher's question. Through the conversation and the construction of the map, participants make explicit the connections between people, places and events in the school space over time. So, for example, at the start of a research project you might ask students:

- to map their social life in the school, indicating the places where they feel comfortable and the places where they don't go or are not allowed to go;
- to draw a map which shows the various social groups that exist within the school and how they use the space;
- to draw a map which shows connections between the school and places in the immediate neighbourhood.

Teachers might also be asked to draw maps which, for example, show the places in which they have pedagogical or disciplinary conversations or where they feel most 'professional' in the school. These kinds of maps can be quickly drawn on notepaper, or they can be more elaborate affairs which use multiple media and large sheets of art paper or material.

There are, however, other kinds of maps – maps that do not simply focus on the physical landscape. In recent years, there has been a growing interest in maps which show social, embodied, aesthetic and/or affective and sensory connections to place: we think for instance of Katherine Harmon's *You Are Here: Personal Geographies and Other Maps of the Imagination* (2004). We also are reminded of political mapping in Avery Gordon's *An Atlas of Radical Cartography* (2008) and Dolores Hayden's *The Power of Place: Urban Landscapes as Public History* (1996), where map-making becomes a way for communities to reclaim their own histories and futures in a place. These kinds of maps are sometimes very different from maps as we are accustomed to think of them. Often hand-drawn, they do not conform to a scale as we might think of it, and they refer to events, metaphors, memories, experiences and emotions.

These kinds of sensory and cultural practice maps have become of interest to educational researchers (e.g. Powell, 2010; Somerville et al., 2015). For example, Margaret Somerville, Jacqueline D'Warte and Lin Brown used mapping in an ethnically, racially and linguistically diverse school that was interested in changing the ways in which it taught literacy. They were committed to identifying students' home and community multi-modal language resources, so that these could be incorporated into day-to-day classes. Children were asked to draw visual and spatial representations that illustrated their everyday language use at home and at school, showing any connections between the two. Teachers and university researchers analysed the results and these became the basis for an action research project.

Researchers usually find that these kinds of participatory mapping activities are helpful in two ways: first, because the conversation that goes on during map-making is often very informative; and, second, because the maps become the focus for further discussion and act as 'triggers' for conversation.

Shadowing students and teachers

The final early method that we sometimes use, if we can, is to shadow a student and their group of friends and/or a teacher throughout a school day. Of course, the student, their friends and the teachers involved all need to give active permission for this to occur. It is thus not surprising that **shadowing** is an activity not often undertaken (although see Harry Wolcott's classic in-depth ethnography of a school principal (1973) which involved shadowing over an entire school year).

Shadowing alerts you to the temporal/spatial arrangements in the school and to the prevailing discourses. Moving from lesson to lesson helps the observer (re)experience the episodic nature of the school day, the proximity or otherwise of rooms, the regularity of disruptions. When we shadowed one girl in one school (it featured in Field Note Two earlier in this chapter) – a girl we named Maggie – at the start of a research visit, we were given a disturbing picture of the ways in which current orthodoxies of teaching produced average exam results rather than actually extending learning and challenging the particular student and her friends (Thomson et al., 2010). We observed, across a series of lessons, the ways in which the girls collaborated to do the minimal amount of work required to meet expectations, as this field note shows:

> The teacher is clearly rattled by her inability to maintain control and by me watching – her voice is at a shout all the time – I can see that she works to connect science to the world; there are teacher-made posters around the room linking the science curriculum to important social issues – nuclear power, global warming, stem cell technologies ... the girls are at the back and are making sure that they all have the answers ready if they are asked. Maggie is slow at finding the words on the page, but uses her 'cheat sheet' (notes from the last time the dummy exam was presented) as backup for the whole class and group activities. When asked to sort out some science questions she simply uses the ones she made up last time. 'Can we do this together?' Lisa asks Maggie. 'I was listening but ... (shakes head). What was that first question we did yesterday?' Maggie shares her work-sheet with her three friends and, work already done, they

> spend time discussing redecorating bedrooms. There is also a discussion about art homework – Maggie says 'I did mine ages ago, I'm a good little girl' (PT field notes, 10 June).

The micro-experiences of shadowing a student across a school day helped us develop an understanding of how underperformance can be produced in school.

Shadowing puts you in the position of the student. As a proxy student, you often see, for example, the ways in which different teachers present lessons in very similar ways. You are also party to the sometimes surprising ways in which students use their learning time slots. You see the ways in which areas of the school are neglected, appropriated by the students, forgotten. You see the ways in which students connect to other groups inside and outside the physical environment. And as proxy teachers you can see the ways in which different groupings of students make it more or less possible to 'teach'. These insights are likely to be valuable in your research.

Final note

No matter how anxious you are to get into the school and start talking to people and making notes, there are benefits from systematically surveying the school first. You do not have to ask the school for much of this kind of information because a lot is in the public arena. Use your skills of searching and you will be surprised what you can find. Your very first impressions of the school can also be very helpful, particularly if you can augment these with guided tours, participatory mapping and shadowing. Understandings of the school as a place orient you to the local and the flows of people, ideas and so on, as well as to the patternings that occur across the wider school system.

Further reading

You may want to read more about discourse and discourse practice. We suggest starting with

Bacchi, Carol (2009). *Analysing Policy: What's the Problem Represented To Be?* Frenches Forest, NSW: Pearson Australia.

Although the book applies to policy, the 'what's the problem' approach applies more broadly to discourse practice.

We also recommend as a good general introduction:

Maclure, Maggie (2003). *Discourse in Educational and Social Research*. Buckingham: Open University Press.

The next two books provide examples of researchers using participatory and a variety of image based approaches to 'reading' the school. The material in these texts does not just apply to the 'getting to know you' stage of the research, but is useful in the more intensive 'knowing all about you' stage too.

Prosser, Jon (ed.) (1998). *Image Based Research: A Sourcebook for Qualitative Researchers*. London: Falmer Press.

Thomson, Pat (ed.) (2008). *Doing Visual Research with Children and Young People*. London: Routledge.

You might also want to read more broadly around methods that can be used to research discourse practice and/or be useful in the early stages of research. We suggest starting with:

Lury, Celia (ed.) (2012). *Inventive Methods: The Happening of the Social*. London: Routledge.

Pink, Sarah (2009). *Doing Sensory Ethnography*. Thousand Oaks, CA: Sage.

It is also helpful to read early on about everyday life and how it is theorized. A helpful survey of various approaches can be found in Moran, Joe (2005). *Reading the Everyday*. London: Routledge.

CHAPTER FIVE

Living with the school

Studies of schools are often completed quickly. A couple of days, perhaps even a week, a recorder full of interviews and a bag full of information and it's back to the office to process what you've got. Of course, there's nothing wrong with doing a short-term study of a school. We've done them ourselves. It's often surprising how much data you can generate in a short space of time. But you do need to be clear about what you can expect to get from this kind of 'snapshot' and what are the limitations of the data.

In this chapter we focus primarily on *time*, by looking at two different approaches to researching a school. We begin by discussing one of our projects and the way in which we approached the making of what we call 'snapshot' case studies. While our study was bigger than the kind that is usually undertaken in doctoral research, some PhD research *is* designed around multiple case studies which are undertaken over a restricted time period. Pat's PhD, referred to in Chapter 1, consisted of twenty case studies conducted over a one-year period. This was what she called a meso-level policy analysis, as it examined what was happening in a number of sites in relation to policy shifts. One or a handful of schools would have been insufficient to say anything about patterns, so a larger number were required. We note that, ironically, even when place-based methods are used in this kind of larger-scale study, place tends to disappear from the final cross-case analysis. Speed also militates against deep engagement with the school.

However, many studies of a single school do begin by surveying a larger number; some researchers go from the many to the one. We therefore go on, in this chapter, to offer some theoretical orientations that can be used to support longer-term, in-depth research in a school. We finish by considering the kinds of strategies and approaches that observant participants might use to get beneath the surface of a school.

Snapshot case studies of 'creative schools'

We undertook a three-year study of school changes promoted and supported by the English Creative Partnerships programme (Thomson et al., 2009). We were interested in the kinds of school change that were occurring (e.g. to school cultures or structures, to teaching and learning practices), who was involved and the level at which any changes occurred (e.g. classroom, whole-school, etc.). Since the Creative Partnerships programme was designed to encourage partnerships between the educational and cultural sectors, we also wanted to know about the models of partnership that schools were using and the impact of these partnerships on capacity-building within the school.

The research was organized into two main phases. The initial phase involved making snapshots of forty schools across England; the second phase focused in greater depth on twelve of the schools. These were not to be representative schools, but schools where interesting things were happening (see Chapter 2). We asked programme staff in the regions to nominate potential schools for us to research. Our final selection was designed to offer some diversity: we chose a balance of primary, secondary, special, rural and urban schools with a diversity of languages and cultural heritages in the school populations. Each of the forty schools participated in a 'research encounter', which occurred over two consecutive days. The first school visits were conducted by pairs of team members, in various combinations, to ensure trustworthiness in the data generation procedures. The bulk of the visits were carried out by single researchers.

Taking snapshots

When applied to a case study developed in a short space of time, the term 'snapshot' emphasizes the fact that an image of the school has been 'taken' rapidly, from a particular perspective and at one moment in the school's history. Our purpose in generating snapshot case studies was to develop a quick collective picture of what was happening across the schools. We also wanted to select twelve of them for more intensive research over three years. A postgraduate researcher might do something similar on a smaller scale – visit six to ten schools first before deciding which ones to study in more depth.

We were thus primarily interested in building up profiles of each of the schools and assuring the accuracy of the data. We built up a lot of material about each school place – using exactly the kinds of techniques outlined in Chapters 3 and 4. We particularly focused on material relevant to our study, so we collected Creative Partnerships material, newsletters, reports to governors, annual reports, documentary evidence on websites and news clippings. Before we began, we knew a lot about each school as a place and its place in the wider region. We conducted individual interviews with the head or a relevant member of the senior leadership team and, where possible, with other individual teachers, a key school governor and the lead creative practitioner. We held focus group discussions with teachers and with students of mixed ages. These interviews were taped and transcribed. We took photographs of the entrance areas, playgrounds and relevant displays. We had informal conversations in the staff room, play areas and offices, observed lessons and extra-curricular activities and kept extensive field notes as records of the visits.

We then had to analyse this data and present them in a common frame so that we had some basis for comparison. We developed synopses of the data from the anonymized schools, no more than 1,000 words long, written to a five-part template that began with some details about school context, identified the origins of the school's involvement with Creative Partnerships, outlined the creative learning projects, discussed the impact of these projects and finished with something about future plans. We illustrated the snapshot with one or two photographs from our data set and made an 'album' of the snapshots on the web so they could be browsed or downloaded. Snapshot 5.1, below, offers an example of one of the forty snapshots.

We presented these likenesses back to the schools to see if they recognized them and encouraged the schools to use them if they wanted to. The process of reducing and summarizing the data imposed a discipline on the research. But the need for brevity and individualized representations of each of the schools limited the scope for analysis, and the invitation to schools to browse the snapshots encouraged us to adopt a standpoint which tended to affirm, rather than critique, the schools' work. However, reading across the snapshots created a picture of the kinds of work that were generally going on in schools under the rubric of 'creativity'.

The school

Rowan Tree Nursery and Infant School is located within a large local authority housing estate on the outskirts of a Midlands city. The area is within a former mining community. Many families are still feeling the effects of the decline of industry in the area over the past three decades and in many cases are finding it difficult to make ends meet.

The headteacher has been in post for eighteen years, and there is high staff retention. There is a high number of teaching assistants as well as a group of arts practitioners on staff. One of the school's creative practitioners is on the board of governors.

Creative Partnerships involvement

Origins

The school has recognized creative approaches to teaching and learning as a necessary part of its commitment to providing significant and individualized learning experiences for its students. The school became involved with Creative Partnerships at the pilot stage and were active in the establishment of partnerships with other schools in their locality.

Projects

Creative Partnerships has funded a number of projects in this school. These include the work of a dancer, a musician and a sculptor. The sculptor has worked collaboratively with children in the nursery on such projects as the sculpture of animals and cardboard furniture;

the current focus is on a bamboo structure in the outside space of the nursery. The dancer has been involved in the development of the skills of the youngest children to an advanced level. Each class within the school has an artist working with them once a week for half a term, reinforcing the continuity of experience, which is at the heart of the school's approach to teaching and learning.

Impact

Creative Partnerships has had a positive impact on school development. Within the school, the arts are seen as a vehicle for experiential learning. Although certain practices have been part of school life for some time, such as a whole day each week devoted to individual learning, Creative Partnerships' involvement has encouraged further modelling of teaching and learning around creative practices. Creative Partnerships' involvement has also opened possibilities for the school to work with a group of artists who have proven to be a great asset and have remained working with the school on a series of projects, to the point where they are now funded by the school itself.

Careful and regular planning takes place between teachers and creative practitioners in order to incorporate creative approaches across the curriculum and to maximize their impact on the students' learning experiences. Examples of the artists' involvement across the curriculum include the teaching of maths and science through the measuring of sculptures and the examination of the properties of the materials used to create the sculptures. The artists' involvement is also seen as part of the teachers' and teaching assistants' professional development.

It is reported that the students' work with the artists has also had a clear impact on their ability to deal more appropriately with personal problems and difficulties. This is partly attributed to an increase in both opportunity and capacity for self-expression. Parents have responded positively to the experience received by their children, attending performances based on project work.

We are getting an awful lot of our curriculum but in a different way and in a more hands-on way, and the language that they will use, as a result of that, is fantastic. To have a six-year-old use the word 'translucent' in the correct context is impressive. (Teacher)

When you look at the sculpture and the progress that the children have made it is more than we could have expected. (Headteacher)

The students are actively engaged in their sessions with artists and acknowledge the way in which the artists bring different experiences to their school day.

It wouldn't be so much fun. We wouldn't do the singing. (Year 1 student, reflecting on what school would be like without the artists)

I wish I was never poorly because I like school. (Year 1 student)

All students are enabled to engage meaningfully in the activities. Artists have built effective relationships with their groups. This is partly due to the consistency in the school's approach to employing the artists to work regularly with all groups.

Future

The school has ambitious plans to continue to base its curriculum around creative teaching and learning. In view of the precarious future of Creative Partnerships' funding, the school has drawn from alternative budgets, such as that for behaviour support or Gifted and Talented funds, in order to maintain the consistency of involvement at its current rate. The main challenges to this approach at the school may be the response of the Local Authority and of Ofsted, although it is hoped by the staff that the school's improving academic standards will demonstrate the effectiveness of the creative approach.

SNAPSHOT 5.1 *A snapshot of Rowan Tree School*

As a representational genre, the snapshot case outline of Rowan Tree is largely descriptive and light on critique, but it does gives a sense of the activities being undertaken and the reasons for doing them. Importantly, it 'places' the activities in their local as well as national context.

We also developed a cross-case analysis across the snapshots. Our analytic approach to the interviews combined discourse analysis (see Chapter 4) with thematized coding (Silverman, 1993). We were interested in what interviewees took as creativity and as whole-school change, which examples they produced, and how they represented the changes that they attributed to Creative Partnerships. We used a schedule to analyse field notes where we recorded information such as the structures supporting Creative Partnerships in the school; the relationship between Creative Partnerships and broader professional development; any changes in student grouping, timetabling, budget or staffing; and the types of evaluation practices carried out. We were particularly concerned to see what steps the school had taken towards making changes sustainable in the longer term when funding for the programme finished.

In this cross-case analysis, we were looking for what Bassey (1999) calls 'fuzzy generalisations' about the kind of school change that was supported by Creative Partnerships. However, our resulting analysis was largely based on self-reporting at the school level, since researcher verification (through, for example, observation over time) was limited by time and design factors. The size of the research team meant that there was little opportunity in the first phase of the project for all of the researchers to work together; it was therefore likely that there would be variations in the data produced simply through differences in approach to school investigation. We did our best to minimize these variations by conducting two separate analyses of the snapshot corpus, but the initial 'researcher effect' could not be ignored. Despite these caveats, certain themes emerged from the analysis, and numbers of schools appeared to have 'things in common' (patterning of places).

We were able to produce a report which addressed five topics: 'What counts as school change?'; 'Who is involved in school change?'; 'Building the capacity for change'; 'Thinking about change'; and a conclusion called 'Making a difference?' Clearly, at this point it was necessary to offer our own understandings and assumptions about 'school change' and clarify how the definitions we had adopted affected the report we were presenting. This was in contrast to the presentation of the snapshot data, which left the reader to browse the accounts and make connections and comparisons. Whereas the snapshots presented individual, named (but anonymized) schools, our report to funders presented synthesized findings in which the schools were referred to by phase rather than picked out separately. This, ironically, made 'place' much less visible. Having thematized the data, it was then mined to find salient examples of the issue or idea. Quotations from the interview transcripts or field notes were used to *illustrate* the analysis; that is, to offer an example or demonstration which helps to clarify or explain the point (see Report 5.2).

In Report 5.2, a Rowan Tree illustration is offered alongside similar comments from teachers in two other schools to illustrate how loose connections were being drawn between student attainment and Creative Partnerships' involvement. We wanted to highlight the status of the evidence for the claim rather than associate the view with a particular school, so the school pseudonyms were not included. The Rowan Tree comment is the first of the three and is presented in bold.

Few schools claimed a causal link between the implementation of CP related changes and the results that the children achieved in statutory tests, but still some were prepared to make tentative connections between the two:

We'd gone into a whole year of sculpture and at the end of that year ...our SAT results had gone up and the second year they'd gone up again, particularly around the boys and we thought this isn't a fluke. So the following year sculpture wasn't done and there was a dip in their maths again. Back came the sculpture and up it went again. So that, in a way, was sort of proving that this was happening and this is what we put in our document because sometimes somebody will read these ... (Teacher, infant school)

> *Going back a few years, you would have only a handful of students doing A level but last year we had seventeen and next year there will be well over twenty who want to do A level maths and in this sort of school that is really unusual.* (Head teacher, secondary school)
>
> *[We had an] unexpected higher achievement in SATs and attributed that to the fact that children had experiences to write about.* (Teacher, primary school)

REPORT 5.2 *Use of data to offer multiple illustrations of teachers' theories*

Rowan Tree became one of our case study schools and we pick up the story of our research with the school later in this chapter. Now, we simply point to the main points that arise from examining this research in some detail.

1. A snapshot approach to a school does yield a surprising amount of data.
2. Much of the data are limited to self-report and official accounts and documents. However, if multiple interviews are undertaken, some different perspectives may emerge.
3. The snapshot is made at a particular time and is immediately out of date.
4. It is possible to generate data around particular categories drawn from the research questions, and this does allow some cross-case comparison to be made.
5. While place is an important part of the data generation, it can become less visible when cross-case analyses (looking for patterns) are written – unless the intention of the case analysis is to focus on place per se.

If, however, you want or need more than this limited lens in order to answer your research question – and we did – then a more sustained engagement with the school or set of schools is probably required. As we noted at the start of the chapter, many researchers do conduct a broader survey in order to select a single or small group to study in depth. They shift from rapid assessment to something much more sustained. And that is what we did. So we move on now to address key aspects of longer-term research with a school. (The next chapter discusses the kind of methods that you might use in longer-term research.)

From the many to the one: Researcher orientations

In this section we present three ideas that are helpful in orienting research in a school over a longer period of time. They are (1) slowness, (2) inhabiting and (3) listening.

1 *Slowness*

Snapshots are quickly undertaken. Speed worries many, including the Slow Science movement. Slow Scientists argue that that quick research is indicative of the kind of accelerated, runaway world we now live in – fast paced, anxious to get to the next thing, continually on the move. Slow Scientists ask, what do we miss when we move fast? Do we simply fail to register the very things that are most germane to understanding the thing we want to understand? Taking their inspiration from the slow food movement, Slow Science argues the need to take time in making sense of a phenomenon. As the Slow Science Manifesto puts it:

> Science needs time to think. Science needs time to read, and time to fail. Science does not always know where it might be at right now. Science develops unsteadily, with jerky moves and unpredictable leaps forward – at the same time, however, it creeps about on a very slow time scale, for which there must be room and to which justice must be done. (http://slow-science.org [accessed 31 October 2015])

Slow research refuses to come to easy conclusions, recognizing that comprehending something can't be done to order. Thinking goes as fast as it goes, sometimes in an instant eureka moment; more often, incrementally and sporadically.

Anthropologists often go slow. Traditionally, anthropological researchers immersed themselves in their field location for at least a year, often revisiting for protracted periods of time. They took copious field notes, but their practice was primarily one of participating, observing and talking with the group they wanted to research. These days, anthropologists rarely see themselves as separate from research 'subjects'. Rather, many anthropologists see themselves as guests who live with a group with whom they collaboratively codify and represent a way of being and doing things in the world (Lassiter, 2005). They often use a range of methods and media in order to generate data and communicate their results.

Anthropologists have, not surprisingly, become interested in the slow movement. Sarah Pink, for instance, has studied 'slow cities' (Pink, 2008; Pink and Lewis, 2014) and she argues that the sensibilities of slowness can usefully inform research practices. She says there are benefits when, for example, a researcher slowly walks together with a participant through a particular location. They stop to talk, look, sense the surrounds (Pink, 2009). In such circumstances, Pink says, memories and narratives are both recalled, and made and remade.

Educational researchers can take a hint from the Slow Science movement. Researchers interested in finding out about a school as a place might think consciously about living in the moment of their investigation, refuse to come to quick conclusions and use all of their available senses to generate understandings about where they are and with whom they are talking and interacting. They might sometimes move slowly around the material place, as well as think slowly about what they are seeing and feeling.

2 *Inhabiting*

It is helpful to think about a lengthy stay in a school as a kind of inhabiting. However, there is a usage of the term that extends and queries common-sense assumptions.

Tim Ingold (2000) discusses living/doing research/making knowledge as a process of inhabiting. His argument consists of several steps and we abbreviate them here in order to make the point in relation to studying a school.

Ingold is critical of the notion of a place as a bounded entity (see Chapters 1 and 3). He argues that a place is not a ring-fenced material location and that none of us actually experience place in this way. 'Lives,' he says, 'are not led inside places but through, around, to and from them, from and to places elsewhere' (Ingold, 2000: 229). Humans are not place-bound – places are sites at which inhabitants meet, and their life trails entwine and enmesh. Human existence thus binds place together through various 'way-finding' lives. Ingold suggests that it is helpful to think of a place as a kind of knot, and our lives as enmeshed in a series of knots, made when our life trails intersect with others. Places, Ingold proposes,

> ... are delineated by movement, not by the outer limits to movements. Indeed, it is for just this reason, that I have chosen to refer to people who frequent places as 'inhabitants' rather than 'locals' for it would be quite wrong to suppose that such people are confined with[in] a particular place, or that their experience is circumscribed by the restricted horizons of a life lived only there. (Ingold, 2009, p. 34)

This is of course how a researcher encounters the school. While it appears to be a bounded site, all manner of things and people move in and out of it every day. Inhabiting the school place, temporarily halting in the knot, is to try to understand the movements and trails through the place and the nature of the practice of knotting that occurs.

According to Ingold, understanding a place is not a matter of seeing it as a network, establishing connections between dots, or seeing it as a set of individualized phenomena. The knowledge of how place happens, he reasons, is not about fact but about narrative. An inhabitant knows a place not as isolated data or events, but as a 'confluence of actions and responses, identified not by their intrinsic attributes, but by the memories they call up ... Every place is a knot of stories' (p. 41).

Science has two practices, Ingold argues, which abstract the knowledge of inhabitants from their paths and places: distillation, which severs the links to narrative; and compartmentalization, which isolates events through codification. To change these science practices, Ingold suggests, scientists need to become inhabitants. Inhabiting helps researchers avoid seeing places as 'containers of elements that are passed on ... from their ancestors, and that ... will in turn pass onto their descendants' (p. 42). Rather, scientists need to live in and through place, and experience it as narrative.

Educational researchers might take from 'inhabiting' a strong sense of being part of, not separate from, the school place that they are researching. They might look for the ways in which being in the school constitutes a narrative, and take pains to record this experience, as well as sinking deeply into what is happening.

3 *Listening*

It is clear that a good researcher listens, and that long-term research in a school means listening a lot. But Les Back (2007) argues that listening is not simply a matter of empathy, or of being quiet while someone else speaks. Nor is it a matter of recording what is said and then replaying it over and over. Rather, Back suggests that sociological listening means 'placing ourselves on the side of the story' being told. This doesn't mean switching off all critical faculties, simply accepting what is being said. According to Back, placing ourselves on the side of the story involves 'artfulness', which he defines as a 'form of openness to others that needs to be crafted, a listening for the background, the half-muted' (p. 8).

Such 'artfulness' is not necessarily what researchers are taught to do, nor what they read in academic journals and books. Back argues that sociology in particular 'has been diverted by an enchanted obsession with the loudest voices, the biggest controversy and the most acute social concern'. He proposes that social scientists focus instead on 'social investigations that utilize a 'democracy of the senses' because we are then 'likely to notice more and ask different questions of our world' (p. 8).

Back advocates a considered form of listening which does not rush to conclusions and which remains open to the world around and through which 'hidden connections can be traced, providing new directions for thought and speech' (p. 1). This means, Back writes, paying

> ... attention to the hidden life of objects and places, the life that is either concerned within those objects or bleached from them by the formalities of power or the forgetfulness of conventional wisdom. It is a practice of scholarship that is committed to a profane illumination, of reading against the grain, which looks for the outside story that is part of the inside story. (p. 9)

Back suggests a mode of thought which is sensitive to time and change, and which validates without romanticism the lives of the people that we work with.

Educational researchers might take from Back's work on listening the importance of being sensitive to what is said and not said, to the forgotten and the relatively obscure, as well as the more obvious aspects of the school place.

These three orientations – slowness, inhabiting and listening – have a great deal in common. They all go to the question of how a researcher positions themselves in the school, and how they behave when they are there. The three orientations are not metaphors, but concern 'being' in a school. These orientations complement activities such as walking and browsing, sitting and watching, feeling and hearing, touching and smelling, as ways to come to understand place. They position you to benefit from being patient, but open to the unpredictable and surprising. You can think of your research as a long encounter with others who are, as Doreen Massey (2005) has it, 'thrown together' in the school as a place and whose stories and encounters you will gradually uncover at the same time as you are writing your own narrative of 'being there'.

We suggest that if you are thinking about research that is something longer than the short-term case study, it could be helpful to consider these three orientations and explore what they might mean for your research.

Thinking about theory and methods

It is often helpful to think at an early stage about the theory or theories you intend to use to analyse your data, since different social theories often point to particular ways of generating data, and it can be tricky to use a particular theory if you haven't generated appropriate data.

It may be the case that you are working with a grounded theory approach (Charmaz, 2006), where you don't want to use any kind of predetermined theoretical framing. However, we suggest that it is still useful to know the kinds of theoretical resources that you may want to use in relation to analysing your data. This is because theories provide 'thinking tools' with which to approach the school. Theorizing should not only happen at the end of your project, but also during it, particularly if you are working on a long-term school engagement. (We discuss this further later in this chapter and in Chapter 7.)

So, you may be interested in looking at some relevant theories quite early on in order to think about how they might shape what you choose to do. We discuss two approaches in some detail here, and then offer some suggestions for other approaches you might check out. We begin with Henri Lefebvre's notion of everyday life, and then go on to the idea of an 'assemblage'.

Everyday life as a trialectic

Many contemporary social scientists are concerned with everyday life (e.g. Augé, 1995; de Certeau, 1988; Elshtain, 1997; Moran, 2005; Smith, 1987). Taking the everyday as a focus is a political stance: there is a democratic impulse in studying what ordinary people say, do, think and feel, and how they understand, experience and talk about their lives and their worlds. There are many theorists of everyday life for you to explore. Each of them provides a way to approach the school as a place where the lives of everyone matters, where it is not just the official that counts, where the focus is on understanding not simply what but also *why* things are as they are. Many theorists of the everyday are also concerned with change and how it might be brought about in order to make life generally better for more people. Here we refer only to the work of philosopher Henri Lefebvre (1947, 1971, 1991, 2004), who was particularly concerned with space, time and place.

Lefebvre wrote extensively about everyday life in space–time. He argued for a scholarly focus on the lives of ordinary people, lives that were residualized by social science and fragmented and dehumanized by the workings of capitalist society, particularly modern cities. Lefebvre was committed to exploring how much ordinary people were in control of their lives, how their capacity to decide and act were limited by economic, social and political structures, as well as how conflict between the rhythms of bodies and seasons and socio-economic relations might be sources for social transformation. Much of Lefebvre's work is applicable to research in schools. We illustrate one possibility by focusing on his notion of the trialectic – not a dialectic – approach to everyday life as spatially-temporally experienced and produced.

Lefebvre suggested that there are three types of space which produce and reproduce everyday life:

1 Conceived space

   In schooling, conceived space is where the discursive work of policy and professional practice happens. This space–time is not a homogeneous 'text', but rather a bricolage of 'bits and pieces ... cannibalised theories, research, trends and fashions' (Ball, 1998, p. 127), rhetorically sutured together. But despite the ad hoc-ery of policy and the inevitable tensions and contradictions that exist within conceived space, there are nevertheless identifiable dominant discursive practices (see Chapter 4) at work in conceived space. In conceived space we find the work of policy intermediaries, policy translations and abstracted bureaucratic procedures and tools (curriculum guidelines, administrative computing platforms and so on).

2 Perceived space

The perceived space of schooling is where everyday meaning-making occurs. Bodies move in perceived space and the materialities of schooling – the buildings, furniture and equipment – frame what can be done. Teaching staff and students mediate and enact the conceived space of policy and professional practices, embodying it and embedding it within taken-for-granted ways of acting, speaking and thinking. This is where, for example, students may talk of 'good', 'bad' or 'boring' lessons, and teachers talk of 'able' and 'wilful' children.

3 Representational space

This is the realm of the symbolic and semiotic, the poetic and the diagrammatic. It can be a source of resistance or a mediating space for the enactment of conceived space – as in the timetable, the school budget and the school map. As lived in schooling, representational space also holds out the possibility of alternative ways of thinking, doing and being. This alternative space is sometimes made material through the provision of semi-permanent 'counter-public spaces' (Fraser, 1997), oppositional spaces which act as a base for thinking and acting in opposition to the official school discourse. These might be student-run art rooms, Aboriginal-led family-rooms and provisions, girls' discussion groups and the like (see Thomson et al., 2005a; Thomson et al., 2005b for discussion of an environmental action group as a counter-public). But alternative representational space most often exists in more fleeting forms, such as the tactical world of daydreaming and subjugated stories (de Certeau, 1988). This is also sometimes called 'third space' (Soja, 1999), a liminal space which transcends subjectivity and objectivity, structure and agency, mind and body (Soja, 1996, p. 56) and which stands in contrast to first and second space.

In order to understand the trialectic at work, Lefebvre argued that time must be seen as both synchronic – what is happening now – and diachronic – what happened in the past. Furthermore, he argues, the synchronic/diachronic can be comprehended best by looking at the rhythms of everyday life. Schools are particularly amenable to what he called 'rhythmanalysis' (Lefebvre, 2004), the study of temporal patterns. There *are* very regular patterns to the school day, term and year: these occur as conceived space, and they serve to organize the rhythms of perceived space, not only for students, but also their families. If we think, for example, of the ways in which parental lives are organized around picking up and dropping off children, we can immediately see the ways in which school rhythms spread well beyond the school gates.

Using Lefebvre's theory of the trialectic orients you to consider what constitutes everyday life in time/space in your chosen and very particular school place. As an educational researcher who is in a school for a length of time, you can experience and understand the rhythms of the school and its various harmonies as well as the discords. You can see the way the school is not a unitary and static organization, but a complex and changing mix of people, things, actions and sayings. Training a lens on conceived, perceived and representational spaces – of the school and its inhabitants, but also the representational space of the research itself – offers a potential explanatory power beyond the descriptive.

Researchers working with a Lefebvrian perspective on the school would look specifically for what happens here, in this place, in relation to:

- the ways in which conceived policy space is brought into and mediated within the school – the way that policy is 'enacted' in place (Ball et al., 2011a). The researcher focuses, for instance, on curriculum practices, lesson plans, testing, timetables, budgets and professional 'handouts' and materials made for teachers to see how policy becomes a practice;
- the ways in which everyday life in the school is experienced – who moves where and when, which parts of the school are used, by whom and when, modes of teaching and learning and talking about them;
- the kinds of multi-media materials that the school generates about itself and the stories that these tell and to whom, as well as the stories, jokes and images that circulate unofficially;

- the various rhythms that occur in the school day, week, term and year and what these mean in terms of the ways in which space/time is variously conceived, perceived and represented.

Seeing a school as a place through a Lefebvrian theoretical lens allows you to explain the 'vernacular' (Thomson et al., 2009) of what happens officially and unofficially, over time, how the lives of those in the school are constructed, how the school is spoken about and experienced, as well as how it might be changed and different.

The school as assemblage

We referred to an assemblage in passing in our discussion on discourse practice in the last chapter. Here we want to unpack the idea a little further and think about what it might offer a place-based school study. An assemblage is usually understood as a collection of things. Thesaurus.com offers as alternatives the nouns aggregation, company, convergence, assembly, congregation and crowd. This definition draws attention to the materiality of an assemblage and also to its potentially arbitrary nature. The antonyms of scattering and dispersal add to this a sense of an assemblage as having been created through some kind of movement in time/space.

We can also think imaginatively about what an assemblage might look like – a mosaic, patchwork, bricolage – as well as some of its properties – heterogeneous, fluid, transitory, mobile, contingent. While this might seen highly indeterminate and potentially difficult to grasp, this is not necessarily a problem. An assemblage might be fleeting, but it might also be ongoing in the sense of continuing to exist as a kind of palimpsest, moving forward through time/space. This notion of assemblage is sympathetic to the notion of a place as something 'thrown together' (Massey, 2005), connected through flows and trails to other places, and neither static nor homogeneous (see Chapter 1).

We take assemblage as a construct which has a methodological use (c.f. Ingold, 2000, 2011; McFarlane, 2011). As Marcus and Saka (2006, p. 106) put it:

> [A]ssemblage functions best as an evocation of emergence and heterogeneity amid the data of inquiry, in relation to other concepts and constructs without rigidifying into the thingness of final or stable states that besets the working terms of classic social theory. ... [A]ssemblage as a conceptual resource has to do with the imaginaries for the shifting relations and emergent conditions of spatially distributed objects of study in the contemporary period of so-called globalization.

The notion of assemblage used here and specifically in relation to school as a place draws from the works of Gilles Deleuze and Felix Guattari (1987), which highlighted the ways in which assemblages are states of becoming. The work of Manuel de Landa (2006) is also relevant: de Landa argued that an assemblage was amenable to analysis through examining the ways in which assemblage components are understood as both material and expressive; that is, they trigger symbolic, sensual, haptic and semiotic interactions and responses. De Landa also emphasized the processes of territorialization, in which assemblage components are stabilized; and deterritorialization, through which destabilization occurs. Finally, he stressed the importance of coding and decoding; that is, the ways in which linguistic resources are deployed to create specific assemblage 'identity'.

How might this approach be applied to the school as a place? As they approach the school, researchers interested in assemblage might have in mind questions such as:

- What are the components of this particular school assemblage? (It is worth spending time brainstorming answers to this question, thinking counter-intuitively.)
- What is the school's 'materiality' – buildings, objects, texts?
- How do these elements of the assemblage support, frame and produce everyday interactions and associations?
- What practices and interactions occur in the school?
- What/who flows 'in and out' – are they local, regional, national, global?
- What traces are there of past practices and interactions, people and things?

- How is the school socio-spatially structured, hierarchized and narrativized?
- If the school is embedded in relations of history and potential, what can I see/hear of the actual and possible? What are the horizons of possibility for people and the school?
- What performances, utterances, images, narratives and events produce the school?
- How does the school assemblage express itself in ways that trigger responses (affiliative, resistant, compliant and so on)?
- What holds this assemblage together and what is making it stable and sustainable?
- What is threatening the stability of the school assemblage?
- How is the assemblage codified and decodified? How rigid/flexible are these processes?

While some of the school as a placed assemblage is easily noticed and will thus be available for use in a snapshot case study, understanding the moving, changing tangle can only happen over time and in time.

Other theoretical options

We hope that these examples of two theoretical resources suggest the potential of using theory to enhance method – to position what you might look for, ask and think about in the school over time. These are not the only options open to you, of course, and you might want to find out about other possibilities, for example:

1 A Bourdieusian approach, in which the school is located within the broader educational field, maps out the various positions, habitus and social relations of the actors in the school, together with the doxa and logic of practices (Grenfell, 2007; Grenfell et al., 2011; Grenfell and Lebaron, 2014).

2. A Foucauldian approach identifies the ways in which knowledges are produced, subjectivities formed and discourse practices operate within the school as discursive assemblages (Ball, 1990; Devine, 1996; Niesche, 2011).
3. An institutional ethnographic approach understands everyday life as framed within relations of ruling, mediated through texts (Griffith and Smith, 2005; Smith, 1993, 2005).
4. A geosemiotic approach focuses on the social meaning of signs and discourses in the material world and the complex interaction of multiple semiotic systems which take their meaning from being situated in a particular place (Nichols et al., 2012; Scollon and Scollon, 2003).

Each of these theoretical approaches suggests particular methods, questions to ask, places to look, people to talk to, and objects and material structures to observe.

We conclude the chapter by considering the kinds of habits that will support you in a long-term school research relationship.

Good research habits in place

We want to build here on the discussion we began in Chapter 2, where we talked about research as a relationship, or, perhaps more accurately, as a set of relationships. The orientations that we have discussed in this chapter suggested the importance of slowness, inhabiting and listening to a place-based study. We then said that it might be helpful to take a theoretical orientation to place as well. How are these things compatible? We explore this question through the concluding section on research habits.

Earlier we addressed the question of how you begin a research relationship and suggested that this was something that had to be worked on, a point we pick up again here. In Chapter 2 we quoted the serendipitous experiences of Jan Nespor at some length. We now go back to Nespor and his two-year immersion in Thurber Elementary in order to begin our discussion of developing good research habits (Nespor, 1997).

Jan Nespor's story

You might remember that Nespor wanted to work in his chosen research school as a collaborator. But this was not easily achieved. This was in part because Nespor was identified as someone *outside* the school, a professor based in a university. This caused ongoing issues with staff. Nespor reports that he was viewed with suspicion because he was

> ... the representative of a powerful institution that directly regulated upward mobility for people like Mr. Watts (the head) in so much as it regulated the acquisition of advanced degrees and indirectly set the agenda for what goes on the schools ... (1997, p. 207)

Some teachers had bad memories of their own teacher education and its apparent lack of direct relevance to actual teaching practice. As Nespor notes, this is not uncommon and is a highly complex issue. In our experience, this attitude to university education staff is quite widespread; it has, in many places, become a rationale for shifting teacher education further and further into schools. Indeed, in a country like England, someone like Jan Nespor would struggle to get a job in teacher education, as subjects like psychology, sociology, history, philosophy and anthropology form ever smaller parts of the curriculum. However, the point is that it is likely that you too will have to deal with existing, perhaps negative, attitudes towards you as an external researcher.

During the first year, Nespor spent a considerable amount of time inhabiting a particular classroom, living with the teacher and her class. This was a class from which a number of children's parents had returned permission slips giving consent for them to be interviewed as part of his research. Nespor notes that his interest in the classroom was

> ... examining the political, cultural and economic flows that determine what is possible within [the] classroom, that shape the identities of the teachers and students who meet there, and that pressure or constrain them to act in certain ways. (p. 210)

However, as the class teacher was one who had negative memories of her own university education and confessed to not understanding what Nespor had said he was interested in when he spoke at the staff meeting, Nespor decided not to dwell on this aspect of his research. Instead he told her

> ... that I wasn't there to observe or judge her teaching but to get to know her students informally before I began interviewing them. She agreed to let me attend on the condition that I didn't take any notes in her classroom. I spent almost every other day in her room until the end of the year. Although most of my work was with the students, I made several overtures for collaboration, Mrs. Jumpers [the teacher] declined these and said she didn't want to 'shortchange' the rest of her curriculum. (p. 210)

In Nespor's matter-of-fact statement about what was possible, we see the kind of negotiation that often occurs in real life research. Research in schools is very often not at all as it is presented in research methods courses. It is also often less than what was initially hoped for, and indeed what was designed. As in any relationship, there are two, sometimes more, parties involved in negotiating what seems reasonable to each of them.

After a year in the school, Nespor attempted to renegotiate his involvement. Once again he attended a staff meeting, and learning from his first appearance where he spoke in terms that were too abstract and removed from the school, he spoke, this time simply, about the possibility of teacher discussion groups.

> Unfortunately my suggestion was a tactical blunder. In spite of my efforts to locate the school in intersections of flows across space and time, I'd neglected to examine the history of the faculty and thus was unprepared when Mrs. Tanner interrupted me to explain that they had already tried what I was suggesting. (1997, p. 211)

Furthermore, because of that history, staff interpreted Nespor's suggestion as a top-down initiative, coming from the university in cahoots with the school administration, rather than emanating from his desire to support teacher learning and democratic discussion.

Nespor writes that he realized that the teachers were 'at the center of a whirl' of policy initiatives, district expectations, national standards agendas and parent hopes. Asking them to spend time away from their classrooms was just another request and seemed like more of the same. While many researchers note the inequitable power relations of research agendas which treat teachers as 'objects', Nespor's attempts to do the opposite were also problematic although for different reasons.

The next year, Nespor offered to work with another class teacher, Mrs Court. He became something of a volunteer in the class, and, for the three days a week he was present, often ran errands, helped individual students and worked with groups. This was a version of the teaching assistant role that we discussed in Chapter 2. Mrs Court asked him if he would work with the class on a language activity – producing a regular newsletter for parents, which would give information about class activities as well as feature children's writing. However, this activity also did not work out quite as planned:

> Ice storms closed the school and made it impossible for me to meet with the student researchers for about a month. Standardized tests ate into class time. Additional schedule disruptions, bad word-processing software, my commitments to have everyone contribute something to the paper, and my willingness to let groups develop long research projects as part of the newspaper activity delayed our editions so long that after one issue the newsletter turned into an end-of-the-year class research anthology. The kids and I had fun doing it, but in some ways it only added to Mrs. Court's worries. It didn't function as the line of communication to parents that she had wanted, and at the same time she felt guilty because she couldn't spare the kids very often to work with me. (1997, p. 215)

Mrs Court was struggling to introduce new ways of teaching and assessing students, and really wanted the parents to understand the process. She also wanted support from other staff, which was not forthcoming, as there were no staff discussion groups since the staff had rejected this suggestion when it had been made by Nespor. At the end of the year, Nespor describes Mrs Court as somewhat demoralized, subject to parent criticism and unable to situate her learning within a supportive professional pedagogical structure. While he could offer 'sympathy and suggestions' (p. 215), Nespor felt that his help was inadequate and that he had inadvertently added to some of the teacher's concerns.

So what can we learn from this story about the conduct of research?

Developing research habits

Nespor's frank, self-critical reflections on his experience are a rarity in methodological writing. But they are very useful for anyone considering inhabiting a school for any length of time, listening and working slowly. They draw attention to the need for:

- tolerance for ambiguity and mess

  Research is often messy. It doesn't always turn out the way that we want. Our presence in the school seems to create tensions and problems, when all we want to do is to help and be positive.

  Nespor's generosity in laying out this situation provides a powerful example of the difficulties of working in schools, of inhabiting the space. Researchers enter a living ecology in which a lot is out of their control. Actions that make it difficult for the research to go on as initially planned are generally quite reasonable responses to histories and presents – rational responses if we bear in mind where the school and people in it have been.

- preparedness to rethink

  Having to renegotiate research while it is going on is not uncommon. While there might be a clear research plan at the outset, this very often changes in response to circumstances, but also in response to what researchers learn as they go along. As Martin Hammersley observes:

  > [T]he issue of how many people to interview, or how many places to observe, is rarely conceptualized by qualitative researchers ... in terms of whether sufficient data will be collected to identify all the relevant themes. This is, in part, because what will be relevant

> themes depends upon analysis of the data and further development and refinement of the research questions, a process that takes place over the course of inquiry. (2015, p. 1)

It seems obvious that in a protracted engagement with a complex organization like a school, initial research plans are likely to change – ideas about what tools to use, for instance, or who to observe and where.

- ongoing practices of reflection

As Jan Nespor's writing elegantly shows, it is important to be reflective and reflexive about the research that you are doing, all the way through the process. To help you in the processes of negotiating, rethinking and making sense of ambiguous situations, it is very helpful to develop routines for writing and talking. Processes of reflection rely on you making time and perhaps also getting some support, particularly if you like to talk through what is happening as a way to begin to sort out your thoughts.

Reflection is also helped by returning to the data that you are generating, re-examining it, asking whether it is what you need in order to answer your research question, and brainstorming options about what you want to do next. You might want to keep a journal or some kind of writing file; blogging can also be extremely helpful in sorting out what is actually going on in a research project.

And it is in your reflections that theory can be very helpful. You can get some distance on your experiences in the school through thinking slowly with your chosen theory. How does the theory help explain what you have seen, heard and done? How might the patterns you have observed and been part of be understood? How does the theory help you to understand more fully the school as a place? What does it not help with? What else might you need to read in order to grasp the phenomena that elude your theory? How can you use your theory to gradually build a nuanced and situated narrative?

Final note

A lot of researchers base their work on quite short engagements with a school. We don't dismiss this, as there is a lot that can be learnt about a school place in a relatively brief space of time. However, settling in for a longer relationship will bring benefits in terms of your grasp of complexities, change and history. We've offered some orientations, and urged you to think about the benefits of working with social theory, as part of the process of getting ready for a longer-term stay in place. Of course, establishing a long-term relationship takes negotiation and work and things don't always run smoothly. Being careful and reflexive in the ways in which you document and communicate with people in the school is a key to success.

Further reading

You might want to follow up some of the literature we have used in this chapter, in particular:

Back, Les (2007). *The Art of Listening*. London: Berg Publishers.
Ingold, Tim (2011). *Ways of Knowing: Essays on Movement, Knowledge and Description*. London: Routledge.

You might also be interested in finding out more about the theories of trialectic and assemblage. We suggest starting with:

On assemblage: Masny, Diana (2012). *Cartographies of Becoming in Education: A Deleuze–Guattari Perspective*. Rotterdam: Sense Publishers.
On Lefebrvre: Middleton, Sue (2014). *Henri Lefebvre and Education: Space, History, Theory*. London: Routledge.

We also suggest reading further about good researcher habits in schools, beginning with:

Nind, Melanie (2014). *What is Inclusive Research?* London: Bloomsbury.

CHAPTER SIX

Multiple perspectives on the school

There are key differences between a short- and a longer-term engagement with a school, as we've already suggested. Being in a school for a long period of time enhances not only the understanding of the school year, with its various regular patterns and irregular happenings, but also the depth of information that it is possible to accrue. People may, in one-off snapshot visits, tell you what you want to hear, or give you the dominant version of events. If you are around for longer, you can see things for yourself as well as ask people to explain things to you – simply because you have the time and you have built connections with them.

While it is possible to get several points of view on a school in the short term, in a longer-term engagement, these can be fleshed out, interrogated and nuanced. Over time, it is also possible to establish relationships with people who are just harder to access in quick visits – parents and carers, frequent visitors, those who are distrustful of research. Another advantage of being around the school for some time is that you begin to see where and how the school is porous – who and what comes in and out of the school and from where. You also get to see the school as a changing, not static, place.

Researchers engaged with a school over a longer period of time seek an enhanced sense of the distinctiveness of place as well as its patternings – they look for events, doings, practices, relations, performances, affective resonances, local meanings and attachments – but to do so, they need a toolkit of procedures. This chapter addresses the place-based researcher's tools for generating and making inventories of 'data'. We consider some of the most common ways researchers go about their work in a school: observing, keeping notes and talking with people. We discuss a range of text and image work. As in previous chapters, we use published research in conversation with our discussion of tools.

But first of all, we take issue with the notion of 'collecting' data – the term we most often hear in relation to data work – and argue instead for the notion of generation.

Generating data

Throughout this book we have used the term 'to generate data'. As we begin another chapter which discusses how we build up a corpus of data (see also Chapters 3 and 4), it is timely to pause briefly to state the reasons for our terminology.

Think first of all about the usual notion of collecting data. What do we most often collect? Mushrooms in the forest. Letters from the postbox. The children from school. In each of these cases, we are collecting something that actually exists as a material *thing* in the world. But data do not exist out there in the world in the same way as mushrooms, letters and children.

This is not to say that there is no material reality; rather, it is to suggest that things/people aren't data until researchers make them data. People don't live their lives as data. Stories are not told as data. Events do not happen as data. Practices don't hang around like mushrooms waiting to be picked – or not. Things aren't data until we make them data.

As researchers generate data, we impose our own set of meanings. We can't help it. We even do this with numbers. We define our terms, we decide what to focus on, what to leave out, what to include, how many, who, where, when and so on. There's no part of a survey that the researcher is not all over, including the choice of statistical approach. The same can be said for interviews. As researchers we decide most of what to talk about with interviewees and we certainly control how to record the interview, how it's edited and how the conversation is represented in and as text. There's no part of an interview that we haven't actually constructed.

If researchers think that the truth is 'out there', lying around like a mushroom, or waiting impatiently like the child at the school gates, then they construct a very significant blind spot in their research. Thinking of *generating* data forces researchers to focus on which tools are to be used for which purposes, and how the research processes of inclusion and exclusion might obscure as much as they reveal. And, of course, different data allow the researcher to 'see and say' different things. Considering what data you want to generate to answer your research question means thinking about the different affordances of different data generation tools.

We don't want to labour this point, but we do think it is important to remind ourselves of the 'researcher effect' before we begin to discuss tools that we might employ throughout a long relationship with a school.

Hanging about with serious intent

Researchers need to find a sensible location in which to begin their investigation of the school. This might be the front office, the staff rooms, a schedule of lessons, the hallway, the detention room. But getting to where you want to be may not be straightforward; our earlier discussion of 'access' and relationships building in Chapter 2 elaborated on the need for continual negotiation about entry to different parts of the school and to different people. This is particularly an issue if you want to research slowly, inhabiting one room, corridor or office for an extended period of time. People may be suspicious about why you want to 'hang about'; while they might have been happy for a one-off visit, they may well require additional conversation, reassurance and promises about what you will and won't do in order to countenance you as a fixture in their lives.

When you do find your first landing place, you need to be armed with your notebook.

Observing and recording

It is likely that observation and recording what you hear, see and experience in the school will be the backbone of your research data. You will use other tools in order to expand and extend your observations, and indeed many research methods texts roll other tools – such as interviews, textual analysis and making images – into their discussion of observation. We want to separate out the observation and recording, because there is often less discussion about the most basic observation practice, namely looking, listening and taking notes.

What you look for will be guided by your research interest. However, our experience is that it is usually best to begin with a period of general observation in your school, and that moving to specific observation 'schedules' comes later – if at all. Hanging around in offices, the staff room, the yard and classrooms with your research questions in mind is likely to be the best way to start. This may feel very indeterminate and unfocused at the start of a project, and this can cause a mild panic that you will never actually get to see what you want. However, our experience is that what you want to see, and where you want to be, gradually come into focus. The most helpful simile we can offer is that this is rather like slowly turning the knob on a projector and seeing things become sharper and clearer as you find – by sight and touch – the right spot to be.

However, even if you are not sure about exactly what in the school is going to be most important, you do need to start making records right from the start. When you do this is important. As Robert Emerson, Rachel Fetz and Linda Shaw (2011, p. 35) put it:

> Field researchers must decide when, where and how to write jottings. Far from simply mundane matters, such decisions can have tremendous import for those in the field. The researcher works hard to establish close ties with participants so that she may be included in activities that are central to their lives. In the midst of such activities, however, she may experience deep ambivalence on the one hand, she may wish to preserve the immediacy of the moment by jotting down words as they are spoken and details of scenes as they are enacted; on the other

> hand, she may feel that taking out a note pad and writing jottings will ruin the moment and plant seeds of distrust. Participants may now see here is someone whose primary interest lies in discovering their secrets and turning their most intimate and cherished experiences into objects of scientific inquiry.

Deciding when and where to make notes is not something that is decided once. It is crucial to keep thinking about what the practices of recording will do to a situation and ongoing relationships. Veteran ethnographer Sara Delamont (2008) warns those new to writing down what they see that they need to be clear about the differences between recording what exists and what happens, and writing down evaluative impressions. She argues that, in the first instance, the job of the ethnographer is to make the best description and account of what is actually happening, rather than focusing on those things which are most obvious, striking or disturbing. She advises researchers to be:

> ... very systematic about observing, and recording, some basic 'facts' in every setting; so for instance, in a school study I would sketch every 'room' or space entered for the first time. Classrooms, labs, staffrooms, library, changing rooms, hockey pitch, sick room, stock cupboard, gym, swimming pool, space for the bicycle racks and so on, and thereafter note where in that space the key actions take place. (p. 43)

Delamont also advises, as we suggested in Chapter 4, documenting what is on the walls; the nature, location and condition of furniture and equipment; and the noise and smells attached to particular locations. In order to guard against feelings of overfamiliarity, she suggests sitting in different places and angles rather than always sitting in the same spot. Because people are more likely to forget details than emotions, memorable events and telling statements, Delmont suggests always focusing recording on the concrete.

> So count things: how many pupils are there in a class? Males? Females? British Asian? African-Caribbean? Turkish? Somali? Are there enough Bibles in RE for every pupil to have one? How many of the Bunsen burners are working? Bodies matter: how are staff and students dressed? Who is clean and who smells?

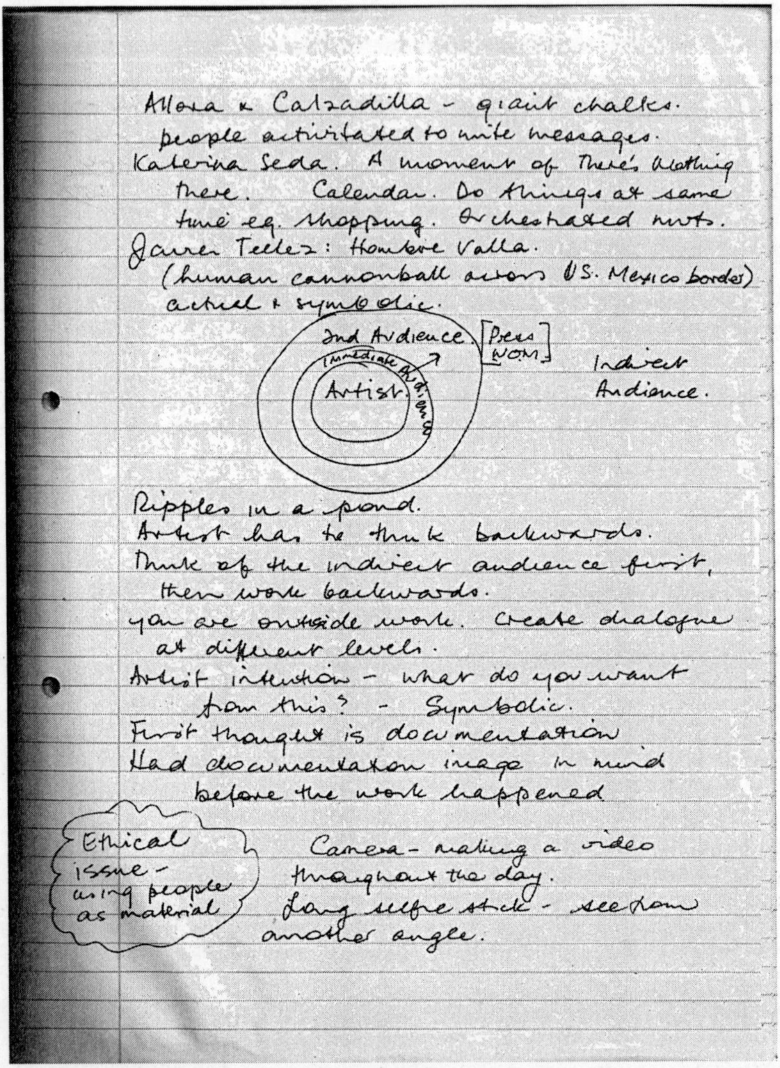

FIGURE 6.1 *Notebook page – field notes*

> What is the state of people's teeth? What youth fashions are in vogue and do they mark out cliques? How many people have all the necessary 'kit'? (p. 44)

We agree with this in general. However, we often find that we have random and associated thoughts that arise when we are making notes in situ, and we usually put those in brackets to discriminate them from the more factual recording. Figure 6.1 shows some of Pat's notes taken during a professional development workshop run by an artist for teachers.

Most of the notes on the page are verbatim extracts of what the artist actually said during a formal presentation about his own work and that of some associate artists. The (rather bad) sketch is of the contents of a PowerPoint slide. However, the comment in the wavy circle at the bottom left-hand side of the page is an evaluative question/comment that has been separated from the rest of the text. It was important to capture the question/comment, but also to indicate that it wasn't part of the actual conversation. The wavy circle is the convention Pat uses in her notes to indicate something that wasn't part of the proceedings. In this case, the note refers to something that she wanted to talk to both the artist and the teachers about later. The wavy circle is her way of signalling 'Follow this up, think about this later, find out more about this.'

What is also apparent from this page of field notes is that these jottings aren't readily comprehensible to other people. The notes are a reminder to the researcher who uses them later to write a more detailed piece. Most field notes are like this. They are not neat and well ordered, as they are inevitably written in a hurry with the researcher trying to capture the most salient points. Delamont describes her own practice as making multilayered notes:

> In situ I write scribbled notes in spiral bound reporter's notebooks – I use abbreviations and mnemonics which I can decipher, and aim to record as much as I can. I do not try to write legibly for anyone else to read these notes, they are an aide memoire for me ... I date each entry, record the time down the left hand side every four to six minutes ... As soon as I get home, or back to wherever I am staying or into a quiet space, I write up those notes into an A4 spiral bound lined book. This is a much more detailed account, based on the field notes, now amplified, and

> with some reflections, commentary and cross-referencing added … these will not be in beautifully grammatical English, but there will be sentences. (p. 47)

We confess that we don't always write amplified field notes and we do secretly envy Delamont her discipline. Even though we can use dictated notes, voice recognition software, or the new smart pens and notebooks, we don't do this nearly as often as we should. We like reading Tricia Wang's blog 'Ethnography Matters' (see http://ethnographymatters.net/blog/2012/08/02/writing-live-fieldnotes-towards-a-more-open-ethnography/ [accessed 30 September 2015]), as she often talks about her use of new technologies for making field notes, but we are still largely analogue in our field noting. We find that tools like voice recognition software are not yet as straightforward or as time-saving as we would like. We are, however, watching the development of new kinds of tech support with some interest (e.g. see Tessler, 2012), particularly those that combine handwriting with auto-text translations. We suspect that very soon we might switch to these, though, as an aside, we note that there is some research (Mueller and Oppenheimer, 2014) which suggests that writing by hand is a particularly good way to both remember and learn.

A field note question which often arises is whether to show your scribblings to people in situ. Some researchers are very cautious about this: Delamont, for example, urges researchers to develop their own shorthand, mnemonics and abbreviations as well as cultivating semi-legible handwriting, in order to avoid the problem of people accidently seeing their notes. It can be more than a little awkward if someone asks to see what you are writing and you don't want to show them. Refusal seems to suggest you really do have something to hide. While we do know of the odd case of researchers who have had problems when people have seen what's in their notes, our position is fairly relaxed. This is probably because we see our own research as being highly participatory and thus we have nothing we really want to conceal. However, we do think it is important to consider the issue of field note privacy and how you might respond to a question to show and tell all.

Delamont keeps a reflections notebook separate from her field notes where she writes about 'ideas for things to follow up, possible papers to write, items to read, reflective commentary on the processes of research'. We can't stress too much how useful this might be – some fieldwork settings are emotionally challenging as well as exhausting. It is as well to have a cathartic outlet even if the confessional writing may never be read by anyone else! Delamont also has a fourth notebook in which she records notes from books and theses, lists of pseudonyms, quotations from field notes and so on: this is a kind of resource book for future writings (2008, pp. 51–3).

We too write very regularly about what we are witnessing and experiencing. Sometimes these writings are more oriented to rich description, where we compose relatively well-crafted pieces about particular settings, events or conversations. These descriptions often refer to other descriptions, events and conversations or they begin to work with analysis or bring an event together with a possible theorization. At other times, the writing is more like 'memos', where we work on specific issues and questions, sometimes experimenting with potential analyses and possible social theory. Rebecca Coles and Pat (Coles and Thomson, 2016) have referred to this kind of writing as 'inbetween writing' – but Emerson and colleagues (2011) just see all of this writing as field notes.

We sometimes blog fieldwork and these posts serve as a kind of audit trail about what happened when and who was involved. Participants can also read the posts to keep up to date with the overall research. Pat has used her own blog 'patter' (patthomson.net) to report her regular work as an 'embedded ethnographer' in the Tate teachers' summer school; participants, artists and curators within Tate have all told her that they found it interesting and useful to have a short, readable record of events with links to relevant online resources. We also use blogs to create an audience for our work. For example, the Tracking Arts Learning and Engagement (TALE) research blog (https://www.researchtale.net) connects with other people interested in research directed at providing evidence about the connections between teachers' and students' learning in the arts. Blogs are a place to test out ideas in public, share possible thinking and stimulate conversation. We think of research blogging as not simply a form of making public the research but also creating a public forum for discussion. This is certainly worth considering, but it does need to be negotiated with the school. It is also important to remember that a public blog will become part of more general school meaning-making resources and will contribute not only to your, but also the wider school's, 'place-making'.

Chatting

Unless you are determined to be completely antisocial – and what kind of relationship building is that? – then you will inevitably end up chatting to people where you are observing. This is an integral part of fieldwork and hanging about. Mostly, because people know that you are in the school doing research and they know what you are doing, it is possible to include an informal chat in your data. You'll just need to find a way to record it before too long, so that you don't forget it later.

Sometimes people will preface their comments with 'This is off the record' or 'You didn't hear this from me' or something similar. If this is the case, then you obviously need to honour their request and neither attribute their comment nor indeed use it. However, you cannot 'un-hear' something. Once you've heard the comment, it sticks in your mind. Our view is that the best way to deal with confidential information is to try to confirm it 'on the record' and use it only if it is confirmed by another person who is speaking in the knowledge that you will use the information. You will also overhear conversations, and this may prove to be both fruitful and an ethical problem. Again, this is a matter of seeing whether there is a way to get the information affirmed on the record, without of course pestering or harassing anyone in order to do so. The edict of doing no harm should always govern how you deal with off-the-record and overheard conversations.

Who do you talk to? Chatting just happens in situ. It's what people do. Sometimes they are silent with each other, but mostly they break the silence. Developing a good line in small talk is a key skill for those who are hanging around schools with serious intent. Chatting is about relationship building. Often the way into a deep and meaningful conversation is via a light-hearted and apparently innocuous exchange. You are building rapport and trust. It's off-putting to people in the school if you sidle up and immediately start quizzing them. They feel under the microscope and just want to get away as quickly as they can. With a chat, a lot of the immediate power is in the hands of the person you are chatting to;

he or she can take the initiative and offer something personal or private or not as they want to. It is important not to get frustrated if chatting with someone you really want to get information from actually doesn't immediately result in anything very significant. A series of chats about the weather might lead somewhere in the end.

We want to look at a piece of published research to see how one researcher used chatting in combination with observation to get a lot of helpful information – to generate her data to enhance her understanding of school as place. Kathleen Nolan examined the discipline practices in one school in the Bronx. She was particularly interested in the ways in which the police were used to control entry and exit to the school, and to patrol the hallways and manage rule infractions that were deemed serious: fighting and theft, but also truanting from lessons. Her research raised serious questions about the increasing similarities between school and prison cultures, and the negative impact this had on students, particularly low-income students of colour. Nolan's book, *Police in the Hallways: Discipline in an Urban High School* (2011) is telling evidence of a complex and not causal, but definitely contributory, school-to-prison 'pipeline'. Her research narrative has considerable overlap with John Devine's ethnography, *Maximum Security* (1996), undertaken fifteen years earlier in another New York school. Together the two in-depth school studies show a frightening progression resulting from the erosion of pastoral care and the imposition of policing practices in New York's education system.

A former teacher and community activist, Nolan was able to select a school close to where she lived, and in which a new principal had apparently reduced the incidents of school violence and improved the school climate. With the support of the local superintendent, Nolan visited the school for about five hours a day, several days a week for a school year. She was also able to see a small group of students outside of school. Nolan describes the corpus of data she generated as follows:

> Along with just 'hanging out' in the hallways, lunchroom, and offices, I attended twelve different classes, four of them on a regular basis, and I conducted audio-recorded interviews with students, school personnel and a few law-enforcement officials. In all, I interviewed thirty three students. I interviewed most students alone, but I also conducted three group interviews.

> Seven students granted me more than one audio-recorded interview. *I had dozens of other lengthy conversations with students during which I took ample notes*. I formally recorded (on audio recordings) six deans, two of them twice, but my knowledge of the deans came mainly from spending time with them and interacting with them in more informal ways. (2011, pp. 8–9, emphasis added)

Nolan also interviewed other school personnel, including those responsible for guidance and safety. She examined school records related to disciplinary incidents and enjoyed conversations with less high-status staff:

> I gained further insight into daily life in the school from speaking with school aides. There were three in particular with whom I became friendly: one stationed in a stairwell, another in the lunchroom, and a third in the detention room. (p. 9)

Nolan confirms the popular mythology that if you really want to know what's going in a school you need to make friends with the non-teaching staff. She accrued information that was highly significant for her study from her informal conversations. She also gained entry to parts of students' lives that she hadn't anticipated:

> One issue that frequently emerged during my conversations with students was the number of summonses they were accumulating. Some were getting summoned to criminal court for incidents that occurred in the school; some were getting summonses for transit court for jumping the subway turnstile or littering in the station. The summons, it turned out, was a fairly prominent theme in many students' lives. So once students began to share their perspectives with me, it seemed (to me at least) a logical next step for me to ask those who had gotten summoned to court whether I could accompany them. Invariably, they thought my request was a bit odd. Often a student would shrug his or her shoulders and say, 'Sure,' but then the student would say something like, 'You know, it's really boring.' (p. 9)

Not all students were willing to chat and not all conversations led to this kind of access to 'non-school' lives (which flow in and out of the school place), but enough did. Nolan clearly showed sufficient interest and trustworthiness to be allowed to participate in non-educational activities. This didn't mean that she hid her views from the students, but it did mean that she recognized and respected their opinions and experiences:

> One day I argued with Carlos at the entrance to the subway. He was attempting to sneak past the turnstile by manipulating his Metro card ... I wanted to pay his fare, but he was refusing to let me do so. My anxiety grew as I imagined a police officer approaching. Carlos finally managed to get past the turnstile without paying. Then, looking back at me, he smiled slightly and said, 'This is the way that we live.' He and I had once discussed the term 'research subject' and he said he didn't like it, so I suggested he come up with another term. He pondered for a while and then decided that he preferred the term 'living proof'. He also liked to think of himself as my 'guide'. Despite my own familiarity with the Bronx, I still had much to learn from all of my 'guides' concerning the social world and the material conditions in which they lived. (p. 10)

In this anecdote the researcher's relationship with Carlos is made clear: he is the expert, she the learner. Their relationship is not of teacher and child, or parent and child. Nolan does not have the authority to compel Carlos to behave legally – and is thus an unwilling witness to a small legal infraction, which would have resulted in a fine or court appearance had Carlos been caught. Nolan does not discuss the ways in which she reconciled her presence at these illegal activities, but this is a dilemma which all researchers working with similar populations must deal with and come to their own ethical decision about. (See also the discussion by Michelle Fine and Lois Weis (1998) on researching with men whose misogyny and domestic violence appalled them.)

Nolan also spent time chatting with young people who were not getting into trouble, and this was important for her study, as she was able to show that all young people in the school lived in fear of the police and prison, and thought they were unfair. She also spoke formally, but more frequently informally, to teachers, and she makes it clear throughout the book that she is at pains to try to present their experiences fairly and show them compassion.

Teachers spoke to her readily. However, she had less luck with police and school safety staff:

> My efforts to gain a police perspective were sometimes frustrated. One September morning, as I was sitting in the dean's office soon after I arrived in the school, several law-enforcement agents ushered a young man into the room. Placing the young man's hands on top of an empty desk, one officer began frisking him, while another searched through the student's backpack. I began taking notes – too brazenly, apparently. The police sergeant whispered to one of the deans to tell me to put away my notebook. He was definitely not comfortable with my presence. It took a few months to develop a friendly rapport with him. Ultimately only Officer Hoffman granted me a formal audio-recorded interview. Several other officers spoke to me informally on a regular basis. (p. 12)

Nolan, like most ethnographers, had to rely on several sources of information. Formal interviews were combined with chats and with her own observations. Nolan's comments on one interview she had with the head of school safety staff nicely illustrate the problem of relying on the formal interview – as well as showing how the Lefebvrian notion of the conceived space of schooling (discussed in Chapter 5) might be relatively quickly generated:

> The head of the safety agents (who worked under the auspices of the police department) did not permit his staff to be interviewed. He himself, however, did grant me an interview, which I could only describe as 'textbook' in that it seemed to reflect the official discourse of the department regarding the training his agents received and official policy. (2011, p. 12)

However, this did not prevent the research:

> Despite limited access I had to officers', and agents', testimonies, their perspectives are not missing. I had the opportunity to see them in action and some of what I learned came from what I saw. (p. 12)

Nespor (1997), whose work we discussed in some detail in

Chapters 2 and 4, reports something similar – his formal conversations with children combined with observations were often more informative than the formal interviews he conducted.

We now want to deal with some other tools you might use to get to know the school as place, in addition to your trusty notebook and your capacity to make conversation with anyone and everyone.

Working with images

Like all parts of modern life, the school is a highly visual place. Researchers can gain a great deal of understanding about the particularity and patterning of place from incorporating elements of visual research in their investigations. We have already discussed some visual tools in relation to getting to know the community – websites, library books and newspapers, for example – in a short-term approach to the school (see Chapters 2–3). Here we expand on this repertoire.

We focus on images which are generated as data. These data might be used as part of later publications, but their initial purpose is as a means of finding out what is going on in the school. It is a way for you to get to know the school as a place better, closer up. We think it is helpful to see visual data through four 'bucket' categories:

1. images that the researcher '*finds*' ready-made in the school;
2. images that the researcher creates as part of his or her research;
3. images that the researcher solicits from people in the school;
4. images that the researcher makes with people in the school.

We address each of these in turn.

You might notice that we have used the term 'finds' in this list and italicized it. We have of course just argued that data aren't found and collected but are generated. Are we being contradictory? Well, we hope not! The 'find' used here refers specifically to artistic traditions of working with 'found' materials – scraps of text, disused items, natural objects (see http://www.artspace.com/magazine/

art_101/art_market/the-history-of-the-found-object-in-art-52224 [accessed 30 September 2015]) – and with ready-made objects, as championed by Duchamp (see http://www.tate.org.uk/learn/online-resources/glossary/r/readymade [accessed 30 September 2015]).

1 *Images that the researcher 'finds' ready-made in the school*

Schools are full of visual material – not simply displays in the foyer, halls, offices and staff rooms and not just on websites and prospectuses (see Chapter 4). There are commercially produced materials and those that are hand-made within the school. Think of the images that students paste on their exercise books and diaries, or the graffiti in the toilets and dark corners of the yard outside. Then there are the doodles that students make in class, the fleeting illustrations that teachers make on whiteboards, the PowerPoints that comprise lessons, the outlines of areas for playing in the yard, the artworks made in and out of class. There might be historical photos in dusty albums stored in cupboards. Any of these images might be worthy of inclusion in a study.

The images in a school can be thought of as *traces* that are left behind of something that happened. They are the marks of activities: activities that are one-off – or regular and patterned. They are the marks left behind of bodies and objects moving, acting and interacting. Approaching a school's visual environment, then, is a little like following animal tracks in the wild. Trackers look for clues in the prints, broken plants, food residues, droppings and flattened ground to determine the species they are looking for, their state of health, their ways of eating and sleeping, and their interactions with other animals. Good trackers can tell a lot simply by reading the traces. This is the mindset that researchers wishing to use found images might adopt. What can be understood simply by looking for visual clues? What happened that resulted in this image?

The image in Figure 6.2, taken in a South African township school, can be understood as a trace of a set of school concerns and activities. However, it also opens up a global health issue and one which takes a particularly brutal turn in the township in which the school is located.

FIGURE 6.2 *A playground trace signalling a bigger issue*

The sign painted onto the school wall is an indication of the approach taken by the school to the wider health issue, one which deals openly with the problem of stigma and isolation. This stands in contrast to the views of some national policymakers and some local township residents. It is perhaps also a model of how a school can face up to a contentious public health issue with courage and humanity. A simple sign is a trace of a discursive practice that could lead to a very substantive researcher discussion and enhanced understandings of place particularity.

Many 'found' images, such as the one above, are integral to the school's **semiotic practices** – that is the ways in which meanings are made within the institution. (Meaning-making is integral to place as we explained in Chapter 1.) Researchers might want to undertake very detailed studies of particular materials in the school if they appear to have particular meaning and significance in the school's everyday life. A researcher might, for example, trace the source of the found visual materials – who bought or made them and why, where are they on show and why here? Asking the question 'What do pictures want?', as does W. J. T. Mitchell (2005), can be a very helpful approach to such materials, alerting us not only to their production, but also the ways in which the image that is produced steers meaning-making.

Some visual/multi-modal material is likely to be more attention-getting than others, and some of more interest to either students or staff. Because people interact with images, researchers might want to pursue how particular visual materials are viewed and understood. Does the image serve a particular purpose – supporting or contradicting a particular way of thinking about the school? For instance, we have often wondered about the display shown in Figure 6.3. This photo is now a historical record of a school that was closed for its 'poor performance', and its leadership team replaced with one considered to be of higher quality. Looking at this image in the light of this intervention makes us wonder how students, parents and visitors variously read the display. Did

FIGURE 6.3 *Attendance records on school wall*

they see it as a signal that the school had a problem with attendance or as a statement that the school had a problem, but was determined to do something about it?

The visual is often not simply an image but a combination of words and images. It is **multi-modal.** In Figure 6.3 there are a lot of numbers and words together with some images of a register, attendance certificate and clocks, perhaps referring to the importance of being on time. The way the overall image is composed is important, as well as the content. Juxtaposition and positioning of the visual in relation to the text is not accidental but designed for a particular purpose – some elements of the overall composition are intended to be the first focus of attention. What most draws our attention is the large heading which stretches across two display boards. The direct address is to the student – your attendance – but the subsequent phrasing immediately raises the question of who the attendance matters to most of all.

We include this example to indicate that the found image often raises as many questions as it answers. However, as part of a corpus of data illuminating meaning-making and discourse practice in place, the found image can be very useful.

2 *Images that the researcher creates as part of his or her research*

Researchers will make their own records of found images – and this recording process is of course part of the data generation process. However, you might want to do more than this. Researchers might produce an archive of photographic still images of events or a location in the school; conduct photographic surveys of displays, students' work, teachers' offices and so on; film/video activities in classrooms, assemblies and school events; or map various material aspects of the school.

Many researchers will be tempted by the apparent simplicity of filming/videoing. We work regularly with both still and moving images, and with professional filmmakers. We also make still and moving images ourselves. There is a range of largely practical questions related to this kind of research and we mention three key issues here.

First, an epistemological point: clearly, a camera is not a lens on reality (Harper, 2013). The person behind the camera decides where to position themselves and which angle to take. He or she decides what should be in the foreground and what in the background, and what should be out of frame altogether. Whatever images are taken, they are always only partial. What one camera operator sees as important, another might ignore altogether. It is possible for two researchers to film the same event and tell completely different stories, simply because they have been recording different things (Reid et al., 1996). It is worth keeping this in mind when thinking about whether to work with professional filmmakers and photographers as they may not see the same things as you.

Second, a practical consideration: it is easy to amass an enormous amount of visual material very quickly. We have often ended up with hundreds of photos after only a few months in a school. It is worth considering early in your research how visual material will be stored and tagged so that it is retrievable. How long will it take to actually watch all of the recordings or to analyse the images? Is it likely that some of this material will be useful in the later stages of research, that is, to communicate your results? If so, is the quality of the image and sound good enough? Have you got the right equipment?

Third, ethical considerations. Many people do not like having their photo taken and you do need to think about when and where you might wield a camera. Intrusive 'snapping' can undo the kind of trust you have created; the school may not be the place to practice street photography. In addition, photographs often give away the what, where and who of the school much more easily than written descriptions. It is not difficult to identify places and people using standard internet searches. There are therefore crucial differences between images you generate and choose to use for your analysis, and those you choose to use in public; this goes back to our discussions of anonymity in Chapter

3 and forward to Chapter 8 for further discussions of publication issues.

We think that mapping is an underutilized approach (see also Chapter 4). Mapping is particularly good for tracking networks, flows, movements and interactions in and around the school. Mapping can also be used to document movements in and out of the school. It can be used to track student and staff social groupings and patterns of interactions. Mapping can help us see some of the 'thrown togetherness' of place. We often use very roughly drawn maps to start conversations – see Figure 6.4.

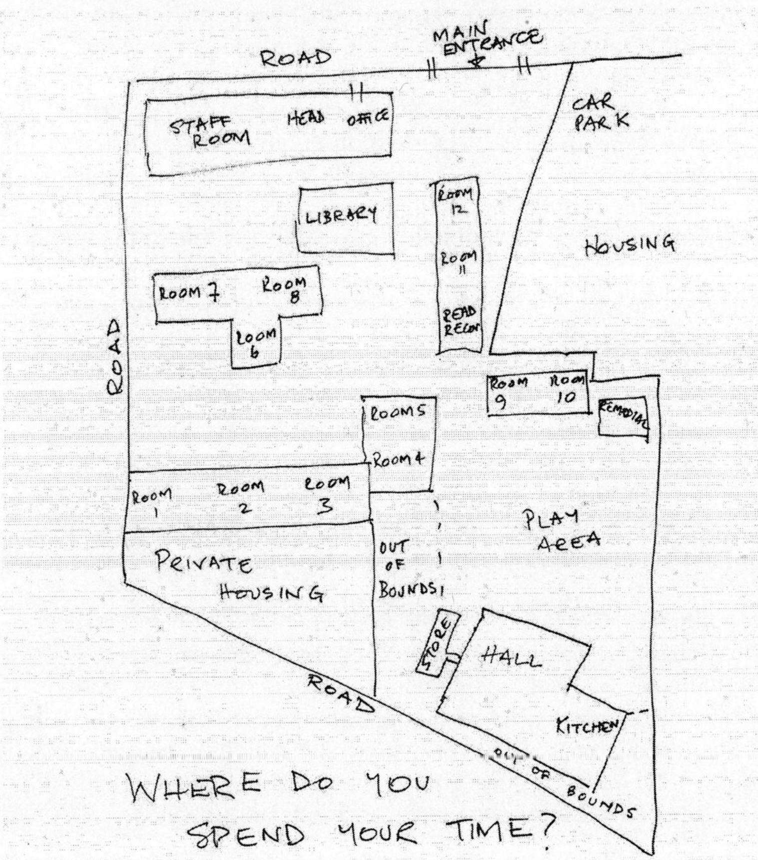

FIGURE 6.4 *Researcher-drawn map ready for a mapping conversation*

Shaun Fielding (2000) used mapping as part of a research project designed to explore the moral geographies of schooling. He examined school rules, and interactions between the head and teachers, teachers and teachers, children and teachers, and among children. He also observed in classrooms. He focused intensively on the movements of individual Year 5 children in lessons conducted by two different teachers with contrasting pedagogic practices. Both teachers worked with the same class and in the same room.

Fielding first of all drew a map of the room showing the position of desks, computer, teacher's table, whiteboards, display, windows and door. He recorded the names of which students sat where. He then mapped one girl's movements on blank copies of the map in two different lessons, as well as listening to her conversations and watching her actions. The results were a stark contrast – in one lesson the student moved around the room and interacted with a number of classmates, while in the other she talked only to students immediately around her, and then somewhat disruptively. Fielding concluded that the inflexibility of the second teacher actually produced inattention, whereas the greater freedom of the environment that resulted from the first teacher's routine classroom practices produced more movement, but also more learning-focused interaction. In a place-based study this approach would support you to think about the ways in which different people have differential experiences of being in the school.

3 *Images that the researcher solicits from people in the school*

The most common way to get participants to produce images is either to ask them to **draw** or paint or to give them a camera. In most cases, this image making is usually a precursor to a conversation. However, even on their own, student drawings can be very interesting – see, for example, the collection of student illustrations about *The School I'd Like* (Burke and Grosvenor, 2004, 2015). Photo-elicitation techniques (Samuels, 2004) – that is, asking someone to make an image which then becomes the focus for a more formal interview – are increasingly used in school research. Many researchers give out cameras and ask participants to produce a small number of images about a carefully delineated topic. Some researchers have also experimented with video diary rooms, adding captions to photographs, adding details to cartoons with blank speech bubbles, making collage scrapbooks or creating installation art or websites.

Researchers unfamiliar with these approaches might assume that children and young people will both want and have the skills to engage happily in image production. In our experience there are always some young people who feel particularly uncomfortable with 'draw and write' exercises and who feel embarrassed about their skills in drawing or in writing or both. We suspect that some researchers might also assume that young people are adept at visual communication and intuitively understand the niceties of composition, simply because they live in image-saturated worlds and take selfies on their phones. Of course, this is not necessarily the case, and students often benefit from some kind of lead-in activity where the elements of visual images are discussed.

For example, as a newly appointed headteacher, Kay Johnson (2008) was keen to explore with her students the ways in which the schoolyard might be improved. She wanted to begin her project by getting a representative group of children from the upper years of the primary school to paint pictures of the spots in the yard that they liked and those that they thought needed to be changed. However, she began the research not with the pictures but by discussing with the children a series of illustrated books which showed perspective, point of view and choice of colour and textures. Page layout and coverage of the page were also talked through. Johnson drew the children's attention to the ways in which these artistic decisions produced particular kinds of meanings and emotional responses. The children used these understandings when doing their own paintings, which were then used as conversation starters. Of course, Johnson had carefully negotiated permission to use the children's artwork in her research.

4 *Images that the researcher makes with people in the school*

It is increasingly common for school researchers to want to work with young people as co-researchers. This is usually more than a choice to avoid children simply being data for research, but rather a positive opting for practices which allow young people's perspectives to influence the process of researching. Research that is co-constructed and co-conducted may well have a visual component. The research methods literatures now include a sizeable body of reports which discuss the practices and ethics of conducting research with children and young people, including the important question of ownership (e.g. Bancroft et al., 2008; Christensen and James, 2000; Clark et al., 2013; Fielding and Bragg, 2003; Warren, 2000). A range of visual methods – making films and videos, taking photographs, and mapping making websites, posters and games – are empirically evidenced in this literature (e.g. Haw and Hadfield, 2012; Stirling and Yamada-Rice, 2015; Thomson, 2008).

Pat and Helen Gunter worked with a student research group examining bullying in a school (Gunter and Thomson, 2008; Thomson and Gunter, 2006, 2007, 2008, 2009). They had initially asked for a representative group with whom they could consult about a survey that they had been asked to design and administer to look at a whole-school innovation. The students tested the survey on themselves and their friends and were then involved in analysing the results. One of the questionnaire responses that concerned them referred to students' sense of a lack of personal safety and they decided that they wanted to investigate this further. They designed a series of photographs which showed ambiguous social situations (see Figure 6.5), and these were used to begin conversations with focus groups of students across the school.

During the process of co-designing this project, the researchers became much more aware of the ways in which

FIGURE 6.5 *Ambiguous photo: a faint or a kicking?*

clothes, bags and shoes, while still regulation uniform attire, worked as signifiers of attachment to various subcultural groups in the school and wider neighbourhood. Neither this place-based information, nor the precise detail about the locations and situations that produced low-level bullying, would have been available to the researchers if they had not been working with visual methods (c.f. Mitchell, 2012).

Working with texts

As with images, schools are replete with texts. We can use school texts to think about how people in the school tell stories about their place and how they make meaning about the place through the process of writing and talking. We can look at texts to see differences within a school – like the school, the texts will not be homogeneous, but will reveal important debates, points of view, allegiances and experiences. We can see both the official and unofficial at work in texts. We can also see how flows of information from other schools, as well as from regional, national and global sources, enter the school. And we can see how school texts might shape action in the place – we refer you back to our discussion of theoretical options in Chapter 4. Institutional ethnography (Smith, 2005) and geo-semiotics (Scollon and Scollon, 2003) are two theoretical approaches that are particularly helpful in orienting you to the ways in which texts produce and reproduce particular kinds of placed actions, interactions, relationships and practices.

As before, in this section we deal with both 'found' and researcher-made texts and again we think of these as traces of activity. These textual traces do particular kinds of work in the school. Our concern is to think about how the texts come to be as they are, how they produce and reproduce social relations, and what work these texts do within and beyond the school.

'Found' texts

We have already considered some of the texts that exist within the school – school displays, websites and prospectuses (see Chapter 4). Schools often have collections of such materials: archives of newsletters, scrapbooks of press clippings and the like. These are all helpful lenses on the ways in which the school seeks to represent itself to the world and build a sense of school identity and ethos (a significant aspect of school as place). Students too produce a range of texts, and researchers particularly interested in curriculum questions will want to collect samples of students' work, teachers' lesson plans and mark books. However, these are not the only texts that researchers might come across in their schools.

Schools routinely produce a great deal of organizational material – policies and guidelines for example. While these are important, they are not the only texts researchers can examine to see the ways in which the school operates and the kind of relationships that exist in the school as place. In fact, simply looking at policies and guidelines can be misleading: what actually happens in the school may not accord neatly with what the school claims as its priorities and practices. Schools produce a range of textual materials that coordinate what goes on in them:

- *The organizational chart* shows the ways in which the school is divided into areas of activity – discipline, curriculum, assessment, liaison with parents, welfare support, professional development and so on. It is possible to see, from an organizational chart, the number of staff who are devoted to a particular area, the level of seniority they have in the school and the number and kind of other staff that they work with. We have recently taken to checking organizational charts in schools we are researching to see how much leadership time is devoted to meeting audit requirements and how much to curriculum and pedagogical development. It is also instructive to see where curriculum and pedagogical expertise is located, who is seen as responsible for discipline and how much of what kind of person is devoted to this activity.
- *The staff list* works with the organizational chart and shows the numbers and kinds of staff – teaching and non-teaching, disciplinary areas, support areas and so on. This is a trace of the decisions that have been made about what is most important in the school, what subjects to offer, class size and the balance of teaching to non-teaching staff.
- *The timetable* shows what subjects are taught in the school. It also shows how teachers are allocated in chunks of time/space to work with particular year levels. Careful reading will reveal which teachers get to teach which kinds of classes. The timetable allows students to make particular kinds of choices and not others, to mix with some people and not others, to use particular kinds of facilities and not

others. The timetable is an integral part of the practice of grouping students into year levels and ability groups. It is also key to whether it is possible for teachers to meet together in planning and learning groups during the school day. Reading the timetable against a school prospectus is often illuminating, as it is possible to see how much time is actually devoted to the activities that get space in the glossy brochure.

- *Room allocations* accompany the timetable. They may be shown on the whole school timetable, but they are often issued separately to each teacher in timetable form, and there is often a master sheet which simply shows room use. This is a clue to the ways in which staff and students move around the school buildings and whether they have 'home rooms' that they can use as a base.
- *The budget* shows how financial resources may or may not be directed to school stated goals and priorities. Budget projections show how the school will or won't be able to meet new policy priorities and how much it is able to spend on 'maintenance activities' such as replenishing library stock. It shows how much contingency fund is available for decisions made during the year, how much is spent on executive salaries and expenses, how much is allocated for potential welfare needs.
- *Staff meeting rosters and agendas* organize the ways in which staff meet together and are involved in school decision-making (Spillane and Zoltner-Sherer, 2004). The balance of transmission to discussion, and of administration to educational issues, is set in the ways in which agendas and schedules are designed – as is the ratio of whole staff gatherings to subgroupings. It is instructive to look at the minutes of staff meetings and consider how many items that were discussed were initiated by staff. Indeed it is helpful to examine these texts asking, 'If I was a staff member with an idea, how would I go about getting it acted on?'

Many of these texts are available in a staff handbook and in governors' manuals. Schools are often unwilling to make these available to short-term visitors, but long-terms guests generally can get access to them. Analysing these administrative texts allows you to better understand local–national frames and interactions, hierarchies, movements, territories and boundaries, and groupings – and thus help you to understand what people tell you about the school.

Researcher produced texts

Research methods texts routinely spend a lot of space discussing the ways in which researchers generate data in textual form – interviews, surveys, focus groups and so on. We will not duplicate discussions of process here, as these are very well covered in the methods literature. Indeed, it would be a peculiar general educational research methods text that did not cover, for example, interviews, and there are several texts which solely address the research interview (e.g. Gubrium and Holstein, 2001; Holstein and Gubrium, 1995; James and Busher, 2009; Salmons, 2010), and permutations of it – life history, narrative, oral history and so on. We want here to consider a few of the better-known tools, together with a couple that are less well used, in the light of when and how they might be useful in studying a school. Like Alison Clark and Peter Moss, we see these more as a **mosaic approach** to data generation (Clark and Moss, 2001) and not as a list of tools that are serially used.

- *Interviews*

  Researchers in a long-term relationship with a school often conduct formal interviews at the start of their investigation. This is primarily fact-finding, but it is also a time when the school checks out the researcher; if the early contact doesn't go well, then it may be difficult for the researcher to do what they want, when they want (see Chapter 2). Researchers also often decide that they want to conduct formal interviews during – and often near the end of – their research in order to answer questions that have arisen, or to probe a particular policy or set of events or to make sure that they have on record a range of different perspectives. Formal interviews have the benefit of being able to be recorded digitally and then transcribed as texts so that they can be revisited and analysed. However, the resulting text is only a partial record of what happened, as none of the embodied responses are captured, unless a video is used. Filming, however, elevates the formality of the interview which may work against frankness. Often, busy school personnel are hard pressed to find the hour or so that is necessary for a formal interview. They may even see the request as an unwelcome intrusion after the researcher has been treated as a guest and thus ought to know the kinds of time pressures that the proposed interviewee is under.

- *Focus groups*

  A focus group allows the researcher to bring together a particular set of people to discuss a nominated topic. Focus groups are thus often used in long-term studies as a means of generating discussion that might otherwise not be available to the researcher. Students can, for instance, be gathered together, school and timetable permitting, to discuss any number of issues – their experiences, their outside school connections, their responses to a particular policy ... But who selects the group is important: is it the researcher or a staff member? Is the group based on friendship, representative characteristics, or prior relationship with the researcher? Where the discussion takes place can affect the process: the researcher needs to know in advance not only which locations are available but also where the group is likely to feel comfortable. For example, the presence of school staff may make students or parents/carers feel reluctant to talk openly.

  There are always up and down sides to focus groups. Problems include some people dominating, the formation of a kind of 'group think' and the disciplinary pressures of the group on members not to be too contrary in their views. These work against the goal of having the group discuss a topic. Focus group discussions are also notoriously difficult to turn into a neat text. Unless the space is miked-up and sound-mixed, then the resulting **transcription** is highly likely to be full of gaps where people mumbled or spoke over each other. And you may not be able to take notes in the group without appearing to distance yourself from the conversation.

- *Records of conversations and interactions*

  Researchers who are interested in fine-grained analyses of the dialogue that goes on in classrooms and other instructional settings, such as gyms and libraries, often want to make highly detailed textual records. This interest might also run to written comments on assignments, notes in daily communication books and discussion at staff meetings. The object of this interest varies, but the records are produced with an analytic process – some kind of linguistic approach – already in mind. With the advent of corpus linguistics software, and software that produces text synced with visual images, these analytic options are now expanded beyond the highly detailed typed transcript.

  Needless to say, the process of turning what the researcher sees and hears into text requires a lot more precision that can be afforded by the field notebook. Very good recording equipment and/or data capture software is required, together with a standard template for formatting any written text, whether it is hard copy or digital. It is also necessary to undertake any recording in as unobtrusive a way as possible. In order to introduce the kind of technical kit that might be useful, multiple cameras and microphones for example, the researcher usually needs to have already built up very good relationships with the relevant people – teachers, students, and specialist and support staff.

- *Surveys*

  Surveys are good for finding patterns that exist at scale – how many, how often, who does this, what kind? – and there may be occasions when a researcher wants to know something like this. A survey might be used initially to see responses to a range of issues in a school: this was how Helen Gunter and Pat started their student research into bullying. Or it might be that a researcher wants to conduct an annual survey of students at a particular year level to see whether there is any change in, for example, their sense of well-being or their career aspirations. Or perhaps there is a survey of staff to test out something that the researcher thinks is happening in the school – a change in attitudes to inclusion, a new set of practices in relation to the use of outside space, some concerns about government policy.

These days, schools themselves conduct quite a few surveys and are accustomed to working with statistical data. This may mean that they have digital software that can be used instead of time-consuming paper and pen exercises. But it will also mean that at least one person on the staff won't be impressed by ambiguous or highly complex wording, poor item design, lack of cross-tabulations, and simple analyses that don't test for significance. However, it is also likely that the school will be interested in the survey results and may want to use the information for itself. If this is the case, producing an executive summary for the school can be a very useful thing to do.

- *Artistic artefacts*

The use of arts-informed methods is becoming more popular in educational research (Leavy, 2009). Researchers might use approaches drawn from the visual and performing arts to engage participants in actions, interactions and conversations, or in the production of objects and ephemeral works, performances and exhibitions. While some of these processes produce texts, many require the researcher, or the researcher and participants, to produce a textual record that can then be curated. **Video methods** and **video dialogues** are often used to allow participants to creatively reflect on their experiences (see, for example, valueliveart.wordpress.com)

Archives of artistic practice are commonplace; live art, for instance, has been producing records of events since the 1960s and 1970s. We thus know some of the major questions involved in their production. How can embodied movement and emotion be captured and recorded? What can possibly be left out of an archived text, and what must be preserved? Who should decide this? If the archive is only

a trace of what has happened, what instructions need to be provided in order for it to be reread later? What is the best medium for recording the activity? Is a play script an adequate record of a performance and how can it be used as data? Is a series of photographs and written sticky notes sufficient to record an interaction with an arts installation piece designed to provoke responses? How accessible and amenable to interpretation are recordings and transcripts of slam poetry written about the school by students? How can we capture what happened when children play in the yard in secret dark places away from adult eyes? (See Figure 6.6.)

Like field notes, perhaps, such texts are incomplete and rely on the researcher to fill in the details of things that are hard to put into words and image – feelings, movement, bodies moving in response to each other.

At the end of this rather long discussion of just some of the kinds of data that researchers can generate from a long-term stay in a school, the question of how this might all be wrestled into some

FIGURE 6.6 *How to show the experience of playing in the seclusion of the 'tree house'?*

kind of shape becomes increasingly problematic. We deal with this in the next chapter.

Final note

A school is a complex organization and requires more than one, two or even three ways to get to know it as a place. Taking a 'multiple' approach to data will produce a rich data set in which the various events and conversations you've experienced are recorded in multiple genres and media. This will allow you to record how various meanings are made in the place and about the place. It will provide you with the means to trace activities, practices, narratives, relationships and flows that happen in the school. You will generate data about the differences that exist within the place, and the ways that what happens there is shaped and influenced by external agents, policies and relationships. In our experience there is never enough and always too much data, and you have to accept that. Even after a really long-term and intense involvement, you are still likely to have questions. Parts of the school will still, and always will be, unknown and unknowable.

Further reading

As you contemplate sinking into a long-term relationship with a school, it is often a good idea to read other people's books and papers about their experiences of doing the same. Here are some research monographs about schools that we enjoy and recommend; they all use multiple data sets and when you read them you should look for the ways in which the data have been generated.

The first set of books examines the heterogeneous nature of schools and the various ways in which student and teacher subcultures are encouraged or marginalized. They show place based micro-politics at work and the ways in which they are classed, raced and gendered.

Datnow, Amanda (1998). *The Gender Politics of Educational Change.* Washington, DC: Falmer Press.

Eckert, Penelope (1989). *Jocks and Burnouts: Social Categories and Identity in the High School*. New York: Teachers College Press.
Livingstone, Sonia and Sefton-Green, Julian (2016). *The Class. Living and Learning in the Digital Age*. New York: NYU Press.
Russell, Lisa (2011). *Understanding Pupil Resistance – Integrating Gender, Ethnicity and Class: An Educational Ethnography*. London: E & E Publishing.
Sefa Dei, George, Josephine Mazzuca, Elizabeth McIsaac and Justine Zine (1997). *Reconstructing Doprout: A Critical Ethnography of the Dynamics of Black Students' Disengagement from School*. Toronto: University of Toronto Press.
Tittle, Diana (1995). *Welcome to Heights High: The Crippling Politics of Restructuring America's Public Schools*. Columbus: Ohio State University Press.

The next two books show longer-term engagements with school through the lens of language and literacy. Again, it is helpful to consider the range of data generation approaches used.

Heath, Shirley Brice (1983). *Ways with Words: Language, Life and Work in Communities and Classrooms*. New York: Cambridge University Press.
Kress, Gunter, Carey Jewitt, Jill Bourne, Anton Franks, John Hardcastle, Ken Jones and Euan Reid (2005). *English in Urban Classrooms: A Multimodal Perspective on Tteaching and Learning*. London: RoutledgeFalmer.

Finally, a book which shows the differences between a neighbourhood school and charter school, and the ways in which they each open up different possibilities for their African-American students. This analysis was only possible through a long-term study and multiple data generation approaches used inside and outside the schools.

Miron, Louis and Lauria Mickey (2005). *Urban Schools: The New Social Spaces of Resistance*. New York: Peter Lang.

CHAPTER SEVEN

Analysing complex data sets

So now you have data. Mountains and mountains of the stuff. What to do with it all? Where to start? Will you ever get through it? Is there a trick to analysis? How do other people do it?

We don't intend this chapter to duplicate what other research methods texts already do. There is a lot of good advice out there about data analysis and various approaches to the task and we list some of them at the end of the chapter. We will instead talk about an orientation to the work of dealing with data, as well as offer some strategies that we have found particularly helpful when trying to make good sense of a school to which we have committed time. Our orientation is geared to helping you develop your understanding of your school as a place and draws on the ways we have discussed place in the first half of the book.

What is 'analysis'?

The word analysis, according to dictionary.com, simply means a detailed examination of something. Its synonyms are words like investigation, examination, inspection, study, perusal. Thesaurus.com lists two types of possible synonym – the first includes dissection, reduction, breakdown, partition, decomposition; the second includes inquiry, clarification, review, summary, synopsis, explanation. These binary synonyms seem to point to two possible paths for analytic processes – one related to the procedures used to dissect, reduce, partition and so on; and the other related to the thinking and writing. The separation of synonyms hints at possible different approaches to analysis as detailed examination: one which is perhaps more procedural and technical and the other which is more reliant on a self conscious process of meaning making.

It is generally the case that analysis of the kinds of data that are produced in school research *does* lend itself to these two broad approaches. One is more technical, consisting of coding and thematizing. It may include, as we have suggested, elements of statistical calculation involving images, words, numbers, networks. Or it may focus on a process of meaning-making through work with words, and reasoning and interpreting. Both of these approaches can be situated within a broad spectrum of philosophical positions – a researcher can use numbers and take up a broadly post-critical stance or work with images and take up a broadly post-positivist position. However, philosophical differences play out in the consideration of what is considered as rigour. As Ann Marie Bathmaker (2010) puts it:

> Discussions and advice about how researchers should go about analysis, how closely qualitative research should emulate what are described as 'scientific' methods, and whether analysis is an art or a science, are reflected in the literature on data analysis. These debates about what constitutes disciplined inquiry, involving considerable differences in conceptualising the research process, mean that different ways of analysing qualitative data cannot be conflated as though they all reflect the same way of thinking about the world. (p. 201)

Bathmaker points out that it is a mistake to read off a philosophical position from the analytic approach taken. Understandings of the actual processes of analysis and the 'results' that emerge – and thus the claims that can be made about them – differ widely. Analysing data is not a neutral process. The way you approach and undertake analysis is embedded in the more general way in which you position your research and yourself as a researcher.

We understand data analysis, as we understand data generation, to be produced by the researcher – a researcher who is creative and interpretive, as well as being thorough and systematic. Analysis involves researchers in:

- getting very familiar with their data, reading and rereading it, perhaps writing about it as a means of the material becoming 'second nature';
- establishing patterns and groupings in the data, working through a variety of processes for ordering, categorizing and connecting isolated nuggets of data;
- making sense of the patterns and groupings that have been created. This is not a matter of simple description, but of putting the patterns and groupings in the context of other research. Researchers must also call on a conceptual or theoretical framing in order to turn their data into results.

This analytic process is thoroughly imbricated in the researcher's subjectivity. It is the researcher who makes the patterns and groups, who decides which goes with what. Out of various possible groupings and patterns, the researcher decides which is the most persuasive and 'true'. It is the researcher who decides which literatures to engage with and what conceptual or theoretical framework is most apt and generative. This requires researcher reflexivity and a systematic process of critically 'testing out' different options to see what seems to be most appropriate, interesting, 'authentic' and rigorous.

Analysing data requires both imagination and the wise and judicious use of other intellectual resources. Researchers must have a commitment to *using* literature, concepts and theories in order make sense of the data that they have generated. Interpretation, particularly with the kinds of data sets that are produced by a long-term engagement with a school, is not amenable to a technical fix. In order to clarify, explain, elaborate and draw out possible implications, researchers must put themselves in the frame. The researcher must take a leap of faith into what often feels like an analytic void where, despite the plethora of books on data analysis, no one will say exactly what mode of analysis will be 'correct'. So, how to start?

Taking the plunge – some early strategies

When you 'finish' ... after you have concluded your intensive period of engagement with the school, after you are no longer committed to being there every day ... Of course you have not really finished, you have simply reached another stage. You will be back in touch with the school. You haven't yet left it. You may have already negotiated how and when you will be sharing your emerging analysis. You may have times when you do some work on data together. You may have agreed that you will be responsible for the analysis but will present a draft of what you come up with. But, for now, you need to take some time out.

It is now that you realize that you have a lot of data. So much. Always too much. Even if you have been doing ongoing analysis throughout your time in school, as we do, there is always the moment of reckoning. How to order all of the material? Is it really possible to make sense of the school that you now know so intimately? What possible analytic approach can you take to do justice to the school, and the people who have gifted their time and their stories to you? How can you do justice to the 'place'?

You are now engaged in place 'making' through data work. How *you* understand the school as a place is highly dependent on what you do now.

Clearing the decks

It can be helpful at the earliest opportunity to do four quite simple things:

1 Map the data set

Make an inventory of what kind of data you have, about what, and in what form. For example:

- Interview with head – audio and transcript. Covers school philosophy, population, school change process.
- Thirty photos of school sports events.
- Twelve newsletters for the year 2015.

And so on ... You get the picture. When it gets to

your field notes, you might want to consider a system where you tag particular issues or information that you have – a map of the school, a map of the classrooms, a conversation between you and a teacher. The idea is simply to try to get a picture of what you have and where it is. You will start to see where there is information about the same thing, generated at different times, perhaps even using different approaches. A simple spreadsheet can help you make some early connections between various pieces of material.

2 Revisit your research question

After being in a school for a long time, it's often hard to remember your research question. It's important to look at it again before you embark on any detailed analysis. Is it still your research question? Does it need a minor refinement?

It's helpful at this stage to keep your question uppermost in your mind. We often suggest to doctoral researchers that they write their question on a large sheet of paper and put it next to their computer and/or where they will be physically doing their analysis. This way it doesn't drift away as you find all of those interesting things in the data. Not all of them are going to be directly useful in answering the question, and some material might need to be set aside so that you can come back to it later.

3 Write your initial impressions of the school

First of all, write a description – the building, details about the composition of the population, the kind of curriculum on offer. Next write down the things that have stuck in your mind about the school – this might just be a list.

And then ...

4 Look at your research question – write about what you think you know that you didn't know when you started.

This activity is a kind of mind-clearing. By writing down all of the things that have been buzzing around, you make sure that you don't lose them, but you also generate a list of things that you can make sure you check out in your forthcoming data analysis. Do these impressions hold up?

You can now set these ideas aside while you approach the data in a more organized way. But the fact that you can already pull out some answers to the question ought also to suggest to you that there is going to be more when you've actually gone through all of the data!

Dipping your toe in the water

Sometimes it's helpful to test out what kind of tools you want to use on a small piece of data. Writing a case study of an individual person in the school, for instance, can show you what you can do with your data and what you can't. Trying to code and thematize one interview can show you something about the level of detail that you might want to use and something about the hierarchies of themes that are possible. Adding another one or two interviews to the initial one may well generate most of the themes that you are likely to get. It's also easy to work on one or a very small group of transcripts to see what gets left out of an initial coding and thematizing – once you see what this is, you may wish to revise what you have.

We also like to try out some analysis in more depth. This can take a number of forms. We offer two examples here:

1 A **document analysis**

This example comes from a study of vernacular change, that is, how a policy was taken on and folded into the ongoing assemblage of one school. As we have explained earlier (see Chapters 1 and 5), understanding the school as a particular place allowed us to investigate the very distinctive ways in which particular people, situated in a specific school with its unique history, geographical location, population and multiple connections and networks, made decisions and modified their practice. A place-based approach oriented us to the ways in which wider scales of activity and flows of information and people added to the particularity of the school. We were also alert to patterns of activities – resemblances to other schools and the various scales and temporalities at work.

We suggested in Chapter 6 that there was mileage in collecting administrative documentation from the school. There are different ways of analysing such material. This next example suggests what might be learnt from a single document that was part of a much wider set of texts that were 'found' in the school. Table 7.1 illustrates the discipline/care staffing complement from a secondary school of 800 or so students. We hoped that this document might begin to help us understand the various official tasks that people did in the school, as well as the leadership team's organizational thinking. We initially saw the organizational chart as a trace of a discursive practice, reflecting both the wider global push for 'distributed leadership' (Harris, 2008) and national flows of funding directed to particular 'poor' and 'special' students. We also knew that this kind of document is required for national inspections and is taken as a sign of good leadership, one of the key categories of external evaluation. This was the framing of the text – we expect to see something of this sort in all English schools.

But we also suspected that this text might help us begin to get to grips with the particularity of place. So we undertook a simple summative content analysis – an approach that involves 'counting and comparisons, usually of keywords or content, followed by the interpretation of the underlying context' (Hsieh and Shannon, 2005). Figure 7.1 shows our first analytic step, the content analysis shown in italics, with some added post-hoc commentary to make the steps in our thinking clearer. You don't need to know all the acronyms in the document to get the overall picture of what is going on in the school. Pay particular attention to the verbs and big headline categories. You will see from the comments in brackets that we also noted things that we needed to follow up in analysing other data.

Table 7.1 School responsibilities for 'student development'

TEACHING STAFF TEACHING AND LEARNING RESPONSIBILITY STRUCTURE

	Leadership	TLR1A (£6,500)	TLR2B (£3,750)	TLR2A (£2,250)
Communication	CTL	1	1	2
Numeracy	CTL	1	1	2
Sciences	CTL	1	1	2
Technologies	CTL	1	1	2
Social Sciences	CTL	1	1	2
Art/PE	CTL	1	1	2
Student Development	CTL	5	2	1

SPECIFIC RESPONSIBILITIES
Student Development Team
(name of team leader)

Post	TLR	Headline Responsibilities
Achievement Leader Year 7	1A	Behaviour, welfare and expectations of students, KS2KS3 liaison, CAT data, identification of specific groups of students and intervention to secure improvements
Achievement Leader Years 8 and 9	1A	Behaviour, welfare and expectations of students, setting and monitoring of progress towards KS3 targets, short course Citizenship, guidance at 14+ transfer to ensure progression
Achievement Leader Years 10 and 11	1A	Behaviour, welfare and expectations of students, setting and monitoring progress towards KS4 targets, key skills, Aim Higher, guidance at 16+ transfer to ensure progression.

Post	TLR	Headline Responsibilities
Achievement Leader 16+	1A	Behaviour, welfare and expectations of students, setting and monitoring progress towards 16+ targets. ALIS, UCAS, transfer at 18+
Head of Learning Support	1A	Leading, planning and evaluating provision for all students with SEN, SENCO, assessing students, needs and ensuring appropriate interventions to secure improvements
Head of Autism Resource Centre	2C	Planning, developing and leading the introduction of the new Enhanced Resource Centre for Autistic students
School Inclusion Manager	2B	Leading, planning and evaluating provision for all students with social, emotional and behavioural difficulties, managing Student Support Centre
Learning for Life Coordinator	2B	Planning, monitoring, assessing and evaluating PSHE/Citizenship/WRL/ Enterprise Education (KS3–KS5)
Skills for Learning Coordinator	2A	Planning, monitoring, assessing and evaluating (in liaison with ASTs) BLP, Key Learning Skills, Key Skills (KS3–KS5)

First of all we looked to see what was included and excluded in 'Student Development':
The area called 'Student Development' brings together discipline, welfare, inclusion, citizenship, enterprise, and special education. However, the term 'development' suggests that all of these are seen by the school leadership as similarly concerned with the formation of student subjects in ways that cannot be effected through the more usual curricula/extra curricular processes. It is perhaps a somewhat strange amalgam. (It is worth trying to find out why this grouping happened.)

Next we looked to see how much resource was spent on Student Development:
There is considerable resource spent on this area. There are six curriculum responsibility allowances shown on the top table, and five for Student Development: four are teachers who work at each year level and are responsible for discipline, welfare and the accumulation and monitoring of various data sets. The fifth is responsible for additional provisions and is the line manager of other staff on the list. This school spends nearly as much on middle level leadership of discipline, welfare, inclusion, citizenship, enterprise, and special education as it does on the rest of the curriculum. (What are the effects of this budget skewing?)

Then we looked to see who did what:
All but one of the positions has monitoring, data or evaluating as a key responsibility. This is indicative of the ways in which performative audit functions – being seen to not simply teach, but also to show that progress in learning or behaviour have occurred – now dominate English schools and their organizational structures. This is a form of surveillance of both staff and students and also the basis for making decisions about what counts as normal/other.

We then focused on what we couldn't find in the document that we might want to find elsewhere in the data:
What we cannot see from this text are any dedicated Student Development staff for which each of these positions is solely responsible. We also cannot see with any clarity the ways in which

students might be categorized in order to fall under the auspices of each position, although it might be surmised that the year level Achievement Leaders identify those students deemed sufficiently needy to warrant remedial support, diagnosis, or behavioural intervention. From then on, the students are probably divided into more specialized categories and become the responsibility of appropriately specialized staff. Undoubtedly, a number of students could well fall into two categories/camps – needing to learn how to behave in an orderly way and how to perform in the required curriculum. (We need to check this out in the interviews.)

We also cannot see from this chart the ways in which students might be sequestered from their peers. One of the characteristics of disciplinary regimes is the use of isolation, and students who are to be 'developed' may well be sat apart from their peers, sent to a separate room, or sent to another part of the school. The annexe in the shed, or the suite of learning support rooms in the temporary buildings at the back of the yard are common in schools. (What happens here?)

It is not clear who makes what decisions. It is likely that the decision about whether a student needed complementary alternative provision would fall to the School Inclusion Manager in consultation with the relevant year level Achievement Leaders. (A set of records in the form of case notes – of behavioral infractions, of meetings with parents and various school staff, of tests and specialist diagnosis – is usually the basis of shifting the student out of some or all of their regular schooling, into something 'other'. This can be further elaborated via checking field notes and interviews.)

FIGURE 7.1 *Content analysis of the organizational chart in Table 7.1.*

A content analysis of this one document revealed some key points about the organization of discipline and welfare in this particular school and the ways in which particular groups of children were separated out for intervention. But this was not enough. The starting point analysis led us to more questions, some of which were factual and some of which were about the discourse practices of the school. The analysis of the document provided clues about the nature of the place that could be followed up. We thus approached other documents, field notes and interviews with questions already in mind about difference and inclusion, about norms, mobilities, territories and boundaries, and how this played out in and as vernacular change.

Keeping track of the cumulative sense-making process of complex data sets – this piece of analysis says X and raises questions Y and Z – is important. We keep an audit trail of analytic notes that help us to trace how we reached a particular view about the school. An analytic audit trail can be referred to later to show others, perhaps the school itself, how particular results were obtained, and is often very helpful when writing about results.

2 A critical incident

We sometimes work with the critical incident analysis developed by David Tripp and explained in his book *Critical Incidents in Tteaching: Developing Professional Judgement* (1993/2011). While initially developed as a way for teachers to interrogate their experiences, the critical incident approach is now more widely used in research analysis. Tripp's view of a critical incident is not the occupational health and safety version, an incident which is a risk to life and limb. His critical incident is an event that, when critically probed, reveals something significant about the wider social relations and institutional procedures. Tripp proposes that an incident can be made critical by asking how the event came to be as it was, what power relations were in play and what could have been done differently.

We often find in a prolonged engagement in school that an event sticks in our mind. It seems important. We often can't say why, but we have learnt that there is often a payoff for 'following our noses' and following up these events. There is some justification for doing this. Michael Polanyi wrote, some fifty years ago, about the ways in which scientific discoveries were often as much about intuition, dreams, hunches and educated guesses as they were about systematic experimentation. He put this down to what he called 'tacit knowledge': understandings that had not yet been brought into language (Polanyi, 1958/1998, 1966). Following Polanyi, then, it is possible that the incident or event that refuses to be forgotten may well be such a phenomenon – something we know in an unknowing way to be significant.

In our first project together we conducted an ethnography of one primary school: Holly Tree Primary (see more about Holly Tree in Chapter 4). During our stay in the school we heard a lot about a particular incident that had happened before we arrived. We used the critical incident approach to investigate it further, as it seemed to be significant (Thomson et al., 2006).

The incident involved a writing project in which children wrote poetry and fiction to produce a published anthology of autobiographies and biographies. A writer and a poet were funded to work in the school for a series of one-day workshops:

> The poet, Ally, worked with the children first of all on a set of poems based around their names. Then the writer, a professional playwright whom we will call Rob, worked with the children to produce filmic word sketches of hypothetical families. A final day was funded so that a subcommittee of children could work with Rob to select and organise the text for publication.
>
> There were some organisational problems with the project. The head-teacher, who had master-minded the project, was not in school while it was being conducted. The staff selected the children to participate and did not make sure that the same children attended each time, so Rob was faced with a slightly different group each time he came. And staff did not always stay in the room with Rob as they were meant to do under grant funding conditions, sometimes leaving him with up to 30 children to work with by himself.
>
> However, the major difficulty was with the final text. Neither the head-teacher nor the staff were prepared to

> publish it. The problem was not with Ally's poems, but with Rob's playscript. They saw it as distinctly odd, and as something that would potentially bring offence to sections of their school community. (p. 31)

> In order to explore what was actually going on, we did four things: (1) we examined the offending text; (2) we conducted an interview with the head and had a conversation with staff; (3) we interviewed Rob, the artist; and (4) we checked the records of our focus groups with children and our field notes to see how the incident was referred to. We also wrote, on and off, about the incident in our extended field notes (see previous chapter) as it seemed to hold some clues as to ways in which the ethos of the school as place operated.

Our analysis of the children's text suggested that it contained numerous references to 'adult themes'. Structured as an episodic soap opera, it drew on familiar televisual tropes as well as the life-worlds of children living in a council estate. We wrote in our paper about the incident:

Readers are presented with small versions of television soaps such as *Footballers' Wives* and *Desperate Housewives* in which many of the characters have exactly such lives and dangerous secrets. There are also a number of references to alcoholism and sex.

> *We see a girl getting ready to go out in the home of the CARTISES. Amy goes out with a boy called Rayorno, who is a gangsta and her mum and dad hate him. Her gran Roseanne loves her job and is very hard working but most nights she comes home at 1.30 or 2.00 am and is always drunk. Amy is missing her friend Emilia.*

> *Amy: She wrote me a letter that made me want to see her even more because she was PREGNANT with a little girl. It's great! I want a baby with Rayorno, yeh cool. Anyway see ya. I am going to try and beg Rayorno for a baby.*

This scenario is clearly challenging. The Midlands city in which the children live does have a recognised 'problem' with teenage

> pregnancy, about which teachers in schools are aware and concerned. This text could be read as an approval of such sexual behaviour, but it could equally be read as a realistic portrayal, as sad, or as something to be disapproved of. (pp. 32–3)

Children did not talk to us a great deal about the project. They wondered what had happened to the publication, and those that did discuss the project referred to it as an enjoyable process in which 'they were allowed to invent things that they thought were funny and dramatic. They had permission to think of themselves as people who wrote scripts like the ones they enjoyed on television' (p. 34). Teachers, on the other hand, were highly critical:

1. Rob exercised poor control.
   Teachers remember the workshops being loud and noisy. They reported that Rob had 'wound up the boys', that he was 'overfriendly – he wound them up and there was nowhere for them to go'. The children 'became silly', 'they couldn't handle it'. Rob was not 'like other artists who could handle them'.
2. Rob did not understand the educational needs of primary school children.
   One staff member said that there was a 'duty of care' issue. 'If children raise things that are unsuitable then you leave it within school, deal with it sensitively as much as appropriate and for their level.' Another noted that there are 'constraints working with under-11-year-olds. You wouldn't show them certain kinds of art that were shocking or harrowing when they don't have the emotional maturity to deal with it.' This staff member noted that 'It's different in literature. Jacqueline Wilson can get away with writing about not perfect home environments – but children can't.'
3. The creative process was flawed.
   One staff member commented that 'as an artist you cannot censor yourself' but 'there should have been more redrafting as part of the creative process – as in working from initial improvisations to a polished public product. Not all that goes on ends up in a final product.'
4. Rob didn't do what he was asked.

The staff were disappointed that there wasn't a publishable product.

5 The ideas were not really the children's.
The staff saw the end product as a stark contrast to the kinds of writing the children did in class. 'Did he set them up? Did he write it himself?' They saw the text as having 'adolescent content': it was 'too mature', was of 'adult interest' and would be 'more suited to secondary school'. It was 'bizarre'. Staff felt uneasy and allowed themselves to speculate that it was possible that Rob had put ideas into the children's heads or that he had written a lot of the material himself or that he had taken away the material and massaged it in ways that somehow corrupted what the children had originally done.

6 The local community would take offence.
The teachers were concerned about the reputation of the school. The text was 'not what we want to promote'. They felt sure that 'if it was sent home, there would be a bad reaction from parents'. They argued that 'the school knows its children and families' and that Rob should have made use of this 'local knowledge'. They commented, 'Control [of products] has to stay in school, artists are just passing through.' (pp. 34–5)

When we interviewed the head, however, she had more mixed feelings. She recognized that the text had some literary merit, but her overwhelming worry was the potential for parent complaint and for the local newspaper to pick it up. The possibility of bad publicity and the knock-on effects on enrolments constituted a risk she was not prepared to take. Rob the artist saw the lack of publication as a relatively straightforward example of censorship.

Through putting these different views in conversation with each other we saw a 'no win' situation. The decision not to publish the anthology of writing was positioned in a particular discursive crucible:

> [T]he project occurred in a specific context – when the policy of parent choice, school marketisation, declining population and

> an aggressive local media might create difficulties for the school (Gewirtz et al., 1995; Cutler and Waine, 1997; Ball and Vincent, 1998). The potential pressures this might cause on any arts or other school activities were not discussed beforehand. But, we suggest that there were other fundamental differences at work which are less easily resolved. We see these as irreconcilable differences between teacherly and artistic discourses. (p. 38)

The critical incident allowed us to see that the teachers worked with a complex set of ideas, which combined: the notion of developmentalism – that children's learning is incremental and tied to age, that some things are age appropriate and others are not; a view of the child as ideally innocent – this has strong roots in both primary education and modernist thought; a notion of the teacher as parent – the idea that the role of teacher is to protect children from harm is a key tenet of the profession; a commitment to keeping the community 'on side' – conflict with the community was a sign of ineffective/poor practice; a strong value attached to control – learning and good behaviour were seen as synonymous; and an approach to writing which included teacher censorship – ideas might come up in a first draft of student work, but should/could be eliminated if they were unsuitable in any way, that is, if they transgressed any of the above. We argued in our paper that

> ... these ideas are strongly rooted in professional histories and training and in dominant policy discourses. Furthermore, they are survival equipment in the current testing and inspection regime. They meet parental and community expectations. We do not see them as wrong or right, but rather as integral to teachers' work in the current climate and context. (p. 38)

These kinds of tensions sit beneath many artists-school activities and have the potential to cause trouble. Yet they are rarely recognized or discussed. These powerful professional discourses came to the surface in this case, and we were able to document them clearly through the use of the critical incident. We concluded from our **critical incident analysis** that the notion that partnerships between schools and artists were simple to set up and maintain was a myth. Partnership was a notion that needed attention at the outset and all the way through artist-in-school programmes.

Analysing this critical incident provided a lens on the workings of the school that we would not otherwise have had. We were able to link back the incident to the flows of policy as the lines of artist, teachers, children and head came together in place. The example illustrates the ways in which working slowly with data – looping iteratively between fieldwork and analysis – is crucial to building an appreciation of placed actions, sayings, beliefs, narratives and actions.

Reaching an overview

It is important to generate some kind of big picture of the school that you are working in and on, and situate it as a place within its historical and broader spatial flows. There are many different approaches to developing an overview of the school. The most common is via some kind of case study method. Here we show some workings from a large-scale study we conducted of forty schools engaged in school change through the Creative Partnerships (CP) programme (see also Chapter 4 for details on our initial snapshot approach) (Thomson et al., 2009). CP offered schools funding for artists to work with teachers so that classroom pedagogy and, eventually, whole schools, might be changed. We followed twelve of the schools in more depth over three school years in order to see what they had taken from CP, how they had used the resources on offer and to what ends.

We understood CP, with its artists, administrative guidelines, reporting processes and regional and national documents, as flowing into each of the schools. Once taken into the school assemblage, there were different 'effects' – these were because of the specificities of each school as a place (or what Pat called 'thisness' – see Chapter 1). The uniqueness of each school, its thrown togetherness, produced what we called 'vernacular change' – that is, change that was specific to each place.

In seeking to condense complex information to make it more available for exploration and interpretation, we set ourselves the discipline of building summary tables that allowed the different features and characteristics of the case study schools to be set alongside one another. This had two main benefits. First, it brought together the analysis of each of the different elements we were interested in, as they related to the individual schools. This allowed us to look again at our interpretation of the way the school had taken up and developed creative learning. This analysis produced a better informed, sharper, shorter version of the earlier school snapshots: it emphasized the features of the individual school and brought aspects of the history and context of the school into play with the actions of key individuals and the take-up of particular ideas and projects. The summary tables were eventually included in our final report, but did not stand alone. They were, however, key to the analysis stage as they guided the accumulation of other material from transcripts, field notes and image banks.

Table 7.2 shows the summary table for Rowan Tree School (which featured in Chapter 4). The categories used in the table were derived from a combination of information from a literature review about school change (Thomson, 2011), readings of our corpus of data and some initial analysis of transcripts, documents and field notes, as outlined above as early analytic stages. The categories were developed through discussions of the entire research team of six people. It will be clear to you that, for instance, the summary description of the 'change modality' as 'devolved' requires the reader to go to the discussion of these labels in the report (see final report on http://www.creativitycultureeducation.org/wp-content/uploads/creative-school-change.pdf [accessed 30 September 2015]).

A caveat. Our analytic categories will not, of course, be those that you use. They are particular to our research about school change. You will develop your own categories to fit with your research question.

Table 7.2 Example of school summary table

ROWAN NURSERY AND INFANTS	Small school in high poverty suburban estate
Context	Experienced head, stable staff, clear philosophy of teaching and learning, strong relationships with local community. Possibility of amalgamation with nearby junior school. Ofsted 'good school'
Priorities for change	Extend early childhood pedagogies. Develop arts curriculum
CREATIVE PARTNERSHIPS	Substantive affiliation
Starting points for Creative Partnerships' related change	Changing the way pupils learn, changing what counts as learning, changing who teaches
Creative approach	Employing artists to work alongside teachers for sustained periods
Creative Partnerships' engagement	Aimed to increase number of adults working in pedagogical roles with children to include artists and thus broaden learning and experiences Rejected teacher apprenticeship CPD model of working with artists
Creative Agent	Community member type, focused on evaluation
Regional focus	Tactical orientation: school-focused and arts-based improvement in teaching and quality of learning
PEDAGOGICAL APPROACH	Exploratory, negotiated and creative approaches
Student voice	Self-expression/identity building. Therapeutic engagement in arts. Academic – collaborative evaluation through discussion and negotiated curriculum

View of community	As assets rich
LEADERSHIP AND MANAGEMENT	Strong bonds between more experienced staff, including head, and strong commitment to bringing newer staff into school community
Change modality	Devolved
Staff participation in decision-making	Emphasis on whole-staff involvement (including artists)
TEACHER LEARNING	Emphasis on learning together within and about the school community. Opportunities for systematic analysis and reflection built in to school schedule. Strong culture of professional inquiry and developed beyond traditional CPD offering, e.g. attendance at Appleby Horse Fair to better understand traveller families' issues
Reorientation	Detailed analysis of artefacts and pedagogies across whole staff including support staff. Full complementarity between teachers and artists

Condensing the data into table form allowed comparisons to be drawn between the characteristics and approaches of different schools. This helped us build theories about clusters of characteristics and actions that influenced change; it also allowed us to present the data in a form which is open to readers to interrogate further. Even in reduced form, the tables are unwieldy, but Table 7.3, an extract from one such comparative table, indicates some of the ways that Rowan Tree might be compared with other schools in the group.

Table 7.3 Extract from cross-school summary table

School	Beginning points	Creative approaches	Affiliation	Pedagogical approach
Oak Tree Primary, large multicultural primary	Changing school organization	Focus on teachers' understanding of creativity	Substantive	Creative approaches primarily to learning environments and extra-curricular activity
Plumtree College Secondary comprehensive serving deprived estate plus older more established middle-class community. Poor building stock	Changing school culture, changing the way pupils learn	Big collaborative productions	Affiliative but opted out	Creative approaches in extra-curricular activities and gifted and talented enhancement
Rowan Tree Nursery, small nursery and infant school in high poverty suburban estate	Changing the way pupils learn, changing what counts as learning	Employing artists to work alongside teachers for sustained periods	Substantive	Exploratory, negotiated and creative approaches
Silver Birch Secondary Catholic secondary school (non-grammar) in area with selective secondary system. Specialist Arts College	Changing school culture	Through big collaborative productions	Symbolic	Creative approaches predominantly, but not exclusively, in extra-curricular activities

School	Beginning points	Creative approaches	Affiliation	Pedagogical approach
Sycamore Secondary. Medium-size specialist business and enterprise college. Located in middle class area but serving nearby estate. Comprehensive in grammar school system	Changing the way learning is organized, changing what counts as learning	Linking creativity, enterprise and entrepreneurialism	Affiliative	Creative skills, creative approaches in extra-curricular and vocational specialism

The comparisons made in Table 7.3 go beyond simply mapping what happened in our schools, as was the case with our interim snapshots. The tables constituted a heuristic approach to change, which we used and extended in our final report. We used categories – and developed a change vocabulary – that we hoped might also be useful to others who wanted to understand the processes of school change. We imagined, for example, that another researcher or a consultant could go into a school and ask questions about 'beginning points' or 'affiliation'. Our representation of change as being patterned, but specific to each school as a place, was intended to be useful to others in synthesizing information and diagnosing school 'stage of change'.

Once you have developed an overview of your data set, which may be like ours or take another form altogether, it is possible to use it to situate more fine-grained analysis.

A slice of analysis

It is hard to provide advice about how to slice the data. Analysis of large data sets often relies on finding a Big Idea around which smaller chunks of analysis can be arranged as an argument. In a thesis, for instance, three or four chapters of results and discussion are held together by the Big Idea. Big Ideas are specific to each project and question. However, in order to illustrate what this might look like, we show a further example from Holly Tree Primary. As you read it, you might ask yourself what the Big Idea about your research school might be.

Figure 7.2 shows a Big Idea about Holly Tree. Our initial research interest was in how this inner-city primary school appeared to include all of its pupils through its focus on the arts. Our analysis of the data suggested that Holly Tree was distinctive in the way it established itself as a unique institution in which everyone was special and different. Our researcher, Lisa Russell, had initially noted this, and her overwhelming 'first impression' was that the school operated in a kind of bubble, with the headteacher working to create a strong barrier between the inside and outside of the school. Outside were potential threats – inspection, poor publicity – but also benefits – possible recognition of achievements and high regard from official sources. Inside the school – and this included parents who had children in the school – an assemblage of practices created a sense of 'home' where everyone was special, could achieve and would be looked after. Central to the sense of home was the head whose influence was everywhere, from the pictures on the walls to the narratives that staff and students told about the school.

Boundary setting within the school appeared, across all of our data, to be a key characteristic of establishing a sense of inclusion – and place. We wanted to explore Holly Tree as an inclusive home because it is exactly these kinds of meaning-making practices that people use to make a material location a place (see Chapter 1).

Based on the Big Idea about Holly Tree, it was possible for us to write a set of papers, slicing through the data and analysis, which showed how aspects of this regime operated. These papers did not arrive out of thin air, but from our interrogation of field notes, from ongoing conversations among ourselves and through various interweavings of theory with our analysis, often captured in 'inbetween' writings (see Chapter 6). We now briefly discuss one of these slices: a paper about the school narratives that worked to both produce and reproduce the idea that there was a Holly Tree Way that was distinctive and different from all other schools.

Our paper, 'Sense-making as a lens on everyday change leadership practice: The case of Holly Tree Primary' (Thomson and Hall, 2011), took a narrative analytic approach (Gabriel, 2000; Riessman, 2008) to the transcripts of interviews and to the records of conversations with teachers, the head and children. We

How does Hollytree primary use arts as a practice for inclusion?

Strong charismatic leadership – long term, well known in community and city

School narratives of distinctiveness, individualism, homeliness, professionalism

Artist in residence from school budget: pedagogies same/ different from teachers

INSIDE: THE HOLLYTREE WAY
OUTSIDE: THREATS AND RECOGNITION

Strong focus on identity work and relationships

External artists may not work so well – critical incident

Symbolic uses of display – good work, good student, good teacher

Management of tensions between creativity and inspection/ test results

School based curriculum development and teacher learning

FIGURE 7.2 *Developing the Big Idea*

asked, 'What are the stories that are told about the school?' We were particularly interested in getting more detail on the 'bubble phenomenon' that Lisa had initially identified, and to understand more about the head's symbolic leadership.

We drew on the work on organizational theorist Karl Weick (1995, 2001), who we had been reading through the fieldwork phase because we suspected that his melding of meaning-making and organizational theory might be helpful to us. Weick agued that people within organizations have various ways of making sense of their work. We identified four dominant plot lines in the stories that we had recorded: *We are an innovative school*; *We do things our way*; *We are child-centred*; *We are a family*. Our paper argued that Miriam, the head, in particular created these stories as a way to make the work in the school meaningful. The extract reproduced below shows how we drew data from interviews and from our observations and field notes:

> Staff continually told us about the ethos of the school. They noted that Holly Tree was the kind of school where they would

want their children to be. They stressed the importance of the relational and associational aspects of the school as a life-world in its own right, not simply as a work-place:

... it's a big family. To me the staff are like an extended family. I love it here. I love the kids. I like how open it all is. (Susan)

When I first came to this school, twenty one years ago, I walked into the school and I can remember it then and I don't think it has changed over the years. It's about respect for each other; it's about teaching children to be confident and independent and showing initiative and it's about listening to children. It's a sort of two-way process. It's just the way that teachers talk to children and children talk to staff and other adults. And that's the ethos. These children are small adults and we try and respect them and they try and respect us. (Colleen)

The routines in the school made it family-like. The Holly Tree day began with breakfast in the gym-dining hall. At lunchtime, staff and children ate school dinner together. Miriam left the local authority catering scheme and took control of her own meal budget, and all food was cooked on the premises by the school's own dinner ladies. The move to local provision allowed Miriam to spend much more per head on food and to tailor-make the menus to suit the children, as well as to provide breakfasts, and lunches for any visitor who happened to be there. No money was required for dinner supervision. The communal meals provided a regular rhythm to the school day, and a pastoral opportunity for staff and children to be together that was abandoned in many English schools some time ago.

This was not the only domestic aspect of work at Holly Tree. Miriam stocked the small staff-room with the kind of furniture, furnishings and pictures that would be found in teachers' homes, not in business catalogues. The staff morning tea and toast roster ensured there was always a reason to come to the staff-room. Staff were encouraged to come to the staff-room to wind down in the calm after the children had left each day. And when innovation was begun, possibilities were discussed in convivial surroundings, and in ways that encouraged interaction: the Spanish curriculum was implemented in part through after-school events with wine, food and singing. (pp. 396–7)

We also had to put this description into conversation with the extant literature in order to specify further the collegiality we had identified. We had to anticipate the kinds of questions that other researchers might ask, given their knowledge of the research that had already been conducted and the tensions and consequences that it might have.

> This was not, as Hargreaves (1990) famously dubbed it, a 'contrived collegiality'. Staff genuinely enjoyed each other's company and cared about each other. One example will stand for the many instances we saw of the extended relationships the school supported. Jill, a staff member, had two children who attended the school:
>
> *My husband used to work here as well but unfortunately he died last year. So I don't have a lot of free time, with being a single mum and working. I've been here so long it's almost like an extended family; we all get on so well. Obviously I've been through a very difficult time recently and everybody's been so supportive. I go to choir and we rehearse on a Monday night and the staff do a rota and take it in turns to come and baby-sit for me. I just think that is absolutely fabulous. It sounds a bit of a cliché but I think our school motto says it all: Happiness. Harmony. Success. Because it is a happy school, we all get on so well together. We're all enthusiastic, even members who have been here for donkey's years. And I think that rubs off onto the kids as well. (Jill)*
>
> This then is a work-place where adults were able to be adults as well as teachers. They had meaningful friendships, and invested in each other, and not just in their own individual development:
>
> *There's always really good banter in the staff room and everybody socialises out of school as well and forms strong friendships and I think that kind of reflects if you're happy where you work you go into your work really positively with lots of energy. And I think that comes across to the children, because they would know if you were a really miserable devil. (Veronica)*
>
> Rath (2006), writing on the connections between friendship and work, noted that when work-places get 'personal' those who work in them talk of 'extended families' and 'happiness'.

> He argued that personal work-places are good for productivity. This perspective reminds us of the darker side of human relations and the ways in which they can be instrumentalised. There is little doubt that the family relations in the school also facilitated staff working hard together to meet performative mandates. (pp. 397–8)

Our paper elaborated our view of the importance of the head's leadership and management practices and the ways in which she had put her stamp on the school to create it as a place. We would always have seen the head as important; indeed, anyone going into the school could see that immediately. What we didn't know in detail before we began this analysis was how her influence and actions played out. The development of the Big Idea positioned our narrative analysis so that we looked for the storied ways in which staff 'signed on' to her vision for the school, and why they remained faithful to the head and the school.

While we did not name this as a place-based analysis in the published journal article, this slice of work underpinned the ways in which our understanding of the school as a place developed. You will see that some elements of a place based analysis are missing from our paper – we did not, for example, locate Holly Tree in its global, national and regional contexts in any detail. But there is a limit to what can be done in a journal article. Our lens in this publication was on the meaning-making aspects of place, but one anchored in a wider place-based analysis.

Theory and analysis

We are not fans of bringing a big theory as a kind of afterthought to data generated through sustained engagement with a school. As we suggested in Chapter 5, it is possible to bring various theoretical resources with you into the school and then into conversation with your lived research experiences. This is how we worked with Weick, for instance, in the example just given. Having a set of possible theoretical frames in your researcher 'toolkit' not only means that you can do some reflective writing along the way to see *whether* a theoretical resource, or *which* theoretical resource, might be useful, but also means that you can ensure that you generate the relevant data.

The research that we have discussed in this book has been conducted by researchers who did not overlay social theory on their data as an afterthought. However, one of them – Jan Nespor – specifically addressed the question of theory and school research in a final chapter in the book *Tangled up in School* (1997). He argues, and we agree, that he feels uneasy about the separation of theory from empirical work – first we report the work, then we theorize it. He suggests that 'theory' is an artefact of the university:

> The academic world I work in is fragmented into regions that struggle to insulate themselves from one another by adopting increasingly specialised academic dialects, tightly drawing the lines of their professional associations and special interest groups, and narrowing the scope of the audiences for their texts. And one reason, or at least one of the things that sustains it, is the acceptance of theory as an autonomous field of discourse, along with the idea that 'merely empirical' work exists only to provide illustrations for, or as a means of generating theory.
>
> Theory-as-an-independent-arena-of-discourse-and-practice is a powerful glue tying together academic networks, but I found at Thurber it pushed me away from people outside academia. This separation of theory (which usually corresponds to writing about other academic texts) from empirical description inevitably privileges the former and distorts or reduces the complexity of the latter. I haven't abandoned theory, but have tried to imbricate my theoretical work with attempts to show what was happening at Thurber. (p. 196)

This is a view with which we have considerable sympathy and the reason we have not offered engagement with theory as a separate stage. Rather, we choose to show, via the example of Holly Tree Primary, the ways in which a framing idea and some of the pertinent literature are woven into an analysis which emerged over time, through the ongoing fieldwork.

There is also of course another way to think about theory, and that is to see empirical study as theory-building. This is an inductive approach – one that works from the specific to the more generalizable. This is a familiar form of educational research. It may indeed be the kind of research that you want to do.

Our research in schools is sometimes of this inductive order. For instance, in our study of vernacular school change we were interested in generating heuristics that might help our funders, school practitioners and other researchers think about the processes of change – in ways that were non-linear and more nuanced than those in vogue with policymakers at the time. However, we also have been engaged in research where building theory is neither appropriate nor possible. Nespor was in just this position after his two-year intensive relationship with Thurber. He explains his reasons for refusing theory building in favour of a question generating approach:

> Webs and networks, after all, don't have conclusions or codas. Untangle them and you have paths leading outward, moving through other intersections, making more connections. You either follow such paths indefinitely, without benefit of a map, or stop somewhere, usually for more or less arbitrary reasons. What you have at the end is a record of itineraries you have worked through, and questions and suggestions for future research. (p. 197)

Nespor offers an example of this kind of analytic work, not theory building per se, but agenda setting and question-posing work. He mobilizes other literature and some social theory in order to achieve a coherent reflection on the work he has undertaken and written about. We quote a small section of his writing here to show how he assembles this mix of questions, literature, social theory and agenda setting. It demonstrates how Nespor works out from the salient points of analysis from his school research to raise wider issues:

> In Chapter 1, I suggested some affinities between the political organisation of the school system and the administrative structure of Thurber itself. What are the connections between inter and intra-school administrative and political structures? The idea of teachers carrying their expertise in their bodies as 'embodied cultural capital' (Bourdieu, 1986) defines the politics of pedagogy as an issue of staffing (the distribution

> of properly endowed bodies around the schools and within a school). We need not endorse this way of thinking about teaching to realise that it points to a need for better understandings of how careers recruitment, hiring and transfer practices distribute teachers from different backgrounds, levels of expertise, ideological perspectives, and fields of specialisation in different schools. What do the staffing mobility patterns in schools look like (cf. Becker, 1980)? How long do teachers stay at school? How do they move? How are they recruited to the school division in the first place? What connections exist between teacher preparation programs and school system personnel offices? How do these influence student-teacher placements and hires? (p. 197)

Nespor does not call these implications arising from his research. He does not suggest that his research has produced some generalizable understanding about these issues. Instead, he offers a set of questions that are important and which might be the basis of a different kind of study. This is an approach that sits well with a single intense engagement with one or a small set of schools.

Final note

Getting a handle on the data that you have generated is a substantive task and one that is always idiosyncratic to the particular study of place you have undertaken and your philosophical position on research. And this is always going to be your interpretation. No matter how thorough you are, no matter how systematic and how transparent your modes of analysis, in the end, this is your interpretation of the school as place. Someone else might look over your data and come to different conclusions. But if you are secure in your analysis and know that you have been self-critical as well as scrupulous, then you will be able to justify and defend your take on the school. Realizing this is both scary and exhilarating.

Further reading

You will want to read about specific approaches to analysing data and there are many resources available. We suggest, however, that it is equally useful for those interested in place to engage with some of the journals where methodological issues are discussed. These often provide more detailed examples of dilemmas and analysis than are given in methods texts. We particularly recommend regular browsing of *Qualitative Inquiry*, the *International Journal of Research and Methods in Education*, the *International Journal of Qualitative Studies in Education*, *Qualitative Health Research* and the *Education Action Research Journal*.

You might also want to follow up the idea of critical incidents:

Tripp, David (1993/2011). *Critical Incidents in Teaching: Developing Professional Judgement*. London: Routledge.

We also recommend these two books which integrate theory in long-term school studies and where theory was integral to the initial design:

Devine, John (1996). *Maximum Security: The Culture of Violence in Inner-city Schools*. Chicago: University of Chicago Press.

Niesche, Richard (2011). *Foucault and Educational Leadership: Disciplining the Principal*. London: Routledge.

CHAPTER EIGHT

Writing the school

Once your analysis is underway, you'll want to start imagining how you might use all of this data. What will you write, and for whom? What else might you do besides write? This is an exciting time in the research and one where you get to be creative. It's also the time when you feel, perhaps even more acutely than before, the responsibility to respect the people who have been hospitable to you for so long. This stage is also the point at which you begin to detach yourself from the school. It has become a place for you too, and will continue to develop as a place as you write and bring your own meaning-making to it. Writing about the school as a place is part of the process of saying goodbye.

This chapter focuses on some strategies to consider when writing the school. It revisits the notion of hospitality, and the importance of taking an appreciative stance in the light of some of the known issues of 'representation'. We then consider the various kinds of audiences that you might want to write for and canvass a range of possible writing genres and media. We conclude the chapter, and the book, by thinking about the entangled processes of 'reporting back' and leaving the school. Much of this chapter is applicable to research more generally, but we do note some particular issues related to place-based studies as we go along. We begin with a note on writing itself.

Writing and text

Writing is not a neutral process, something that occurs after the real research is over. Researchers don't just 'write up' what they already know. Writing continues the process of interpretation of events, experiences and conversations; it is an integral part of the analysis of data. Writing is also the primary way in which researchers communicate to readers what they have seen and done in the school.

Writing is not an exact science. Words are not a mirror on the world. They are cultural artefacts, approximations of the material world and everyday life. In most places in the world, for example, the word 'table' will be understood to refer to some kind of structure on which things are placed. However, the size, height and dimensions of tables differ and there are significant differences between, for instance, a low Japanese table and the standard Western table found in most English-speaking countries. A word, and the thing that it refers to, can mean very different things in different locations; even in the same location a word may mean different things to different people (Fish, 1980). Because of the lack of equivalence between the material and the word, and its openness to interpretation, it is common to hear research writing talked about as a 'representation' (Hall, 1997).

When words are strung together in sentences, paragraphs and pages, their meanings become even less predictable. While writers might try to convey their own understanding through their writing, readers will always bring their own understanding to the text. In a very real sense, once the text is written it becomes a separate object and no longer the same as it was when it was in the hands of the writer (Barthes, 1967).

Margaret Atwood (2003), writing about writing, describes the book (also read 'academic paper') as an intermediary between reader and writer. She imagines the page as a messenger, an envoy between two unseen parties:

> The writer communicates with the page. The reader also communicates with the page. The writer and the reader communicate only through the page ... pay no attention to the facsimiles of the writer that appear on talk shows, in newspaper interviews, and the like – they ought not to have anything to do with what goes on between you, the reader, and the page you are reading, where an invisible hand has previously left some marks for you to decipher. (p. 113)

What the reader does with the text is out of sight, as well as out of the control, of the writer.

Academic writers (ourselves included) know from the way in which their work is cited that readers often make different sense of writing from what they intended. Any text, including scholarly varieties, once written, stands apart from the writer and becomes available for interpretative reading work.

However, perhaps because an anonymous reader is a forbidding prospect, Atwood suggests that writers always write for someone. When we write diaries we are writing for ourselves as reader, for letter writers it is another person who is known to the writer: these are known readers. The problem for writers comes, Atwood suggests, when they have to send their writing out to an unknown reader – to Them. Doubt sets in. For successful fiction writers like Atwood, doubt and fear coalesce around the possibility of disappointing Them in some way. For academic writers, doubt arises not so much about disappointing readers, but about the kinds of judgements that They might make about the quality of our ideas and argument, about our scholarship and about our writing. Some of what They think is communicated back to writers in the form of reviews, while much, of course, will remain always unknown – and always therefore potentially negative.

Atwood considers a number of instances where writers have addressed their fear of what readers might make of the text. She talks for instance of Victorian writers who address their 'Dear Reader', of writers who have written about writers and their fears, and of writers who address their own concerns about how readers will deal with their creation. One of these is John Bunyan, who in *The Pilgrim's Progress* (1678) makes his book into a person. As Atwood puts it:

> Bunyan gives his book a list of detailed instructions; but the book becomes frightened of its assignment, and begins to answer back. Bunyan reassures it, and replies to its objections by telling it what to say in various difficult situations; and finally, he tells it, or her, that no matter how wonderful she is, there will be some people that won't like them, because that's just the way it is ... Useful and bracing advice for any book, I think. (p. 131)

Atwood suggests that the duty of the book is thus to bear whatever the reader makes of it, even it if desires something else. She proposes that writers have an obligation to words to let them go. When we send our words out into the world, we are moving from our most intimate reader – ourselves – to Them. We are committing words and writing to interpretations we cannot predict.

We do not do words a good turn by keeping them always to ourselves. Perhaps it sounds rather fanciful to say that words want something from us as writers and readers, but if you think about it, there is an element of a truth in this idea. Words that are not used fall out of fashion, they no longer live, they reside in dictionaries and old books but are no longer common parlance. Words mean nothing until we take them up and write them, and then they mean nothing again until they are read. While they are infinite in their supply and malleable, they rely on us to animate them.

Thinking about what words and writing need from us as writers (and readers), while perhaps odd, does position us to think about how we might work with words so that they leave our screens with a fighting chance of being read sympathetically, empathetically, critically, imaginatively. If words are organized so that it is hard for readers to bring them to life, then we have failed the words we have made use of. They have been, to steal another metaphor from Atwood, sent to the dead letter office rather than being put into circulation. If words and writing want to be read, then we owe it to them to make whatever changes we need to so that they can be taken up and savoured by readers. This is doing justice not only to our ideas, but also to the words we take up. It is sending out our messenger as well equipped as possible.

We thus need to think of ourselves as crafting with words in the hope that the reader will take from them the kinds of meanings that we intend. This is a particular responsibility for place-based researchers who have spent extensive periods of time enjoying the school's hospitality; we want our readers to understand as much about the school as place as is possible. How we write the text is thus very important.

Crafting the text

Writing about a long encounter with a school requires a serious engagement with the craft of putting words together. Representing the school in ways that position readers to appreciate the people and the place does not come from a hurried 'writing up' approach. Honouring the time you have spent, and the hospitality shown to you, means allowing time to work on the text, and adopting a crafting approach. This means being prepared to draft and revise, as well as working on the actual textual features – voice and style, the balance of description and exposition and the inclusion of visual materials. This is 'slow' writing.

There are now a plethora of books about academic writing and how it might be made 'stylish' and 'less stodgy' (Billig, 2013; Pinker, 2014; Sword, 2012). The advice always suggests that writers avoid the overuse of passive voice, heavily nominalized text, lengthy sentences and massive amounts of citations. This is all very sensible and we do urge you to look at some of this kind of advice. However, there are three other sources of useful resources about research writing, produced by:

1. ethnographers concerned with the ethical practices of authorship, and the necessary combination of rigorous reflexive scholarship and a well-crafted text (Behar and Gordon, 1995; Clifford and Marcus, 1986; Geertz, 1988; Narayan, 2012);
2. narrative researchers who explore story and the use of settings, plot, characterization, metaphor and metonymy, collage and montage, linearity and non-linearity (e.g. Ah Nee-Benham and Cooper, 1998; Clandinin and Connelly, 2000; Czarniawska, 1997; McLaughlin and Tierney, 1993; Riessman, 2008; Thomas, 1995);
3. and arts-informed research practitioners who advocate and experiment with the use of research-based poetry, fiction and theatre, as well as performance, exhibitions, films and dance (e.g. Denzin, 2003; Jones, 2006; Leavy, 2009; Piantanida et al., 2003; Richardson, 1997).

Dipping into these resources shows the sheer variety of possible ways to think about writing the school. It also strongly suggests that writing is something to be taken as seriously as methods, and to be studied and practised with the same kind of continuing and thoughtful application.

We can't stress enough the importance of working on the writing about your school, trying out various approaches, revising and polishing the text until it gets somewhere near good enough.

Writing about other people and their place

Writing is a responsibility. Now, this is not what usually strikes you when you think about writing. Writing is often discussed in terms of its difficulties – the problems that researchers experience in terms of structuring their text, or the problems they have getting over wanting their first drafts to be perfect, or the problems of finding the time to sit down to compose. And writers who write about academic writing usually stress that writing is a social practice shaped by disciplines, conventions and hidden rules. You have to know what these are, you are told, in order to get published.

We don't want to deny any of this, but these are not our concerns in this chapter. We want to return to the twin ideas of hospitality and appreciation that we discussed in Chapter 2. There, we suggested that a school was being a generous host in allowing any researcher 'inside', particularly for any length of time. We argued that this meant that the researcher needed to attempt to understand and be empathetic with the school and its people: to look first for what was essentially good about the place, rather than set out to find all the negatives. This was not a plea for 'balance' in approach, but rather an ethical position based on the understanding of the researcher as a special guest being given unprecedented access to family doings.

We proposed that learning from the school, as well as about it, meant looking first for the positives, and then for the difficulties and dilemmas. This is the critical stance taken by Sara Lawrence-Lightfoot (1984) in her work on school portraiture. We also argued in Chapters 1 and 3 that it was important to put the school in its wider context, and to understand the ways in which what happened in the school was produced and framed by wider flows of people, information, resources, narratives, practices and ideas. Getting the bigger picture allows a nuanced understanding of the school as a place and why things are as they are.

These perspectives come to the fore again when you begin to think about how to write about the school. That's because you've been a guest of the school for a long time. And this was not a quick visit for a meal with strangers. You don't get to give frank comments to the camera, out of sight and hearing of the host, about his or her performance. This is not an occasion to allocate the host a score when you leave, or to settle any scores. Now is the time to be the good guest and to leave as politely and, yes, as humbly as you came into the life of the school.

Questions of anonymity and confidentiality come to the fore when writing about place and your experience in the school. You've thought about these things before, but now they are back with a vengeance. How much detail can you give before you give the school or people within it away? But how much detail do you have to provide to help the reader understand not only the patterns, but also the particularity, of the place? Honouring place in the place-based study does present particular challenges, as Nespor (2000) points out (and see our discussion in Chapter 3).

There may well be some issues that you want to discuss that you know will be difficult for people in the school and which may damage the good relationships that have been built up over serial shared activities and conversations. We discuss these later in the chapter. However, it's important that your intention, and the stance from which you write, is not designed to find out what is *wrong* with school but instead *how the school works* and *why it is as it is*. We take the view that your research, and the writing that comes from it, is in a very crucial sense co-constructed. You have, together with the school community, experienced everyday life in this particular place. Acknowledging the co-constructed nature of the research data that you have thus raises the question of how the writing process might continue this dimension of working together. We will explore this through four ideas: (1) putting yourself in the text, (2) representing other people fairly, (3) co-writing, and (4) textual choices and tactics.

Putting yourself in the text

We probably don't really need to say that all researchers shape the research that they do, that there is no neutral stance and that all research is thus situated, partial and particular. We do, however, need to address the thorny question of how this is communicated to readers. Academic writing comes in many forms and it is now widely accepted that either a first- or third-person narrative can be used. The question therefore is not about whether it is right to write as 'I' but rather is it appropriate and, if so, when and where? Unfortunately there is no right answer to this question either!

Writers often feel that they need to use 'I' in order to signal that this is their version of the school. There might be others, written by different people. 'I'-conscious writers often discuss the decisions that they made about their research, and its various ebbs, flows and bumps. Writing in the first person lets the reader know that this was research that entailed numerous methodological and ethical decisions. We have used these kinds of first-person accounts throughout this book, particularly from Jan Nespor, who provides an exemplary approach to research practice writing (see Chapters 2 and 6 in particular).

This extract from Stephanie Springgay's (2008) ethnography, *Body Knowledge and Curriculum: Pedagogies of Touch in Youth and Visual Culture*, offers another example. Springgay explored contemporary art practice with students in a single school. She writes in the first person to convey something of the process of her research and the ways in which she thought about it:

> As the six-month semester in the school unfolded, my research methodology, the visual exploration with the students, student and researcher understandings, and ongoing analysis of student work emerged simultaneously. There were many days when I would arrive home from school, and as I prepared myself for the following day, uploading videos, reading the day's notes in my visual journal, or designing a lesson on a contemporary artist, I would find myself frustrated, panicked and scared. I had nothing. I would convince myself that I had collected 'no data'. The research was going nowhere. And yet something propelled me forward; a nagging voice echoing in my ear, 'What did it all mean?' As the videotapes piled up on my apartment floor and the students' art explorations propelled class discussions, I realised that I was right in the middle of things, in the space marked by meditation and complexity. (p. 8)

Springgay's concern was to express something of the 'unknowing' that she experienced during the research process; her concern was not to present a neat narrative, with all loose threads woven tightly together. She wanted the reader to know that this was not simply an experience, but was the way in which Springgay the researcher and her research came into being. This is an ontological point, as well as an experiential description.

Sometimes, the authorial decision to use 'I' is made because the writers have decided the reader should see through their eyes, walk along with them as an unseen presence, relive the events, conversations and interactions together with them. This is often achieved through the use of rewritten field notes and exegesis. This extract from Margaret Somerville's (2011) research (see recommended reading in Chapter 4), on a primary school wetlands-based curriculum programme, shows how these two modes of writing are typically combined:

> Walking out of the scrub at the edge of the field there's a big puddle of water lying since recent rains. My heart rises the first time I see this water appear after drought. The second time there is already an amazing chorus of frogs. My son tells me they sing in unison so the females can choose a mate. But where do they come from? Where do they go? There have been no frogs singing since that first day at dawn. Why aren't they singing? Is it the time, or are they all gone again? It's Sunday morning so I wander over the little wetland again, I think about knowing a place day in and day out, over seasons and years to really know what is going on, I think about what places teach us.
>
> It was on a visit to a school on practicum that I entered the world of frogs. I had visited the crowded portable classroom earlier in the day and watched the children navigate desks, chairs, boxes, hanging artworks, and other objects that make up this decidedly working class primary school classroom, I thought about Lefebvre's contention that the whole of social space proceeds from the body (1974/1991). The social space of this classroom is produced by these movements, bodies and objects, producing, in turn, the subjectivities of the children there. My attention was especially drawn to Mary, a child with Down Syndrome, moving awkwardly in this cramped space accompanied by an integration aide. It seemed that there was

> just nowhere she could fit in this crowded space with her extra human attachment.
>
> When I returned after school the teacher and the integration aide, still working in the well-worn classroom, invited me to watch a short DVD of the rehearsal for the Christmas concert. There on the interactive screen, the children came to life as frogs, dancing their frog dance to music made entirely of frog calls. The children get to know the frogs in the wetland. They learn how frogs live and move, and the sounds of the distinctive calls of each species. The classroom, cleared of clutter, becomes the space of the wetlands. Children dance to the frog calls, moving frog limbs, fingers splayed, jumping, leap-frogging, becoming-frog to music. Mary in particular loves the performance, moving freely in this frog collective, unaccompanied by her integration aide. In one brief sequence towards the end she smiles pure pleasure at the camera, her body liberated in her frog dance. I learn that this is just a very small part of an integrated program involving visits to the local Morwell River Wetlands. (pp. 67–8)

Somerville weaves her own understanding of water in the dry Australian bush with her narrative of research in a primary classroom. In the first part of the paper we have cited, her own experience is represented through a worked over field note – a combination of memory, experience and reflection – and then an encounter narrative. There is a reference to a particular theory of spatial relations (Lefebvre) which signposts the theoretical underpinning of the description to come. Later in the chapter, Somerville brings both of these strands together, working with both her own experiences and those of the class, using spatial theory as the means of harmonizing her sense of self as a researcher and her interpretation of the wetlands programme.

The first person is not the only way to put the researcher's self in the text. Sometimes the inclusion of the reader in the text is achieved by the use of the inclusive second person. In Sara Lawrence-Lightfoot's portrait of John F. Kennedy High School she chooses to use both 'you' and 'I' in order to achieve both the sense of the reader being there, and the recognition that this is her interpretation of the school. Lawrence-Lightfoot begins with three pages that introduce the reader to the neighbourhood; she writes of the drive to the Bronx from New York City:

> As you drive down the winding hills of Riverdale into the valley below, the landscape shifts from the orange and yellow colors of fall to the grey concrete of city streets, you are in the valley of Riverdale when you turn up 230th Street toward John F Kennedy High School. The texture and pace of life are transformed. The traffic becomes congested, the sidewalks crowded, and the noise level increases, five or six gas stations, their neon signs blaring, come into view. Fast-food joints, drug stores, dry-cleaning establishments, laundromats, and corner grocery stores line the streets. (Lawrence-Lightfoot, 1986, pp. 57–8)

The use of 'you' puts the reader in the position of the driver. Lawrence-Lightfoot's evocative description provides just enough detail to trigger the reader's imagination so that we can see the autumn colours turning into concrete grey city streets in our minds. It is as if we are looking out of the front windows of our own car.

Lawrence-Lightfoot then switches to 'I'. The reader is now lurking behind her as she enters the school for the first time:

> A friendly security guard, dressed in regular street clothes, inquires casually about my destination, and writes out a visitor's card for me. As I try to follow his abbreviated directions I feel lost in the swarm of students moving through the halls. Bodies are pressed close. For a moment my feet are lifted from the floor by the crowd's momentum as we move en masse up the escalator. (p. 58)

Lawrence-Lightfoot now situates this personal narrative by providing some key statistical information about the size of the school, before switching back to description of what this actually means for getting around the building, a necessary everyday activity:

> There are 5,300 students in Kennedy High School, and during changeovers between classes close to 4,000 students crowd onto the escalators that rise two floors at a time. On each step of the moving stairs, there are three, sometimes four, students packed together. When the escalator reaches a floor, hundreds of people get stacked up as they try to make the swing onto the next escalator. Along the walls above the escalator are

> colorful murals drawn by Kennedy art students, painted signs direct you to offices and activity centers in the building. Other murals offer words of encouragement – cheering students on in their pursuit of 'educational excellence'. The most prominent message, shouted in bold colors, says, 'Catch the Kennedy spirit.' The inspirational, lively drawings sharply contrast with the dull institutional grays and greens that dominate the building's walls and ceilings. (pp. 58–9)

Lawrence-Lightfoot then returns the reader to the immediacy of her response to the mass of students, the movement, the building itself:

> Since I have never been in a school of this large a scale and never seen an escalator in a school building, my first associations are of rising from underground at a subway station, or traveling upwards in a big department store. Although I feel vaguely displaced and uneasy, everyone else seems to be totally used to the body crunch and unconcerned about the crowded conditions. I see no pushing and shoving or gestures of impatience even though the momentum of the crowds often throws people against one another. A short, vivacious girl with a head full of tight curls and a ready smile may have noticed my disorientation and turns around to me as we reach the next landing. 'There are many ways up,' she says cryptically, and then inquires, 'Why don't you take the teachers' elevator?' Her first comment, probably meant to convey modes of transportation to the upper floors, echoes through my head for the rest of my visit to Kennedy High. It seem an apt metaphor for the rising expectations and goals of Kennedy's teachers and students; a first sign of the optimistic, spirited references that pervades the language of the school's inhabitants. (p. 59)

In this passage, the reader is given important information about the school: despite its hustle and bustle, there is both physical and verbal consideration between people. Lawrence-Lightfoot does not feel unsafe. She also points early in this school portrait to a first impression that is later confirmed – the student's statement that 'there are many ways up'. Without labouring the point about diversity and difference, she flags up that this is at the heart of the school's successes.

Lawrence-Lightfoot's skill in combining information, first-person writing and carefully crafted description is one model that might guide the way in which the first person can be used to enhance the reader's understanding. She does not lapse into a total 'I' narrative – me, all about me. The portrait is not about her, but about letting the reader understand the school place as she encountered it. You might also take from this example that thinking about the balance and nature of description is as important to a reader's introduction to the school as place as the use of the first person.

Representing other people fairly

We have already referred to the need to be critical. Your job is to be a researcher and not a public relations officer or a journalist working for a tabloid newspaper interested only in a sensationalist story. However, being a researcher can sometimes be difficult. Without even wanting to, we can unwittingly say things in ways that are worrying or offensive to the people we have spent so long with. Things that were okay to laugh and joke about in private can become something quite alarming when they appear on the page, about to go out into the world.

At a time when many schools are very sensitive about the ways in which they are perceived, it is very easy for even the most careful researcher to say something in a way that causes offence. Relations that were good for the entire time you were in the school suddenly become tense and difficult. The worst-case scenario is that the school, or someone in it, may withdraw from the research. Any participant has the ethical right to withdraw consent from participating in the research at any time, so getting the writing stage of the research right is very important.

There is no doubt that it can be very difficult to say something that is overtly critical. This is a dilemma well known to ethnographers. Caroline Brettell's (1996) edited collection is tellingly entitled *When They Read What We Write*. Brettell invited ethnographers to offer narratives of occasions when their participants reacted negatively to the researchers' written interpretations, many of them made back 'at home'. The contributors have no easy advice to offer. However, they report that the advice that they were given was to negotiate with their research participants.

Negotiation is an obvious strategy for the researcher to try, particularly a place-based researcher whose commitment has been to relationships and open communication. At a practical level, this means keeping in contact with the school while the analysis and writing are going on, and offering verbal reports of work in progress, or drafts for people to comment on. We have done this ourselves, but we also often find that people cannot find the time or energy to find out about our interim ideas – unless we also tell them that there are some things that they may find difficult. And being told that there may be a problem doesn't necessarily create a positive environment conducive to open discussions!

The ways in which any potentially contentious issues are presented has an effect on the way in which they are understood, discussed and resolved. In multi-sited case studies, potentially tricky questions can be abstracted from the particularities of each place, and discussed as cross-case issues. However, dealing with a single school and the particularities and eccentricities of place means that it is more difficult to abstract the possible difficulties away. Researchers might:

- situate the potentially contentious problem in the widest possible context – focus on the global and national flows and frames – so that its production can be seen as not simply that of individuals, or of the school by itself;
- offer a multi-voiced account which shows the various points of view and how they interact to produce the potentially contentious problem – show the school as a heterogeneous place and not a monolith. One textual form which accomplishes multi-vocality is Readers' Theatre (Donmoyer and Yennie-Donmoyer, 1995) – a genre in which people's actual words and the major points that they make are scripted as a play, and then performed.
- fictionalize the account so that the potentially contentious issue is discussed (Clough, 2002), but not particularized – create an imaginary place which shares some key characteristics with the material.

The authors in Brettell's anthology do not have a shared view on which strategies are most effective. On balance, most seem to suggest that the researcher must try to negotiate but must ultimately be prepared to stand by his or her interpretations. This view is not shared, and many researchers do feel that if their most trusted participants do not want some things written about, then they are prepared to omit those aspects of the place from any writing they produce.

Facing the difficult can be important, even transformative. While the following extract is not about research into a school, we think that Laurie Richmond's (2013) commentary on her work with the Sugpiaq peoples living in Old Harbor, Alaska, is instructive.

> When I first mentioned (over the phone) to Laurence that I might want to write about him, he said, 'piss on you', and hung up fairly soon after. His reaction affected me deeply. I felt like I had betrayed him and our trust. I began to seriously question my role and purpose as an academic scholar in an indigenous setting. As a researcher was I basically a glorified spy? How could I do this job and honor my relationships? In the immediate future, I was prepared to give up on this writing and project altogether.
>
> The next time that Laurence called, I discussed our relationship and the writing process with him in a way that I never had before. In a way, this particular project sparked a new kind of openness and communication between us – both about what I was doing in Old Harbor and about what our relationship means [sic] to each other. I told him that I was looking at fisheries issues and that through him and the people in Old Harbor I had begun to learn that fishing regulations are more than mere policies or changes to protect fish – they also affect the lives of fishermen in deeply personal ways. I wanted to be able to convey this kind of personal story in my writing. I then told him that I would never write anything about him that he didn't want me to and would drop the idea completely. He told me that he was glad I brought it up and that he had been thinking about it a lot. He said that he would think about it some more and get back to me.
>
> A few days later he called me back and said that he had considered it and that he felt I was right about the fishing policies and that what happened in Old Harbor with the loss of fishing was really bad. He said that when I come to visit I should

> bring what I wrote and that he had a few other things that he wanted to tell me. (pp. 81–2)

Richmond's story shows the ways in which place-based meanings are sometimes kept secret, and revealed only when necessary to prevent the researcher making representational blunders. The example also suggests that the quality of relationship established in the first instance, and the ways in which it is maintained, position the researcher to resolve representational issues. The same principles of respect, appreciation and honesty that are involved in beginning and sustaining a relationship are vital to resolving writing-related difficulties.

Co-writing

Many anthropologists and participatory researchers see that the reciprocity implied in the notion of partnership extends to co-writing anything written about a place and its people (Lassiter, 2005). They see the co-writing and the shared meaning-making as a place-making practice, with the text itself continuing to work after publication to continue the process of place narrativizing.

There are of course lots of things that can go wrong in co-writing and it is as well to anticipate some of them in advance – one party consistently misses deadlines, one partner has unreasonable expectations of others, one produces sloppy and/or hard to understand writing and this has to be dealt with without damaging relationships. So if you decide to co-write – and this is something that we sometimes do – then it is important at the start to agree on the process, that is who will write what; the ways of handling differences and disagreements, that is, who has the last say; and the order of authorship, that is, who goes first and last.

There are three main ways in which co-writing is achieved:

1. Type-talk: where two or more people sit side by side at the computer and write together.
2. Cut it up and put it back together: where two or more people divide the paper into sections and write these separately, then one person puts the draft together.

3 First cut: where one person takes the lead and writes the first draft in its entirety and the others add, subtract and amend (Thomson and Kamler, 2013).

Working with people who are not as used to writing as you are, or who may feel daunted about writing with a researcher, means that you may need to adopt either type-talk or first cut strategies.

Type-talk has the advantage of allowing you to 'scribe' what your school co-author is saying. However, having hold of the keyboard is also a powerful position, and it is important to avoid the situation where you are busily writing away while your alleged co-author says nothing and is not invited to do so. On the other hand, having you do all the talking while your school co-author does the keyboard work means that he or she is reduced to a secretarial role. Type-talk is also time consuming and people in schools may not have the time available to do this kind of authoring.

First cut has the advantage of not demanding too much from busy people in schools. You simply ask them to tell you what you've got wrong, what you've left out, what wasn't obvious to them and where you might change things. Being able to say this to you depends on your school co-author feeling confident about contributing.

Of course, cut it up and put it back together again, which has different people writing different sections together, is also possible. We have written together with our school partners in this way. The key issue when using this strategy is to make sure that the text reads as if it is written by one person, or to use a device like writing in separate 'voices' in the text, to show the different perspectives, and value the different ways of writing (see Chapter 9 in Thomson and Kamler, 2013, for further discussion of co-writing).

All three co-authoring strategies depend on the quality of the relationship between the writers. The practice of writing together, and the negotiations about text, can be understood as dependent on 'relationships-based' ethics. As Sarah Banks and her colleagues (Banks et al., 2013) put it.

> Relationship-based ethics, including the ethics of care (which focuses on responsibilities attached to particular relationships) is as important as principle-based ethics (which focuses on

individual rights and duties) in conceptualising and understanding the ethical dimensions of the research. (p. 274)

Relationship-based ethics is an everyday practice, rooted in the researcher's stance, interactions and processes. We highly recommend the guidelines produced by Banks et al., *Community-Based Participatory Research: A Guide to Ethical Principles and Practice* (Centre for Social Justice and Community Action, 2012). They suggest the following as helpful in participatory research – and we extend this to place-based studies – mutual respect; equality and inclusion; democratic participation; active learning; making a difference; collective action and personal integrity (p. 8). While working with these principles will not resolve problems per se, they may provide better grounds for problem resolution than the more difficult-to-determine ethical principle of 'doing no harm'. These relationship ethics can also guide agreements about the distribution and archiving of materials emanating from place-based research – that is, who should keep which elements of the research data, who should have access to it and where it should be stored.

Textual choices and tactics

The key question when writing the school is 'Who is the reader?' It is important to consider the range of people and organizations who might want to know about the research. Understanding the potential reader and how you might tell him or her about the school as place leads you to consider what kinds of writing and other artefacts and materials might be produced. It may not be enough simply to produce a research report; you may need to write several different pieces for different readers. Potential readers include:

- The school staff and students. You might offer to talk about the research and its results at a staff, student council or a governors' or parents' meeting. You could write about the research and its results for the school newsletter or you could place a version of the research results on the school intranet.
- The local community/ies. Consider writing something for the local newspaper and/or appearing on the local radio.

It is important not to forget that these can be risky media where it is possible for words to be taken out of context. Getting some help from your university press relations staff is often a good idea.

- Professionals. Teachers and trainee teachers, social and youth workers, for example, might all be interested in your work. More journalistic academic outlets and mainstream media research magazines are often interested in a short research précis, especially if it has wider appeal than a specialist audience. These kinds of platforms also provide journalistic support for you to write in the appropriate house style.
- Policymakers and key players in organizations in the field. Not all school studies have immediate policy implications. You may find, however, that your work dovetails with other research and that together there is something important to say. You may be able to offer a briefing, or write a specific short research summary, for relevant people.
- Funders. If your work has been externally funded then you will have to write a research report. This is generally tailored to the specific interests of the funder, and it is often published by them. It is also good to put these reports online so that they are more widely available. In our experience a research report can act as a kind of 'base line' text from which other texts drawn so it is worth spending time on getting reports right.
- Other researchers. You can write for academic colleagues through a range of media, including blogs. The usual way to reach other academics is through publishing an academic book or a series of journal articles. These days at least some of these texts can be made more accessible through the use of sites such as researchgate.com and academia.edu. It is important not to assume that people in schools are indifferent to academic publications. Our experience is that many are delighted to see their place not only in more popular texts but also in publications used largely by academics.

There are of course other ways to communicate your research. These days, it's not just about writing. We've already mentioned blogs, and other forms of social media might also be useful for your particular research. However, you might also consider film (particularly if you have been using visual methods), an exhibition or a website. As we have already noted, questions of confidentiality and anonymity always need to be renegotiated if you are using images and/or any platform that is highly visible. But it is also important to recall that it is now very difficult to retain anonymity when so many details can be so easily searched online. It is vital that you ensure that everyone is aware of any potential issues involved in going public, no matter what the medium.

We are particularly interested in the ways in which our research can be made into materials useful for teaching purposes and we often develop heuristics specifically for that purpose, or work with schools and school staff to develop ways in which they can tell their own stories – see, for example, our website getwet.org.uk about an action research project which developed an interdisciplinary primary and secondary approach to learning about water (this project had a water pumping station as a place). We worked first of all on this website, and then attended to more scholarly publications related to the project when the website was completed.

The long farewell

It is as important to leave as to enter the school – the place you now know intimately – well. Closing off your research may not be the end of the relationship, but it certainly marks a shift in it. Once you have begun the writing and things are being published and are out in the world, it is time to formally conclude your connection with this place.

You may have grown fond of the school and the people in it. You've spent a lot of time there. It may be sad to leave, and your routine of being there on a regular basis is about to end. There are people with whom you may want to keep in contact, and maybe even a few others that you are happy to not see again! We often keep in touch with people after we have been in their professional lives and their place for an extended period of time. Sometimes this is simply through social media or it might be more organized social get-togethers. We also often find that we go back to particular places over and over as our research relationship has been so productive. Some of our research participants have become our friends. Our relationship is more than about the research.

But whatever the particulars of the situation in the place where you've been, the reality is that it is good to do something formal to mark the occasion of leaving. It is crucial to avoid the equivalent of the midnight flit, sneaking out of the place and people's lives without saying anything. You were there one day and then whooof, you've vanished. At the very least, there is a thank you to say for the hospitality. There might be a small gathering in the pub or a goodbye at a staff meeting. You can anticipate this moment and plan for it.

Leaving worthwhile materials and publications is part of the process of saying goodbye. Publications and materials are tangible mementoes of the time you've spent in the school. They are important for you, but also for the school that has hosted you. Don't underestimate the importance of this last stage.

'Have you read the book about our place?' people might ask the next researcher to come knocking at the school door. 'Read that first to understand who we are and where we've been.'

Further reading

Brettell, Caroline (ed.) (1996). *When They Read What We Write: The Politics of Ethnography*. New York: Praeger.

Centre for Social Justice and Community Action (2012). *Community-Based Participatory Research: A Guide to Ethical Principles and Practice*, National Coordinating Centre for Public Engagement, Durham University, https://www.dur.ac.uk/resources/beacon/CBPREthicsGuidewebNovember20121.pdf (accessed 16 July 2015).

Ghodsee, K. (2016) *From Notes to Narrative. Writing Ethnographies That Everyone Can Read*. Chicago: University of Chicago Press.

Thomson, Pat and Barbara Kamler (2013). *Writing for Peer Reviewed Journals: Strategies for Getting Published*. London: Routledge.

APPENDIX

Data featured in this book is drawn from the following projects:

AHRC Connected Communities Scoping Study: 'Performing Impact: Narratives, Texts and Performances in Community Theatre', http://performingimpactproject.wordpress.com.

Arts Council England/Creative Partnerships: 'Creative School Change', http://www.creativitycultureeducation.org/creative-school-change.

Creative Partnerships: 'Case Studies of 30 Leading Schools'. See the David Fulton Creative Teaching/Creative Schools series, https://www.routledge.com/series/CTCS.

Culture, Creativity and Education: 'Evaluation of Knowledge Transfer in the Royal Shakespeare Company Leading Practitioner Network', http://www.creativitycultureeducation.org/a-study-of-the-learning-performance-network-an-education-programme-of-the-royal-shakespeare-company.

Culture, Creativity and Education: 'Signature Pedagogies: Ethnographic Studies of Artists at Work', http://www.signaturepedagogies.org.uk.

ESRC RES-000-22-0834: 'Promoting Social and Education Inclusion Through the Creative Arts', http://www.leeds.ac.uk/educol/documents/190288.pdf.

Get Wet: The Papplewick Water Literacies project. Esmee Fairbairn, Garfield Weston Trust, http://www.getwet.org.uk.

Pupil researcher projects in Ridley Grove Primary and Knutsford High School.

BIBLIOGRAPHY

Achilles, C. (1999). *Let's Put Kids First, Finally*. Thousand Oaks, CA: Corwin Press.

Achilles, C., J. Finn and H. Bain (1997). 'Using class size to reduce the equity gap'. *Educational Leadership* 55 (4): 40–3.

Ah Nee-Benham, M. and J. Cooper (1998). *Let My Spirit Soar! Narratives of Diverse Women in School Leadership*. Thousand Oaks, CA: Sage.

Ainscow, M. (2015). *Towards Self-Improving School Systems: Lessons from a City Challenge*. London: Routledge.

Alderson, P. (2011). *The Ethics of Research with Children and Young People: A Practical Handbook*. 2nd edn. London: Sage.

Anderson, G., K. Herr and A. S. Nihlen (2008). *Studying Your Own School: An Educator's Guide to Qualitative Practitioner Research*. 2nd edn. Thousand Oaks, CA: Corwin Press.

Anderson, M. and K. Freebody (2014). *Partnerships in Education Research: Creating Knowledge That Matters*. London: Bloomsbury.

Appadurai, A. (1996). *Modernity at Large: Cultural Dimensions of Globalisation*. Minneapolis and London: University of Minnesota Press.

Armstrong, F. (2003). *Spaced Out: Policy, Difference and the Challenge of Inclusive Education*. Dordrecht: Kluwer Academic Publishers.

Atkins, W. (2014). *The Moor: Lives, Landscape, Literature*. London: Faber & Faber.

Atwood, M. (2003). *Negotiating with the Dead: A Writer on Writing*. London: Virago.

Auge, M. (1995). *Non-Places: Introduction to an Anthropology of Supermodernity*. London and New York: Verso.

Baars, S., A. Bernardes, A. Elwick, A. Malorie, G. Mcaleavy, L. Mcinerney, L. Menzies and A. Riggall (2014). *Lessons from London Schools: Investigating the Success*. Centre for London. https://www.cfbt.com/~/media/cfbtcorporate/files/research/2014/r-london-schools-2014.pdf (accessed 3 August 2015).

Bacchi, C. and J. Bonham (2014). 'Reclaiming discursive practices as an anaytic focus'. *Foucault Studies* 17 (April): 173–92.

Back, L. (2007). *The Art of Listening*. London: Berg Publishers.

Back, L. and N. Puwar (2013). *Live Methods*. London: John Wiley & Sons.

Badcock, B. (1997). 'Recently observed polarising tendencies and Australian cities'. *Australian Geographic Studies* 35 (3): 243–59.

Bailey, S. (2013). *Exploring ADHD: An Ethnography of Disorder in Early Childhood*. London: Routledge.

Ball, S. (1981). *Beachside Comprehensive: A Case Study of Secondary Schooling*. Cambridge: Cambridge University Press.

Ball, S. (1990). *Foucault and Education: Disciplines and Knowledge*. London: Routledge.

Ball, S. (1998). 'Big policies/small world: An introduction to international perspectives in education policy'. *Comparative Education* 34 (2): 119–30.

Ball, S., M. Maguire and A. Braun (2011a). *How Schools do Policy: Policy Enactments in Secondary Schools*. London: Routledge.

Ball, S., M. Maguire and A. Braun (2011b). 'Policy enactments in the secondary school: Theory and practice'. ESRC end of award report, res-062-23-1484. Swindon: ESRC.

Ballas, D., D. Dorling and B. Hennig (2014). *The Social Atlas of Europe*. Bristol: Policy Press.

Bancroft, S., M. Fawcett and P. Hay, eds (2008). *Researching Children Researching the World: 5x5x5 Creativity*. Stoke-on-Trent: Trentham Books.

Banks, S., A. Armstrong, K. Carter, H. Graham, P. Hayward, A. Henry, T. Holland, C. Holmes, A. Lee, A. McNulty, N. Moore, N. Nayling, A. Stokoe and A. Strachan (2013). 'Everyday ethics in community-based participatory research'. *Contemporary Social Science* 8 (3): 263–7.

Barthes, R. (1967). 'The death of the author'. *Aspen* 5/6 (Fall/Winter), http://www.ubu.com/aspen/aspen5and6/threeEssays.html – barthes (accessed 12 February 2014).

Barton, D. and M. Hamilton (1998). *Local Literacies: Reading and Writing in One Community*. London and New York: Routledge.

Bassey, M. (1999). *Case Study Research in Educational Settings*. Maidenhead and Philadelphia, PA: Open University Press.

Bathmaker, A. M. (2010). 'Dealing with data analysis'. In *The Routledge Doctoral Student's Companion: Getting to Grips with Research in Education and the Social Sciences*, ed. P. Thomson and M. Walker, London: Routledge: pp. 200–12.

Baum, S. and R. Hassan (1993). 'Economic restructuring and spatial equity: A case study of Adelaide'. *Australia New Zealand Journal of Sociology* 29 (2): 151–72.

Behar, R. and D. Gordon, eds (1995). *Women Writing Culture*. Berkeley, Los Angeles, CA, and London: University of California Press.

Billig, M. (2013). *Learn to Write Badly: How to Succeed in the Social Sciences*. Cambridge: Cambridge University Press.

Brettell, C. B., ed. (1996). *When They Read What We Write: The Politics of Ethnography*. New York: Praeger.

Burke, C. and I. Grosvenor (2004). *The School I'd Like: Children and Young People's Reflections on an Eductation for the 21st Century*. London: RoutledgeFalmer.

Burke, C. and I. Grosvenor (2015). *The School I'd Like Revisited: Children and Young People's Reflections on an Education for the Future*. London: Routledge.

Casanova, U. (1991). *Elementary School Secretaries: The Women in the Principal's Office*. Newbury Park, CA: Corwin Press.

Centre for Social Justice and Community Action (2012). *Community-Based Participatory Research: A Guide to Ethical Principles and Practice*. National Coordinating Centre for Public Engagement, Durham University, https://www.dur.ac.uk/resources/beacon/CBPREthicsGuidewebNovember20121.pdf (accessed 16 July 2015).

Charmaz, K. (2006). *Constructing Grounded Theory: A Practical Guide Through Qualitative Analysis*. Thousand Oaks, CA: Sage.

Cheney, G., L. Christensen, C. Conrad and D. Lair (2004). 'Corporate rhetoric as organizational discourse'. In *The Sage Handbook of Organizational Discourse*, ed. C. Oswick, L. Putnam, C. Hardy, N. Phillips and D. Grant. Thousand Oaks, CA: Sage, pp. 79–103.

Chouliaraki, L. and N. Fairclough (1999). *Discourse in Late Modernity: Rethinking Critical Discourse Analysis*. Edinburgh: Edinburgh University Press.

Christensen, P. and A. James, eds (2000). *Research with Children*. London and New York: Falmer.

Cipollone, K. and E. A. Stich (2012). 'Attending to issues of access in contemporary times: Centring a significant side issue'. *Ethnography and Education* 7 (1): 21–38.

Clandinin, D. J. and F. M. Connelly (2000). *Narrative Inquiry: Experience and Story in Qualitative Research*. San Francisco, CA: Jossey Bass.

Clark, A., R. Flewitt, M. Hammersley and M. Robb, eds (2013). *Understanding Research with Children*. London: Sage.

Clark, A. and P. Moss (2001). *Listening to Young Children: The Mosaic Approach*. London: National Children's Bureau.

Clifford, J. and G. Marcus (1986). *Writing Culture: The Politics and Poetics of Ethnography*. Los Angeles, CA: University of California Press.

Clough, P. (2002). *Narratives and Fictions in Educational Research*. Buckingham: Open University Press.

Cochran-Smith, M. and S. Lytle (1993). *Inside-Outside: Teacher Research and Knowledge*. Columbia, NY: Teachers College Press.

Cochran-Smith, M. and S. Lytle (2009). *Inquiry as Stance: Practitioner Research for the Next Generation*. New York: Teachers College Press.

Coles, R. and P. Thomson (2016). 'Between records and representations: Inbetween writing in educational ethnography'. *Ethnography and Education* 11(3) 253–66.

Comber, B. (2015). *Literacy, Place and Pedagogies of Possibility*. London: Routledge.

Comber, B., P. Thomson and M. Wells (2001). 'Critical literacy finds a "place": Writing and social action in a low income Australian grade 2/3 classroom'. *Elementary School Journal* 101 (4): 451–64.

Connell, R. W. (1995). *Masculinities*. Cambridge: Polity Press.

Cordingley, P. (2005). *The Impact of Collaborative Continuing Professional Development*. London: EPPI-Centre, Institute of Education.

Cresswell, T. (2004). *Place: A Short Introduction*. Oxford: Blackwell.

Czarniawska, B. (1997). *Narrating the Organization: Dramas of Institutional Identity*. Chicago, IL: University of Chicago Press.

Dahl, R. (1989). *Matilda*. London: Puffin Books.

Davis, M. (1992). *City of Quartz: Excavating the Future in Los Angeles*. London: Vintage.

Debord, G. (1956/1958). 'Theory of the dérive'. *Les lèvres* nues 9 (Paris, November 1956). Reprinted in *Internationale Situationniste* 2 (Paris, December 1958). Translated by Ken Knabb. http://www.cddc.vt.edu/sionline/si/theory.html (accessed 14 September 2015).

de Certeau, M. (1988). *The Practice of Everyday Llife*. Los Angeles, CA: University of California Press.

Delamont, S. (2008). 'For Lust of Knowing – Observation in Educational Ethnography'. In *How to do Educational Ethnography*, ed. G. Walford, 39–56. London: Tufnell Press.

de Landa, M. (2006). *A New Philosophy of Society: Assemblage Theory and Social Complexity*. London: Continuum.

Deleuze, G. and F. Guattari (1987). *A Thousand Plateaus: Capitalism and Schizophrenia*. Minneapolis, MN and London: University of Minnesota Press.

Denzin, N. K., ed. (2003). *Performance Ethnography: Critical Pedagogy and the Politics of Culture*. Thousand Oaks, CA: Sage.

Devine, J. (1996). *Maximum Security: The Culture of Violence in Inner-city Schools*. Chicago, IL: University of Chicago Press.

Dixon, J. and K. Durrheim (2000). 'Displacing place-identity: A discursive approach to locating self and other'. *British Journal of Social Psychology* 39 (1): 27–44.

Donehower, K., C. Hogg, E. Schell and R. Brooke (2007). *Rural Literacies*. Carbondale, IL: University of Southern Illinois Press.

Donmoyer, R. and J. Yennie-Donmoyer (1995). 'Data as drama: Reflections on the use of readers theater as a mode of qualitative data display'. *Qualitative Inquiry* 1 (4): 402–28.

Driver, S. and A. Martell (1997). 'New Labour's communitarianisms'. *Critical Social Policy* 52 (17): 27–46.

Earl, A. (2015). 'Are we all foodies now? An ethnographic exploration of food experience in primary schools'. Nottingham: University of Nottingham.

Ellard, C. (2015). *Places of the Heart: The Psychogeography of Everyday Life*. London: Bellevue Literary Press.

Elshtain, J. B. (1997). *Real Politics at the Centre of Everyday Life*. Baltimore, NJ and London: Johns Hopkins University Press.

Emerson, R., R. Fetz and L. Shaw (2011). *Writing Ethnographic Fieldnotes*. 2nd edn. Chicago, IL: University of Chicago Press.

Emmel, N. (2008). *Participatory Mapping: An Innovative Sociological Method*. ESRC National Centre for Research Methods, http://eprints.ncrm.ac.uk/540/2/2008-07-toolkit-participatory-map.pdf (accessed 18 July 2015).

Erstad, O. and J. Sefton Green, eds (2013). *Identity, Community and Learning Lives in the Digital Age*. Cambridge: Cambridge University Press.

Fairclough, N. (2003). *Analysing Discourse: Textual Analysis for Social Research*. London: Routledge.

Fielding, M. and S. Bragg (2003). *Students as Researchers: Making a Difference*. Cambridge: Pearson.

Fielding, S. (2000). '"Walk on the Left": Children's Geographies and the Primary School'. In *Children's Geographies: Playing, Living, Learning*, ed. S. Holloway and G. Valentine, London: Routledge, pp. 199–211.

Fine, M. and L. Weis (1998). *The Unknown City: The Lives of Poor and Working Class Young Adults*. Boston, Boston MA: Beacon Press.

Fish, S. (1980). *Is There a Text in This Class? The Authority of Interpretive Communities*. Cambridge, MA: Harvard University Press.

Foucault, M. (1972). *The Archeology of Knowledge* (1995 edn). London: Routledge.

Foucault, M. (1980). *Language, Counter Memory, Practice*. New York: Cornell University Press.

Foucault, M. (2001). *Fearless Speech*. New York: Semiotext[e].
Fraser, N. (1997). *Justice Interruptus: Critical Reflections on the 'Postsocialist' Condition*. London: Routledge.
Frazer, E. and N. Lacey (1993). *The Politics of Community: A Feminist Critique of the Liberal–Communitarian debate*. New York: Harvester Wheatsheaf.
Gabriel, Y. (2000). *Storytelling in Organisations: Facts, Fictions and Fantasies*. Oxford: Oxford University Press.
Geertz, C. (1988). *Works and Lives: The Anthropologist as Author* (1994 edn). Stanford, CA: Stanford University Press.
Gertler, M. (2001). 'Best practice? Geography, learning and the institutional limits to strong convergence'. *Journal of Economic Geography* 1 (1): 5–26.
Giddens, A. (1990). *The Consequences of Modernity*. Cambridge: Polity Press.
Giddens, A. (1991). *Modernity and Self Identity*. Stanford, CA: Stanford University Press.
Gonzales, N. and L. Moll (2002). 'Cruzanda el puente: Building bridges to funds of knowledge'. *Educational Policy* 16 (4): 623–41.
Gonzales, N., L. Moll and C. Amanti (2005). *Funds of Knowledge*. Mahwah, NJ: Lawrence Erlbaum.
Gonzales, N., L. Moll, M. Floyd-Tenery, A. Rivera, P. Rendon, R. Gonzales and C. Amanti (1993). *Teacher Research on Funds of Knowledge: Learning from Households*. National Centre for Research on Cultural Diversity and Second Language Learning, http://ncbe.gwu.edu/miscpubs/ncrcdsll/epr6.html (last accessed 13 August 2004).
Gorard, S., C. Taylor and J. Fitz (2003). *Schools, Markets and Choice Policies*. London: RoutledgeFalmer.
Gordon, A. (2008). *An Atlas of Radical Cartography*. New York: Journal of Aesthetics and Protest Press.
Green, B. and M. Corbett, eds (2013). *Rethinking Rural Literacies: Transnational Perspectives*. London: Palgrave Macmillan.
Gregory, E. and A. Williams (2000). *City Literacies: Learning to Read Across Generations and Cultures*. London and New York: Routledge.
Grenfell, M. (2007). *Pierre Bourdieu*. London: Bloomsbury.
Grenfell, M. and M. Lebaron, eds (2014). *Bourdieu and Data Analysis: Methodological Principles and Practice*. Oxford: Oxford University Press.
Grenfell, M., D. Bloome, C. Hardy, K. Pahl, J. Rowsell and B. Street (2011). *Language, Ethnography and Education: Bridging New Literacy Studies and Bourdieu*. London: Routedge.
Griffith, A. and D. Smith (2005). *Mothering for Schooling*. New York: RoutledgeFalmer.

Gubrium, J. and J. Holstein (2001). *Handbook of Interview Research: Context and Method*. London, Thousand Oaks, CA, and New Delhi: Sage.

Gunter, H. and P. Thomson (2008). 'Learning about student voice'. *Support for Learning* 22 (4): 181–8.

Hall, J. (2001). *Canal Town Youth: Community Organisation and the Development of Adolescent Identity*. Albany, NY: State University of New York Press.

Hall, S. (1997). 'The work of representation'. In *Representation: Cultural Representations and Signifying Practices*, ed. S. Hall, 13–74. Milton Keynes: Open University Press.

Hamilton, I. and D. Roberts (2014). *Walking the Literary Landscape: 20 Classic Walks for Book-lovers in Northern England*. London: Vertebrate.

Hammersley, M. (2015). 'Sampling and thematic analysis: A response to Fugard and Potts'. *International Journal of Social Research Methodology*, http://www.tandfonline.com/doi/pdf/10.1080/13645579.2015.1005456 (accessed 8 April 2016).

Hamnett, S. and R. Freestone, eds (2000). *The Australian Metropolis: A Planning History*. Sydney: Allen & Unwin.

Harmon, K. (2004). *You Are Here: Personal Geographies and other Maps of the Imagination*. New York: Princeton Architectural Press.

Harper, D. (2013). *Visual Sociology*. London: Routledge.

Harris, A. (2008). *Distributed School Leadership: Developing Tomorrow's Leaders*. London: Routledge.

Hattie, J. (2008). *Visible Learning: A Synthesis of over 800 Meta-Analyses Relating to Achievement*. London: Routledge.

Haw, K. and M. Hadfield (2012). *Video in Social Science Research: Functions and Forms*. London: Routledge.

Hayden, D. (1996). *The Power of Place: Urban Landscapes as Public History*. Cambridge, MA: MIT Press.

Hayward, V. and P. Thomson (2012). 'Performing Health: An Investigation of Emotional Health and Wellbing (EWHB) in a High Performance School'. In *Performativity and Education – a UK Perspective. Ethnographic Effects, Outcomes and Agency*, ed. B. Jeffrey and G. Troman, London: Tufnell Press.

Hirschman, E. (1970). *Exit, Voice and Loyalty: Responses to Decline in Firms, Organizations and States*. Boston, MA: Harvard University Press.

Hodkinson, P. and H. Hodkinson (2003). 'Individuals, communities of practice and the policy context: School teachers' learning in their workplace'. *Studies in Continuing Education* 25 (1): 3–21.

Holstein, J. and J. Gubrium (1995). *The Active Interview*. Thousand Oaks, CA, London and New Delhi: Sage.

Hopkins, D., M. Ainscow and M. West (1994). *School Improvement in an Era of Change*. London: Cassell.

Hsieh, H.-F. and S.A. Shannon (2005). 'Three approaches to qualitative content analysis'. *Qualitative Health Research* 15 (9): 1277–88.

Ingold, T. (2000). *The Perception of the Environment: Essays in Livelihood, Dwelling and Skill*. London: Routledge.

Ingold, T. (2009). 'Against space'. In *Boundless Worlds: An Anthropological Approach to Movement*, ed. P. W. Kirby, 29–44. New York: Bergahn Books.

Ingold, T. (2011). *Being Alive: Essays on Movement, Knowledge and Description*. London: Routledge.

James, N. and H. Busher (2009). *Online Interviewing*. London: Sage.

Johnson, K. (2008). 'Teaching children to use visual research methods'. In *Doing Visual Research with Children and Young People*, ed. P. Thomson, 77–94. London: Routledge.

Jones, K. (2006). 'A biographic researcher in pursuit of an aesthetic: The use of arts-based (re)presentations in "performative" dissemination of life stories'. *Qualitative Sociology Review* 2 (1): 66–85.

Jones, S., C. Hall, P. Thomson, A. Barrett and J. Hanby (2013). 'Re-presenting the "forgotten estate": Participatory theatre, place and community identity'. *Discourse* 34 (1): 118–31.

Kelly, A. (2009). 'In defence of anonymity: Rejoining the criticism'. *British Educational Research Journal* 35 (3): 4331–45.

Kerr, K., A. Dyson and C. Raffo (2014). *Education, Disadvantage and Place: Making the Local Matter*. Bristol: Policy Press.

Kmetz, M., K. Donehower, C. Hogg and E. Schell (2012). *Reclaiming the Rural: Essays on Literacy, Rhetoric, and Pedagogy*. Carbondale, IL: University of Southern Illinois Press.

Kretzmann, J. and J. McKnight (1993). *Building Communities from the Inside-Out*. Chicago, IL: Asset-Based Community Development Institute.

Lahman, M. K. E., K. L. Rodriguez, L. Moses, K. M. Griffin, B. M. Mendoza and W. Yacoub (2015). 'A rose by any other name is still a rose? Problematising pseudonyms in research'. *Qualitative Inquiry* 21 (5): 445–53.

Lassiter, L. E. (2005). *The Chicago Guide to Collaborative Ethnography*. Chicago, IL: University of Chicago Press.

Lawrence-Lightfoot, S. (1984). *The Good High School: Portraits of Character and Culture*. New York: Basic Books.

Leavy, P. (2009). *Method Meets Art: Arts-Based Research Practice*. New York: Guilford Press.

Lefebvre, H. (1947). *Critique of Everyday Life* (Vol. 1 of 1991 edn). London: Verso.

Lefebvre, H. (1971). *Everyday Life in the Modern World* (1994 edn). London: Transaction Publishers.

Lefebvre, H. (1991). *The Production of Space*. Oxford: Blackwell (orig. pub. 1959).

Lefebvre, H. (2004). *Rhythmanalysis. Space, Time and Everyday Life*. London: Continuum.

Leithwood, K., C. Day, P. Sammons, A. Harris and D. Hopkins (2006). *Successful School Leadership: What it is and How it Influences Pupil Learning. Research report RR800*. London: DfES.

Lewicka, M. (2008). 'Place attachment, place identity, and place memory: Retsoring the forgotten city past'. *Journal of Environmental Psychology* 28 (3): 209–31.

Lipman, P. (1998). *Race, Class, and Power in School Restructuring*. New York: State University of New York Press.

Lupton, R. (2003). *Poverty Sstreet: The Dynamics of Neighbourhood Decline and Renewal*. Bristol: Policy Press.

Maguire, M., J. Perryman, S. Ball and A. Braun (2011). 'The ordinary school – what is it?' *British Journal of Sociology of Education* 32 (1): 1–16.

Mannion, G. (2012). 'Intergenerational education: The significance of reciprocity and place'. *Journal of Intergenerational Relationships* 10 (4): 386–99.

Marchington, M. and I. Grugulis (2000). '"Best practice" human resource management: Perfect opportunity or dangerous illusion'. *International Journal of Human Resource Management* 11 (6): 1104–24.

Marcus, G. and E. Saka (2006). 'Assemblage'. *Theory, Culture & Society* 23 (2–3): 101–6.

Marsden, P. (2014). *Rising Ground: A Search for the Spirit of Place*. London: Granta.

Marx, G. (2006). 'What's in a name? Some reflections on the sociology of anonymity'. *Information Society: An International Journal* 15 (2): 99–112.

Massey, D. (1994). *Space, Place and Gender*. Minneapolis, MN: University of Minnesota Press.

Massey, D. (2005). *For Space*. London: Sage.

McDonald, P., B. Pini and R. Mayes (2012). 'Organisational rhetoric in the prospectuses of elite private schools: Unpacking strategies of persuasion'. *British Journal of Sociology of Education* 33 (1): 1–20.

McFarlane, C. (2011). *Learning the City: Knowledge and Translocal Assemblage*. London: Wiley-Blackwell.

McGregor, J. (2003). 'Spatiality and teacher workplace cultures'. In

Space, Curriculum and Learning, ed. R. Edwards and R. Usher, Greenwich, CT: Information Age Publishing, 45–58.

McKnight, J. (1995). *The Careless Society: Community and its Counterfeits*. New York: Basic Books.

McKnight, J. and J. Kretzmann (1996). *Mapping Community Capacity*. Evanston, IL: Institute for Policy Research, Northwestern University.

McLaughlin, D. and W. Tierney, eds (1993). *Naming Silenced Lives: Personal Narratives and the Process of Educational Change*. New York and London: Routledge.

Menter, I., D. Elliott, M. Hulme, J. Lewin and K. Lowden (2011). *A Guide to Practitioner Research in Education*. London: Sage.

Metz, M. and R. Page (2002). 'The uses of practitioner research and status issues in educational research: Reply to Gary Anderson'. *Educational Researcher* 31 (7): 26–7.

Mitchell, C. (2012). *Doing Visual Research*. Thousand Oaks, CA: Sage.

Mitchell, W. J. T. (2005). *What do Pictures Want? The Lives and Loves of Images*. Chicago, IL: University of Chicago Press.

Moran, J. (2005). *Reading the Everyday*. London: Routledge.

Mueller, P. and D. M. Oppenheimer (2014). 'The pen is mightier than the keyboard: Advantages of longhand over laptop notetaking'. *Psychological Science* 25 (6): 1159–68.

Murray, L. and B. Lawrence (2000). *Practitioner-Based Enquiry: Principles for Postgraduate Research*. London and New York: Falmer.

Narayan, K. (2012). *Alive in the Writing: Crafting Ethnography in the Company of Chekov*. Chicago, IL: University of Chicago Press.

Nespor, J. (1997). *Tangled up in School: Politics, Space, Bodies, and Signs in the Educational Process*. Mahwah, NJ: Lawrence Erlbaum.

Nespor, J. (2000). 'Anonymity and place in qualitative inquiry'. *Qualitative Inquiry* 6 (4): 546–69.

Nespor, J. (2002). 'Studying the spatialities of schooling'. *Pedagogy, Culture and Society* 10 (3): 483–92.

Nichols, S., J. Rowsell, H. Nixon and S. Rainford (2012). *Resourcing Early Learners: New Networks, New Actors*. New York: Routledge.

Niesche, R. (2011). *Foucault and Educational Leadership: Disciplining the Principal*. London: Routledge.

Nolan, K. (2011). *Police in the Hallways: Discipline in an Urban High School*. Minneapolis, MN: University of Minnesota Press.

O'Reilly, M., K. Karim, H. Taylor and N. Dogra (2011). 'Parent and child views on anonymity: "I've got nothing to hide"'. *International Journal of Social Research Methodology* 15 (3): 211–23.

Obama, B. (2006). *The Audacity of Hope: Thoughts on Reclaiming the American Dream*. New York: Random House.

Peel, M. (1995). *Good Times, Hard Times: The Past and Future in Elizabeth*. Melbourne: Melbourne University Press.

Penuel, W. R., M. Riel, A. A. Krause and K. Frank. (2009). 'Analysing teachers' professional interactions in a school as social capital: A social network approach'. *Teachers College Record* 111 (1): 124–63.

Piantanida, M., P. McMahon and N. Garman (2003). 'Sculpting the contours of arts-based educational research within a discourse community'. *Qualitative Inquiry* 9 (2): 182–91.

Pink, S. (2008). 'Sense and sustainability: The case of the slow city movement'. *Local Environment: The International Journal of Justice and Sustainability* 13 (2): 95–106.

Pink, S. (2009). *Doing Sensory Ethnography*. Thousand Oaks, CA: Sage.

Pink, S. and T. Lewis (2014). 'Making resilience: Eveyday affect and global affiliation in Australian slow cities'. *Cultural Geographies* 21 (4): 695–710.

Pinker, S. (2014). *The Sense of Style: The Thinking Person's Guide to Writing in the 21st Century*. New York: Allen Lane.

Plank, D. (1996). 'Dreams of community'. *Journal of Education Policy* 12 (1–2): 13–20.

Polanyi, M. (1958/1998). *Personal Knowledge: Towards a Post Critical Philosophy*. London: Routledge.

Polanyi, M. (1966). *The Tacit Dimension*. Garden City, NY: Doubleday.

Powell, K. (2010). 'Making a sense of place: Mapping as a multisensory research method'. *Qualitative Inquiry* 16 (7): 539–55.

Power, S., G. Rees and C. Taylor (2005). 'New Labour and educational disadvantage: The limits of area based initiatives'. *London Review of Education* 3 (2): 101–16.

Prosser, J. (1999). 'Visual sociology and school culture'. In *School Culture*, ed. J. Prosser, 82–97. London: Paul Chapman Publishing.

Putnam, R. (2000). *Bowling Alone: The Collapse and Revival of American Community*. New York: Simon & Schuster.

Reckwitz, A. (2002). 'Towards a theory of social practices: A development in culturalist theorising'. *European Journal of Social Theory* 5 (2): 243–63.

Rees, G., S. Power and C. Taylor (2007). 'The governance of educational inequalities: The limits of area-based initiatives'. *International Journal of Comparative Policy Analysis* 9 (3): 261–74.

Reich, R. (1991). *The Work of Nations: A Blueprint for the Future*. New York: Simon & Schuster.

Reid, J.-A., B. Kamler, A. Simpson and R. MacLean (1996). '"Do you see what I see?" Reading a different classroom scene'. *Qualitative Studies in Education* 9 (1): 87–108.

Richardson, L. (1997). *Fields of Play: Constructing an Academic Life*. New Brunswick, NJ: Rutgers University Press.

Richardson, T. (2015). *Walking Inside Out: Contemporary British Psychogeography*. New York: Rowman & Littlefield.

Richmond, L. (2013). 'Anagyuk (Partner): Personal Relationships and the Exploration of Sugpiaq Fishing Geographies in Old Harbor, Alaska'. In *A Deeper Sense of Place: Stories and Journeys of Collaboration in Indigenous Research*, ed. J. T. Johnson and S. C. Larsen, 73–84. Corvallis, OR: Oregon State University Press.

Riessman, C. K. (2008). *Narrative Methods for the Human Sciences*. Thousand Oaks, CA: Sage.

Rose, G. (2001). *Visual Methodologies*. London, Thousand Oaks, CA, and New Delhi: Sage.

Rowling, J. K. (2003). *Harry Potter and the Order of the Phoenix*. London: Bloomsbury.

Sahlberg, P. (2012). *Finnish Lessons: What Can the World Learn from Educational Change in Finland?* London: Routledge.

Salmons, J. (2010). *Online Interviews in Real Time*. London: Sage.

Samuels, J. (2004). 'Breaking the ethnographer's frames: Reflections on the use of photo-elicitation in understanding Sri Lankan monastic cultures'. *American Behavioural Scientist* 47 (12): 1528–50.

Schatzki, T. (2001). 'Introduction'. In *The Practice Turn in Contemporary Theory*, ed. T. Schatzki, K. Knorr Cetina and E. Von Savigny, 1–14. London: Routledge.

Schratz, M. (2009). 'Leading and learning as a transcultural experience: A visual account'. *International Journal of Leadership in Education* 12 (3): 283–96.

Scollon, R. and S. W. Scollon (2003). *Discourses in Place: Language in the Material World*. London and New York: Routledge.

Sikes, P. and A. Potts, eds (2008). *Researching Education from the Inside*. London: Routledge.

Silverman, D. (1993). *Interpreting Qualitative Data: Methods for Analysing Talk, Text and Interaction*. London: Sage.

Slater, N. (2003). *Toast: The Story of a Boy's Hunger*. London: Harper Perennial.

Slee, R. (2011). *The Irregular School: Exclusion, Schooling and Inclusive Education*. London: Routledge.

Smith, D. (1987). *The Eeveryday World as Problematic: A feminist Sociology*. Boston, MA: Northeastern University Press.

Smith, D. (1993). *Texts, Facts and Femininity: Exploring the Relations of Ruling*. London: Routledge.

Smith, D. (2005). *Institutional Ethnography. A Sociology for People*. Lanham, MD: Alta Mira Press.

Smith, E. (2008). *Using Secondary Data in Social and Educational Research*. Buckingham: Open University Press.

Soja, E. (1996). *Thirdspace: Journeys to Los Angeles and Other Real-and-Imagined Places*. Oxford: Blackwell.

Soja, E. (1999). 'Thirdspace: Expanding the scope of the geographical imagination'. In *Human Geography Today*, ed. D. Massey, J. Allen and P. Sarre, 260–78. Cambridge: Polity Press.

Somerville, M. J. (2011). 'Becoming Frog'. In *Place Pedagogy Change*, ed. M. J. Somerville, B. Davies, K. Power, S. Gannon and P. De Carteret, 65–80. Rotterdam: Sense Publishers.

Somerville, M. J., J. D'Warte and L. Brown (2015). 'Mapping students' everyday mulitmodal language practices in a high needs school'. University of Western Sydney, http://www.uws.edu.au/__data/assets/pdf_file/0009/857367/SOMERVILLE,_DWARTE,_BROWN_for_reduced_Website.pdf (accessed 16 July 2015).

Spillane, J. and J. Zoltner-Sherer (2004). 'A distributed perspective on school leadership practice as stretched out over people and place'. Paper presented at *American Educational Research Conference*. San Diego.

Springgay, S. (2008). *Body Knowledge and Curriculum: Pedagogies of Touch in Youth and Visual Culture*. New York: Peter Lang.

Stirling, E. and D. Yamada-Rice (2015). *Visual Methods with Children and Young People: Academics and Visual Industries in Dialogue*. London: Palgrave Macmillan.

Sword, H. (2012). *Stylish Academic Writing*. Cambridge, MA: Harvard University Press.

Teddlie, C. and D. Reynolds, eds (2000). *The International Handbook of School Effectiveness*. London: Falmer.

Tessler, S. (2012). 'From field notes, to transcripts, to tape recordings: Evolution or combination?' *International Journal of Qualitative Methods* 11 (4): 446–60.

Thomas, D., ed. (1995). *Teachers' Stories*. Buckingham: Open University Press.

Thomson, P. (1999). 'Doing justice: Stories of everyday life in disadvantaged schools and neighbourhoods'. PhD, Deakin University. Accessible via the Australian Digital Thesis programme.

Thomson, P. (2000). 'Like schools, educational disadvantage and "thisness"'. *Australian Educational Researcher* 27 (3): 151–66.

Thomson, P. (2002). *Schooling the Rustbelt Kids: Making the Difference in Changing Times*. Sydney: Allen & Unwin (Trentham Books, UK).

Thomson, P., ed. (2008). *Doing Visual Research with Children and Young People*. London: Routledge.

Thomson, P. (2011). *Whole School Change: A Reading of the Literatures* (2nd edn). London: Creative Partnerships, Arts Council England.

Thomson, P., A. Barrett, C. Hall, J. Hanby and S. Jones (2014). 'Arts in the community as a place-making event'. In *The Routledge International Handbook of Arts and Education*, ed. M. Fleming, L. Bresler and O. T. John, 295–304. London: Routledge.

Thomson, P., L. Ellison, T. Byrom and D. Bulman (2004). *An Investigation of Queries that School Offices Receive from Parents/Carers*. London: Department for Education and Skills, http://dera.ioe.ac.uk/5028/1/RR575.pdf (accessed 7 July 2016).

Thomson, P. and H. Gunter (2006). 'From "consulting pupils" to "pupils as researchers": A situated case narrative'. *British Educational Research Journal* 32 (6): 839–56.

Thomson, P. and H. Gunter (2007). 'The methodology of students-as-researchers: Valuing and using experience and expertise to develop methods'. *Discourse* 28 (3): 327–42.

Thomson, P. and H. Gunter (2008). 'Researching bullying with students: A lens on everyday life in a reforming high school'. *International Journal of Inclusive Education* 12 (2): 185–200.

Thomson, P. and H. Gunter (2009). 'Students' participation in school change: Action research on the ground'. In *The Handbook of Educational Action Research*, ed. B. Somekh and S. Noffke, Thousand Oaks, CA: Sage, pp. 409–19.

Thomson, P. and H. Gunter (2011). 'Inside, outside, upside down: The fluidity of academic researcher "identity" in working with/in school'. *International Journal of Qualitative Methods* 34 (1): 17–30.

Thomson, P. and C. Hall (2011). 'Sense-making as a lens on everyday change leadership practice: The case of Holly Tree Primary'. *International Journal of Leadership in Education* 14 (4): 385–403.

Thomson, P., C. Hall and K. Jones (2010). 'Maggie's day: A small scale analysis of English education policy'. *Journal of Education Policy* 25 (5): 639–56.

Thomson, P., C. Hall and L. Russell (2006). 'An arts project failed, censored or ...? A critical incident approach to artist–school partnerships'. *Changing English* 13 (1): 29–44.

Thomson, P., C. Hall and L. Russell (2007). 'If these walls could speak: Reading displays of primary children's work'. *Ethnography and Education* 3 (3): 381–400.

Thomson, P. and V. Hayward (2014). 'Managing performance: The implementation of the English Healthy Schools Programme'. In *Deconstructing Educational Leadership: Derrida and Lyotard*, ed. R. Niesche, 63–83. London: Routledge.

Thomson, P., K. Jones and C. Hall (2009). *Creative Whole School*

Change: Final Report. London: Creativity, Culture and Education, Arts Council England.

Thomson, P. and B. Kamler (2013). *Writing for Peer Reviewed Journals: Strategies for Getting Published*. London: Routledge.

Thomson, P., V. McQuade and K. Rochford (2005a). '"My Little Special House": Re-forming the risky geographies of middle school girls at Clifftop College'. In *Problem Girls: Understanding and Supporting Troubled and Troublesome Girls and Young Women*, ed. G. Lloyd, 172–89. London: RoutledgeFalmer.

Thomson, P., V. McQuade and K. Rochford (2005b). '"No-one's a good or bad student here": An active citizenship project as "doing justice"'. *International Journal of Learning*, http://ijl.cgpublisher.com/ (accessed 30 September 2015).

Thrupp, M. (1999). *Schools Making a Difference: Let's be Realistic! School Mix, School Effectiveness and the Social Limits of Reform*. Buckingham: Open University Press.

Thrupp, M. and R. Lupton (2011). 'The impact of school context: What headteachers say'. London: Centre for Analysis of Social Exclusion, London School of Economics.

Tittle, D. (1995). *Welcome to Heights High: The Crippling Politics of Restructuring America's Public Schools*. Columbus, OH: Ohio State University Press.

Tonnies, F. (1957/1887). *Community and Society (Gemeinschaft and Gesellschaft)*. East Lansing, MI: Michigan State University Press.

Tripp, D. (1993/2011). *Critical Incidents in Teaching: Developing Professional Judgement*. London: Routledge.

Tuan, Y.-F. (1977/2011). *Space and Place: The Perspective of Experience*. Minneapolis, MN: University of Minnesota Press.

Tuck, E. and M. McKenzie, eds (2015). *Place in Research: Theory, Methodology and Methods*. New York: Routledge.

Tyler, D. (2015). *Uncomon Ground: A Word-lover's Guide to the British Landscape*. London: Guardian Faber Publishing.

Vartanian, T. (2011). *Secondary Data Analysis*. Oxford: Oxford University Press.

Walford, G. (2006). 'Research ethical guidelines and anonymity'. *International Journal of Research and Methods in Education* 28 (1): 83–93.

Walford, G., ed. (2008). *How to do Educational Ethnography*. London: Tufnell Press.

Walford, G. (2010). 'Site selection within comparative case study and ethnographic research'. *Compare: A Journal of Comparative and International Education* 31 (2): 151–64.

Wanat, C. (2008). 'Getting past the gatekeepers: Differences between access and cooperation in public school research'. *Field Methods* 20 (2): 191–208.

Warren, S. (2000). 'Let's do it properly: Inviting children to be researchers'. In *Researching Children's Perspectives*, ed. A. Lewis and G. Lindsay, 122–34. Buckingham: Open University Press.

Weber, S. and C. Mitchell (1995). *That's Funny, You Don't Look Like a Teacher*. London: Falmer.

Weick, K.E. (1995). *Sensemaking in Organizations*. Thousand Oaks, CA: Sage.

Weick, K.E. (2001). *Making Sense of the Organization*. Malden, MA: Blackwell.

Wilkins, A. (2011). 'School choice and the commodification of education: A visual approach to school brochures and wesbites'. *Critical Social Policy* 32 (1): 69–86.

Wolcott, H. (1973). *The Man in the Principal's Office: An Ethnography*. Prospect Heights, IL: Waveland Press.

Woods, P. (1983). *Sociology and the School: An Interactionist Viewpoint*. London: Routledge.

Zaretsky, E. (1977). *Capitalism, the Family and Personal Life*. New York: HarperCollins.

Zeni, J., ed. (2001). *Ethical Issues in Practitioner Research*. New York: Teachers College Press.

INDEX